gourmet food with all of the flavor and none of the guilt

THE GUILT FREE GOURMET
Low Fat & Calorie Cookbook - Volume 1

Follow me online at:
The Web: www.theguiltfreegourmet.net
Connect: @dhallakx7
Facebook: The Guilt Free Gourmet LLC.
Instagram: TheGuiltFreeGourmet ... No, seriously... Follow me on Instagram!!
Youtube Channel: The Guilt Free Gourmet ... I'll be uploading a lot of fun cooking vids soon! Subscribe please!
You can find this book, as well as my Low Point Cooking Guide, on Amazon.com
(not to be confused with that 7 year old vegan, gluten free, hippie dessert book of the same name... That's not mine)

Copyright 2019 by Daniel Hallak
Book design by: Daniel Hallak
Edited by: Mary Geiler
Photography by Daniel Hallak
Raspberry White Chocolate Cake photography by: Randy Van Winkle Photography *randyvanwinklephotography.com*
Nutritional Information provided by Lindie Kusky ... aka: @cake.riot
The Guilt Free Gourmet is privately owned, so feel free to buy me out, baby!! Daddy needs a new pair of shoes.
The Guilt Free Gourmet, Low Fat & Calorie Cookbook: Volume 1 - 1st Edition 2019
The Author grants permission to reprint this publication **for personal use only**

LEGAL DISCLAIMERS:

The Guilt Free Gourmet® 2019

Though we have copyright protection over this publication and the materials here-in, we at The Guilt Free Gourmet want to make sure you understand that **you have our full and complete permission to have this material printed for your private use**! **If you are a home cook or a cooking enthusiast, please know that we wish for you to be able to print this material, either at home, or at a business that offers printing services, such as Staples, Office Depot, Kinkos, etc.**

If you try to take this to a printing center and they say that they can't print it, PLEASE tell them to look at the disclaimer cited above. The Author has expressly stated that he (me) has given permission for you to print it... Then poke him/her in the chest to establish dominance. Howling loudly while pointing at their copy machine.

Weight Watchers International & WW ®

The Guilt Free Gourmet is not affiliated with, nor is it endorsed by Weight Watchers International, Inc. (now WW®). Weight Watchers has not reviewed this publication for accuracy or suitability for WW members.

Weight Watchers, WW®, Point, Points, Smart Points, SP's and Freestyle are all registered trademarks of Weight Watchers International, Inc. Authentic information about the program is only available at your local WW workshop or online through the WW website and mobile app. The information and recipes contained within this guide are based solely on the recollections and assumptions of The Guilt Free Gourmet. The information and recipes are not warranted for any purpose by the author other than for educational purposes and for reference under fair use doctrine.

All readers are encouraged to go to a WW Workshop or the WW website for actual WW information and to also enter the listed ingredients of my recipes themselves into the Recipe Builder. Point values for certain ingredients change and are updated periodically by WW®, which may change the point values we are suggesting to be accurate for our recipes <u>at this time</u>.

This guide is in **NO WAY** meant to be a replacement for the WW Program. It is merely developed and intended for use as a collection of privately developed recipes, designed to complement the instructional materials and resources provided by WW to its members... BECAUSE WW IS AWESOME!

Any non-generic recipes within this guide were developed by me. All Point values were determined by entering the ingredients, measurements and servings into the Recipe Builder within the WW mobile App that is only available to paying members of the system. I strongly encourage anyone interested in developing a healthier lifestyle to join and follow the strategies for healthy living provided by Weight Watchers International (WW®).

All use of the terms Weight Watchers, WW, Point, Points, Smart Points, SP's and Freestyle in the following cookbook are used SOLELY for reference purposes, as is appropriate and allowed under fair use doctrine.

     I dedicated "The Low Point Cooking Guide" from last year, to my wife, so I feel like I should dedicate this bad boy to the person who is ultimately responsible for it... my son, Jesse. Excuse me while I monologue.

     Jesse, I know you won't be able to read this for Lord knows HOW long, but thank you. I wish with all of my heart and soul that I could send a message now, back to myself when you were born. I wish that I could go back and calm my fears, calm my worries and smack the selfish angriness out of myself. I wish that I could go back and show old-me a glimpse of the joy that you have brought to our lives. I wish that I could go back and tell myself of just how much you would end up changing me into a better person. All of this is because of you. At first, I had a lot of anger and selfish resentment in my heart about it... but you're the best thing that's ever happened to me. From the day you were born, you've forced me to change, to not think about myself first, to have to care unconditionally and unselfishly.

     I know that I still can't communicate with you verbally yet... but someday you'll be able to read this and you'll know that you are the most joyous part of my every day. Your smile, laughter and constant need for hugs, makes my soul sing. Know that I am constantly calling you "sunshine with feet", to 100,000+ people, on an almost daily basis. Because of you, my heart is content.

- Dad
09-11-19

Table of Contents

2019 | Cookbook Volume 1 - 1st Edition
Recipe Point Values based on the WW Freestyle program

Introduction
My personal weight loss journey and why I started trying to cook healthier ... *page 6-7*

My Cooking Philosophy?
Trying to explain why I go to such insane lengths, to cook as crazy as I do ... *pages 8*

Important Kitchen Gadgets
An explanation of some of my most commonly used kitchen tools. Geared towards folks who are newer in the kitchen ... *pages 9*

Foundation Recipes
Recipes for items that serve as the "base" for appetizers found in this book ... *page 10 - 25*

Ground Meat Seasoning Recipes
10 recipes to transform ground turkey into a healthy stand-in for different flavorful types of meat and sausage ... *page 20- 25*

Dips & Spreads
Recipes for 16 amazingly low calorie, fat and "point" delicious dips and spreads... *page 26 - 43*

Salad Dressings
Recipes for 15 low point, calorie & fat salad dressings, each with a generous 1/4 cup serving size ... *pages 44 - 53*

Appetizers
20 delicious and gourmet, low calorie and fat appetizers, that are SURE to turn heads at your next gathering ... *pages 54 - 95*

Dessert Intro & Cupcakes
18 low sugar, low fat, low calorie extravagant cupcakes, that are guaranteed to keep you from feeling deprived ... *pages 96 - 141*

Cakes
Simple steps for converting some of my cupcake recipes into full sized gourmet cakes ... *pages 142 - 151*

Nutritional Information
A 2 page spread, with the nutritional values for every recipe in the book. Info. provided by the lovely and sometimes insane, @cake.riot ... *pages 152 - 153*

Acknowledgements & A Bad Mental Image
Like a good Ice Cream Sundae, all good things must come to an end ... *pages 154 - 155*

Introduction
Nothing about my intro. has really changed? Who woulda' thunk it.

Alright, for you folks that already have "The 2019 Low Point Cooking Guide" or follow me on Connect, this is going to be preeeeetty repetitive. Sorry *shrugs*
This is mainly for the folks that don't know me yet.

Hi there, my name is Daniel, but most of you know me from **WW Connect** as dhallakx7. As of the writing of this cookbook, I'm a 42-year-old stay at home dad to my 2 special needs kidlettes, Rachel (Autistic) and Jesse (Down Syndrome). Prior to this, I worked as a Graphic Designer & Web Developer for a really great company. I had just received a promotion, but when Jesse was born preemie and his diagnosis was finally confirmed, our priorities had to change, so I became Mr. Mom.

I still remember the night in 3rd grade when I turned from liking food, to wanting to gorge on food. My best friend Bart and I went to a high school soccer game with my older brother. At that game I saw something that I'd never seen before. A food vendor showed up in the bleachers pushing a food cart. He was using it to make hot, sugar coated mini cake donuts, fresh to order. I remember running down to that cart with my friend, looking at the fresh donuts, then immediately running up to my brother and asking for the money to buy some... then to buy some more... then to buy some more. And that's where it started.

I spent the better part of the next 30 years going from "husky" to overweight, eventually becoming heavy enough to be classified as obese. I only went swimming 3 or 4 times in the past 25 years out of shame for how I looked. I would make excuses not to see friends who were visiting from out of town, whom I hadn't seen in years. Heck, I wouldn't even change in the same room as my wife because I was

The new and improved 2019 Dad Bod GTO. Now available with dual child carriers, improved mileage and extended warranty

embarrassed about my body. Yet, did it make me want to change and lose weight? Nope, I figured it wasn't worth it.

In order to lose weight, I was going to be eating nothing but rice cakes and tasteless diet food. I would have to start going to the gym, running and stop eating all the foods that I loved to eat. People on diets are always so miserable and complain about what they can't eat, how their diet de jour doesn't allow them to have sugar, or they are cutting all carbs, or they are doing "cleanses" or whatever insane dietary deprivation is the current trend. Why in the heck would I want to do that? I'd rather be fat and eating than be skinny and surviving on rice cakes, bean curd and sadness. But, when I finally hit my mental rock bottom, I stumbled upon an article online late at night. It was written by a female blogger who tried Weight Watchers for one month without doing any exercise and without giving up eating regular food. She ended up losing 5 pounds over the course of the month without working out, while still eating normal foods and staying within her Weight Watchers daily allotment of "Smart Points". I figured it was worth a shot as I had no

Cont.

Introduction

desire to stop eating normal food and no desire to exercise (at that time). The first few weeks were difficult but manageable. I was losing weight, I wasn't working out, but dear Lord, there was so much food that I missed eating that I couldn't have because it was so high in points. Then it happened... I found the "recipe builder' tool, within the WW mobile phone App, that pretty much changed everything.

I immediately realized the full possibilities the tool offered. I bought a cooking magazine from the grocery store, that had a recipe on the cover for a skillet full of baked rolls covered in tons of cheese, marinara sauce, pepperoni and Italian sausage. The type of meal there is NO WAY you could ever eat on Weight Watchers and stay within your points.

I scoured Connect for ingredient swap ideas and even came up with a few ideas of my own. I started swapping out regular cheese for fat free cheese and mixed in some plain yogurt for added creaminess. I adjusted spice amounts, checked how much wine I could cut with water to reduce the points and still taste it in a sauce. I tried getting as creative as I possibly could to make the skillet as low fat and low calorie as possible. Each time I did that with a new recipe, it became more and more fun, like challenging myself to solve a difficult puzzle. Now I can look at almost any recipe and think of ways to almost immediately start cutting the calories, while retaining the flavor.

Now, I absolutely LOVE doing this. I wake up every day, genuinely looking forward to "what am I going to try and make today?" I love logging in to the WW mobile app to check and see if there's anyone that needs a question answered, or needs help with a recipe... I love getting tagged by people who are looking for help.

After being stuck in a house, changing diapers, vacuuming, or being a taxi all day... getting to interact with adults who value you and want to chat, even if it's digitally, is such a relief.

My Food Philosophy

You might be tempted to gloss over this and go straight to the recipes, but please don't. This is very important. Before you dig into these recipes and get an extremely confused look as you exclaim, "Why in the good Lord's name is he doing this and (or)that?..." You need to understand the reason for my mad scientist-ness.

The most important factor is that I love, love, love to try challenging myself to think of new ways to do things. My primary goal in anything that I make, is to make it taste great while cutting down the fat, calories and WW Points. My goal is to turn EVERYTHING into an ultra low calorie version of itself. Cooking with that mindset is what allowed me to lose so much weight, so fast, without ANY excercise... and while still eating well. I didn't even go for 1 single walk during my march from start, till I hit my goal weight. I dropped weight like a brick, while eating lasagna, pasta dishes, casseroles and desserts. My style of cooking relies upon the principle of "Calorie Density."

The basic principle of Calorie Density, is that by modifying recipes to be lower in calories, you can consume the EXACT SAME AMOUNT OF FOOD, by weight, as someone else, but with a drastic reduction in the amount of calories you consume in a day. It's like choosing to eat a 1 pound Lean Cuisine dinner, while your buddy eats a 1 pound Stouffers dinner. You're both eating the same exact amount of food... but your meal is leaner and healthier.

When you're trying to eat healthier and lose weight, do you reach for "Hungry Man XL" frozen dinners, or do you reach for "Healthy Choice" Steamers"? You eat the Healthy Choice meal because it's a responsible amount of food, but lighter in fat, calories, carbs and sugars.

It's weight loss 101, folks. No matter what fad diet you follow, they all have the same basic principle. If you eat more calories than your body uses in a day... you're going to gain weight. Most people try to cut calories by starving themselves. THAT slows your metabolism and makes you actually gain weight once you start eating again. BUT..... by manipulating your food to so that you eat just as much, just as often, but at half the calories. There is no starving, no slowing of your metabolism... you're still eating like a normal person, just leaner.

That's the basic principle for why I go crazy-mad-scientist in the kitchen, to the extent that I do. It allows me to have a larger portion size, even seconds, most of the time... and still able to lose or maintain my weight. While other people are constantly being told "Just eat the normal, full fat, full calorie dish... just have a much smaller portion... this is a lifestyle!", I say forget that. Who wants a "lifestyle" that revolves around having fat-filled little hockey puck sized "responsible" entrees and desserts. I don't want to feel like I'm on a diet or have to eat a portion of food that's sized for a toddler.

My "Low Point & Calorie Cooking Guide", that I published last December (2018), is a treasure trove of tutorials, tips, and building block recipes, that was meant to teach you to start manipulating your food with all of my food hacks and tricks. If you don't have it, it is a 100% FREE download off of my website. Yes... you can purchase a hard copy on Amazon, but you can download it, in its entirety, completely and utterly for free. It's my gift to you, because I want you to succeed.

The principles and recipes that I explain in that book are the foundation for this one. This cookbook takes what was taught in my cooking guide and shows you how you can make amazing dishes out of those tips and base-recipes. You now have ALL of the tools you need, to start making your own crazy and gourmet dishes, that are lean, low calorie, low fat, but full flavor.

For most of you folks that cook a lot and have spent years trying new things in the kitchen, these Gadgets & Gizmos are nothing new to you. But this particular page is directed more towards people who aren't as comfortable in the kitchen yet and are wondering what some of the things are that I mention a lot in my posts. I've often heard people say "what's a food processor,?" or "Immersion Blender?" Well I thought it'd be a good use of a page to point out what some of the primary things are that I use, and what their purpose is, for the newer cooks in the kitchen.

1. Food Processor

Think of a food processor of a giant, wide bottomed blender. There are quite a few dips and dressings that are in this cookbook that rely heavily on using a food processor. ESPECIALLY the guacamole and the hummus. Sweet Lord in Heaven, it's worth it to get an inexpensive food processor for the Hummus recipe alone.

You don't need to buy an expensive model. Even just an inexpensive one from Big Lots will do the job. It is a necessity for a couple of the recipes.

2. Pasta Makers

Fresh pasta, if made the way that I teach, is lower in points and calories than store bought dried pasta. The Foundation recipe section will have my updated Pasta making guide in it. In this book, fresh pasta is used in the Lasagna al Rotolo appetizer. It allows us to make a pasta sheet, half the size of a sheet pan, for 3 points.

3. Wire Strainers

These are used EXTENSIVELY in my cupcake and cake recipes, as well as in a few of the dips and sauces. You don't need an expensive set. I got mine at the 99 cent store and they've lasted for years.

4. Immersion Blender

YOU NEED THIS IN YOUR LIFE! It's essentially a small blender at the end of a stick. It is used in all of the recipes for my "creamy" dressings. Throw all of the dressing ingredients into the cup, use the immersion blender... you have dressing in 15 seconds. You can also use a regular blender as well, but it takes up a lot more counterspace. You can purchase an inexpensive one at walmart for $20. You don't need the ultra expensive brands that have more gadgets than a swiss army knife.

5. Stock Pot with Steamer Inserts

This sounds like something that would be crazy expensive, but I've seen them at Ross and Marshalls for $20-$30. They are so worth it. I use the deep insert to steam cakes inside of a Corningware ceramic round dish, as well as using it to steam my Weight Watchers friendly Tamales and Seafood Boils (shrimp, corn, 0sp sausage). I use the shallower steamer insert to steam 2 ingredient dough for my Bahn Mi Sliders. It is also used to steam the Tamale balls for my Tamale appetizers. Want even more reason to get one? My steamed chocolate cake recipe requires one, as well as my Tamale Ball apetizers. Well... ok, you can get away with using a small steamer for the Tamales, but you'll have to make them in multiple batches. It'll take forever. There are ultra expensive ones, however, mine was a cheap one from Ross (if I remember correctly) and it's lasted foreeever.

FOUNDATIONS

Recipes for miscellaneous food items used as the building blocks for other meals

What are Foundation Recipes, and why do they need a section? To me, any recipe that is used as the base, or, dare I say..... Foundation for a dish, needs special mention. For example, there are a few recipes in here that contain my low point and calorie Rice Krispies breading. They are an important part of that dish, however I don't want to type out the ingredients and directions for that one single component, eeeevery time that a recipe calls for it. I'd much rather say "1 batch of my breading, pg 16."

These are the foundational components of a dish (like pasta for my lasagna rolls) that have a few ingredients and would require typing out a lot of steps, so... here they all are, tossed into one spot.

To answer an obvious question... Yes. With the exception of the new breading recipe, as well as the new and improved Ground Meat Seasoning recipes, all of these recipes can be found in my old Cooking Guide, in that book's Foundation section. However, I have only included the ones that pertain to dishes found in this book. I'd rather include some of them here again, rather than have the following text in a recipe:

"... for this recipe, make a 1 cup batch of a recipe that's back in my other book ..."
- Sincerely,
Mr. That'd Suck.

Foundation Recipes

Low Point & Calorie Breading ... pg 12
Fat Free Cream Cheese Substitute ... pg 13
Masa Dough and Tortillas ...pg 14-15
Pasta: Fresh, Low Calorie, Low Point ... pg 16-19
Ricotta Gnocchi ... pg 18
Seasoning Mixes for Ground Meat ... pg 20-25

IMPORTANT NOTE:
All recipes in this book were developed over the course of 15 months. They have all been designed and optimized, by me, for use with the "Freestyle" program. Know that WW periodically adjusts the point values of certain ingredients within their database. As a result, there may be a 1 point difference between what my recipes were when they were developed, versus what their point values are "now". You are all encouraged to enter these recipes into your app, to double check the current accuracy of their listed points at this present date.

Guilt Free Breading

In my Low Point Cooking Guide, I have a recipe for breading using a mix of dried mashed potato flakes and breadcrumbs. I came up with that recipe roughly 18 months ago. I came up with this one about 1 month ago and now, I definitely prefer this one. @*andmatsmom*, actually got me thinking about this, when she meantioned using Rice Krispies for pie crust

Breading:
- 1-1/4 cup crispy rice cereal (like rice krispies). Place it in a ziplock bag and crush it. You'll end up with around 2/3 cup.
- 1-1/2 tsp plain breadcrumbs
- 2 tsp panko breadcrumbs
- 1/4 tsp salt
- 1/4 tsp black pepper
- 1/4 tsp garlic powder
- 1/4 tsp onion powder
- 1/2 tsp italian seasoning

Egg Wash:
- 2 large eggs
- 1-1/2 tsp self rising flour
- 1-1/2 tsp cornstarch
- 1 tsp dijon mustard
- 1/2 tsp water

Servings Info.:
Yield: about 3/4 cup breading
Servings: n/a
Serving Size: n/a

Point Values:
4 total points

Note:
- This recipe is just meant to give you a recipe for low point breading. How you use it, how many servings you get out of it, as well as how many points it is in total, is completely dependent on what you make.
- This breading is used in a few of the appetizers later in this book.
- This versatile breading works great on anything. Zucchini, banana bites, chicken strips, clams...

Directions:

1. Prepare the egg wash. Whisk together the 2 eggs, set aside.
2. In a small dish, stir together the flour, cornstarch, dijon mustard and water into a smooth, thick paste. Whisk into the beaten eggs. It will slightly thicken the egg wash.
3. In a large ziplock bag, crush the rice krispie cereal until it has the same texture as plain breadcrumbs. Pour into a bowl.
4. Add the panko, regular breadcrumbs, salt, pepper, garlic powder, onion powder and italian seasoning (optional). Stir to mix.
5. Now it's pretty self explanatory Dip things in the egg, let the excess run off into the bowl. Then lightly coat with the breading.
6. Spray the breaded items with cooking spray, on a foil lined pan.
7. Once breaded, I typically use this to bake things at 425 degrees for around 15 minutes, or until browned.

Turning Greek Yogurt into a fat free Cream Cheese Substitute

DIY Fat Free "Cream Cheese" Substitute

First off I need to give credit where it's due and thank "*@mickeydoyle5*" from Connect for tipping me off to this ingredient hack that I had never heard of before. Once I heard about it I HAD to try it considering how much fat free cream cheese I go through with my cupcakes. THIS STUFF IS AWESOME!!! Make sure that you use a Greek Yogurt with a very mild "tang" to it, as a lot of Greek Yogurts have a very sharp taste that sucks the life & happiness out of desserts normally. I used Chobani Fat Free Greek Yogurt, though my ABSOLUTE FAVORITE is FAGE 0%, Fage is a little pricier but it has the least amount of yogurt tang of all the major brands. It is an almost perfect match to a slightly softened cream cheese with juuuust a tiny bit of bite to it. I personally think that it works as a wonderful sub for cream cheese in dips, spreads and in appetizers. Some folks have been using this in cheesecake recipes with success, which inspired me to start using it in place of cream cheese for my frostings.

Yields: 3.5 cups of Cream Cheese Substitute
Points: 0 Points

What You'll Need:

- 35oz FAGE (or other mild) Fat Free Greek Yogurt
- Cheese Cloth (or paper coffee filters)
- Strainer
- Large Bowl
- Plastic Wrap

Directions:

1. Attach or set a plastic or metal strainer onto a large bowl or pot in such a way that the strainer will not come in contact with any liquid that drips to the bottom.
2. Line the bowl of the strainer with 6-8 layers of cheesecloth or paper coffee liners (much cheaper).
3. Pour all of the Greek Yogurt onto the cheesecloth.
4. Cover it all with plastic wrap and set in the refrigerator for at least 24 hours (mine was fine at 24).
5. Store in an air tight container for up to 1 week and use in place of regular cream cheese.

Note:

- If you are unable to get cheese cloth you can line your strainer with a few layers of paper coffee filters.

0 point creamy awesomeness

Foundation Recipes • Page 13

Masa & Tortillas
The Latin American Dough For Tortillas, Tamales, Sopes, & more

Latin American cuisine would be nowhere without Masa, a dough made from very finely ground corn, which is used to make Tortillas, Tamales, Gorditas, Sopes... it is everything in Latin cooking. Think of it like the all purpose flour that you're used to using for biscuits, rolls, pizza dough, and other common baked goods. The flour required to make Masa is in most all grocery stores, typically found in either the Latin/Ethnic section or by where the Cornmeal is sold, sometimes labeled as "Maseca, Instant Tamale Mix." Note, this is NOT a traditional recipe, this is my version. I like my tortillas a little softer, so I add yogurt in place of lard. This makes the masa softer and also helps the texture should you choose to make tamales by adding the additional baking powder.

Ingredients:

- 2 cups Masa Harina, Maseca, or other brand Instant Corn Masa (corn flour NOT cornmeal!!)
- 1-1/4 cup Water
- 1/2 cup Fat Free Plain or Greek Yogurt
- 1/2 tsp salt
- Additional water if needed for mixing
  *** *(add 2tsp baking powder if being used to make Tamales)*

SERVING SIZE & POINTS:

- Varies. The servings and points for tortillas made in this manner are completely dependent upon how many you make from your dough. It is portioned exactly the same as you would 2 ingredient dough.

Directions:

1. In a large mixing bowl, combine the corn flour, 1-1/4 cups water, yogurt, and salt. Mix thoroughly until you form a semi-firm dough ball. If dough appears dry while mixing, add additional water as needed.

2. Remove dough to a cutting board, and cut into 2 equal sized 1 cup dough balls. Then portion each 1 cup dough ball in to 1/4's and then into 1/8's sized portions.

3. Roll each one of the 16 small dough sections into a circular ball. Then, on a flat surface, use your palm and fingers to press the dough balls into tortilla sized rounds.

4. For perfectly uniform tortillas, you can use a traditional tortilla press to form them. They are fairly inexpensive and can be purchased at most ethnic grocery stores, walmarts, or online, for around $10-15. Get a metal one.

5. To cook the tortillas, heat a skillet, griddle, or large pan on medium-high heat. Cook each tortilla for around 45 seconds on each side.

6. Keep tortillas warm by placing them in a covered container, or place them on a plate covered with a dish cloth. Tortillas are best served warm... unlike revenge.

A FEW DIFFERENT USES:
A) Sopes - Traditionally, the base is made from a circle of fried masa with sides pinched up to resemble a shallow cup. However for WW purposes you should spray it with cooking spray and then bake it. This can then be topped with any number of toppings. Bake the shells at 350 degrees for 10-15 minutes.
B) Tamales - If you are a WW member, you can view a video in Connect where I show how to make 3 point Tamales. Searching for #dhallaktamales and scrolling down to my DIY Tamale video.
C) Arepas - Arepas are awesome. For best results use a 3 point 1/4 cup section of the Masa dough, form it into a 1/2" thick tortilla round. For the non-fried WW version, cook it on a hot griddle or pan for 45 seconds on each side, and then remove it from the heat and slice it ALMOST completely in half down its length like a big pocket. Stuff it with fillings of your choice, then return it to heat.
D) If you need me to explain what a Taco is... put down this book. Put it down. No really, put it down. No food for you.

COOKING TIP:
- You can easily HALF this recipe if you don't want to make a big batch.
- If you plan to make Tamales OR Arepas, make sure to add 1 tsp of baking powder to each cup of flour that you use to help them fluff up a little bit.
- If you would like to NOT use the yogurt in this recipe due to dairy allergies, you can replace it with an equal amount of silken tofu.
- If you would like an even MORE chewie tortilla, you can substitute 1/4 cup of the corn flour with 1/4 cup of all purpose flour. I personally love the texture that way... but I'm a full-on Gringo.
- If you buy a tortilla press, I would recommend a metal one. They are a few dollars more, but they are more durable. I've broken 2 plastic ones from the hinges breaking with too much pressure.
- Instead of a tortilla press you can put one of the balls of masa between 2 layers of plastic wrap and press down with a pot.
- For more savory tortillas add 1/2 tsp garlic and onion powder to the flour.

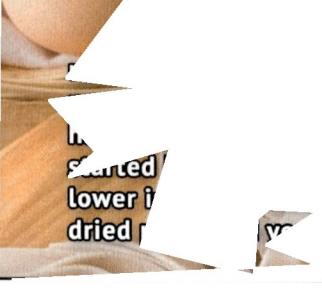

Ingredients:

- 2 cups of all purpose flour (or your flour of choice)
- 3 large eggs
- 1/2 tsp salt (optional)
- 2 Tbsp water
- 5 sprays, olive oil cooking spray
- additional water for mixing, as needed, 1 tsp at a time
  ** *additional 1-1/2 tsp flour, plus cooking spray for dusting*

Directions:

1. In a large mixing bowl or stand mixer, combine the flour, eggs, salt, olive oil cooking spray and 2 Tbsp of water to form a dough ball. The mixture will be dry, so add water as needed to help the dough come together. We aren't adding all of the water all at once because we want to cut down on how much flour we have to use for dusting later on. Wet dough = bad.

2. Remove dough to a cutting board, and cut into 2 equal sized 1 cup dough balls. I typically wrap and keep 1 of them in the freezer so that I can thaw it out and have ready-made pasta dough at a later time. For this recipe, we will assume that you are doing the same.

3. Take 1 of your 1 cup pasta dough balls, and cut it into (4) 1/4 cup portions, just like when you section 2 ingredient dough. Next, roll each one of the 1/4 cup sections into 4 small dough balls.

4. The dough balls vary in points. The first 1/4 cup balls is 3 points, the 2nd ball is 7, the 3rd is 10 and the 4th ball is 13. If you want slightly more pasta, roll the 1 cup ball into a log, then cut it into 3 equal 1/3 cup servings, rather than (4) 1/4 cup servings. Adjust your points accordingly.

5. Use your hand and a rolling pin to flatten one of the 1/4 cup pasta balls into a roughly rectangular flat shape. **(Read Notes for instructions for dusting the dough)****

6. You are trying to shape your flattened dough balls to fit length-wise across most of the pasta makers guide-track.

7. With the pasta-width adjustment at its widest setting, run the pasta through the sheet rollers 3-4 times, then adjust the knob on the machine to make the rollers 1 step closer together.

8. After every 3-4 passes through the rollers, continue to make the pasta sheet thinner and thinner, stopping after the 2nd from the thinnest setting.

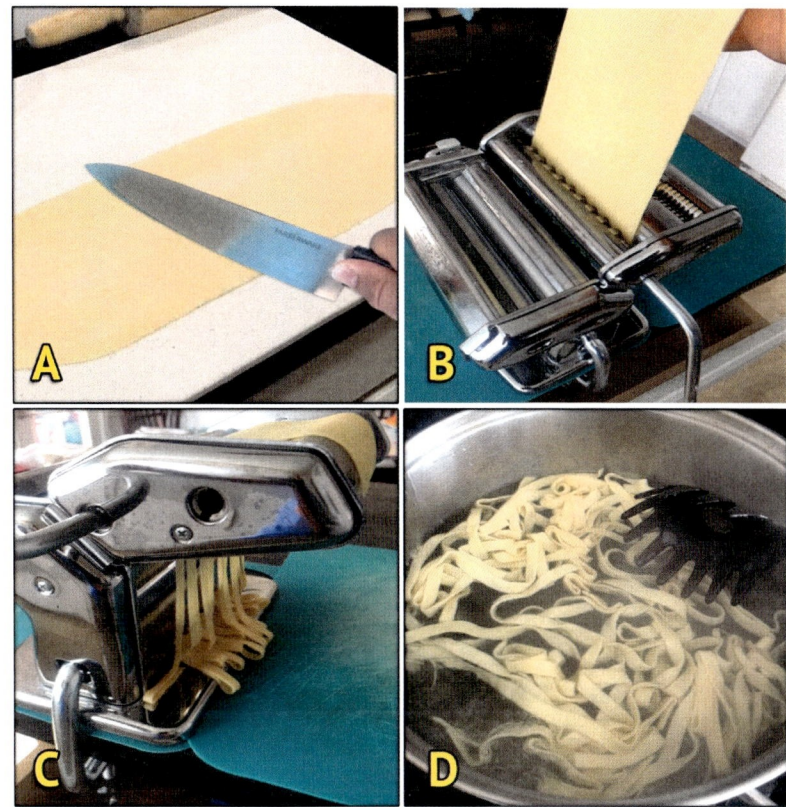

9. Yeah... I know this machine looks different. These 4 pics were taken today, 7 months later, with a new pasta maker 🧑‍🍳 **(A)** Use a knife to cut your pasta sheet in half, then use a few taps of the remaining flour in your wire strainer, to lightly dust the pasta sheet on both sides. **(B)** Move hand crank to the hole for the linguini cutter. Hold one of the pasta sheet halves over the unit, positioning the bottom of the sheet against the cutting blades. **(C)** Turn the hand crank, while lowering the pasta sheet into the blades. **(D)** As soon as the noodles are cut, drop them into a pot of boiling water. Use a utensil to stir and separate them. Boil for 2 minutes then remove from water and strain. Repeat until all of the pasta is rolled out, cut into noodles and boiled. Use immediately by stirring them into a sauce. If you need to save them for later, rinse the noodles off with cool water and store in a ziplock bag in the fridge. Reheat by putting them back into boiling water for a few seconds.

COOKING TIP:
- **DUSTING:** Traditionally, chefs don't "dust" dough with flour, they freakin DUMP fist fulls of flour onto it. For this recipe, take 1-1/2 tsp of flour and put it into a fine mesh wire strainer. When you need to dust your dough with flour, lightly tap the strainer over the dough instead. Also, you can lightly spritz the dough with cooking spray, as seen in my Youtube video for making low point pasta dough and noodles.
- If you are making lasagna I would highly recommend boiling the pasta sheets first then rinsing them off. Boiling them will make them get MUCH bigger, plus it will give them a slightly firmer texture.
- If you do not have a stand mixer to mix your dough you can either mix it by hand in a mixing bowl, or you can actually mix the dough VERY quickly in a food processor. Check out my video in **Youtube** channel, *"The Guilt Free Gourmet"* to find the food processor pasta dough video.
- If you are allergic to gluten, Bob's Red Mill has a great certified Gluten Free, Celiac-friendly, All Purpose Flour, available at most major markets.

Ricotta Gnocchi

Making fresh Ricotta Gnocchi with...

As much as I enjoy making pasta from scratch, most folks in WW don't. Let's face it... it's intimidating. I needed to figure out a way to show people how easy it could be to make their own delicious pasta, without needing any special equipment or pasta machines. Well, now all people have to do is make dough, roll it into ropes, cut it into nuggets and boil. Done.

The KEY to these dumplings is that you want to cut them small. They are not meant to be the bulk of a dish. Fortify them with lots of 0 point veggies, meats, and a low point sauce. You want to stretch the 1/4 cup servings as far as you can. They are the star of a dish, not the bulk of it.

Point Value:

(1) 1/4 cup section = 3 points (2) 1/4 cup section = 7 points
(3) 1/4 cup section = 10 points (4) 1/4 cup section = 14 points

Yields: (2) 1 cup Dough Balls, (16) 1/4 cup servings. Each 1/4 cup serving yields around 70 small dumplings per 1/4 cup

Ingredients:

- 2 cups All Purpose Flour *(or your preferred flour)*
- 1 tsp baking powder
- 2 large eggs
- 1/2 cup Fat Free Ricotta Cheese
- 1/2 tsp salt
- olive oil cooking spray
- additional water to mix (around 1/4 cup)

Directions:

1. In a large mixing bowl, combine the flour, baking powder, eggs, ricotta and salt to form a dough ball. Add extra water as necessary to just help the ball come together. The dough should be the texture of semi firm play dough. Not too firm, but still soft.

2. Cut the 2 cup dough ball into 2 equal sized 1 cup dough balls. Wrap one in plastic wrap and store in the freezer for later use if you only want to make a 1 cup batch. Otherwise prepare both sections.

3. Cut the 1 cup dough ball section into (4) 1/4 cup, then cut those in half into small 1/8 cup sections.

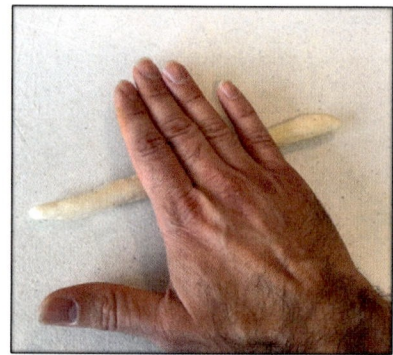

4. Roll each 1/8 section into long ropes, about as thick as your pinky finger. Lightly spray with cooking spray to help prevent sticking.

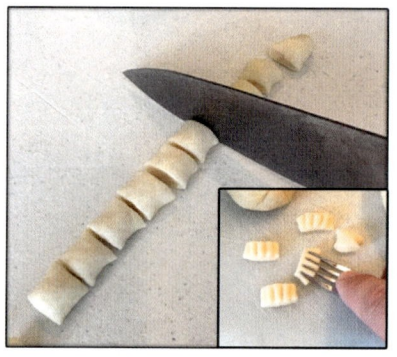

5. Cut each strand into small gnocchi. You should be able to get around 60-70 small gnocchi per 1/4 cup section. Then, lightly press down on each dumpling with a small fork, to give them a gnocchi "look" and make them slightly larger.

6. Drop dumplings into boiling water and cook for 2-3 minutes. Toss with your sauce immediately, or rinse with cold water and store in a ziplock bag in the fridge for later.

Pictured is 3 points of cooked, store bought lasagna noodles, next to 3 points of cooked fresh pasta, made from a single 1/4 cup dough section. The fresh pasta sheet is approx. only 10 more calories, while being 3-4x the size.

This image shows the difference between 13 points of cooked of fresh linguini, next to 13 points of store bought spaghetti

HELPFUL TIPS:

- *No Pasta Maker? No Problem:*
  Though it's ideal to try and make pasta with a pasta maker, you CAN make it without one. Sure, the finished pasta isn't uniform, but you'll definitely get your fit-points in while making it. Use a rolling pin to roll out the 1/4 cup sections of dough to be as wide/long/thin as you can. It won't be as great as with a machine, but it's doable. Dust your flat-ish dough with a little flour, using the wire strainer trick, then gently roll it into a long pinwheel. Use a sharp knife to cut thin slices into the rolled up dough. Once opened up, they will be long noodles.

- *Minimize Points from Dusting:*
  When making your dough, try to not add too much liquid at once. Your goal is to have the dough just come together (for the regular pasta dough, not the gnocchi). Too wet, and you'll have to add more flour, which will up the points. As mentioned earlier, place 1-1/2 tsp of flour into a fine mesh wire strainer. If you HAVE to dust your dough, gently tap the strainer while holding it over your dough, so that it gets a very light dusting. That 1-1/2 tsp will last a long time this way. If the dough is a little too dry, spritz it with a light mist of olive oil cooking spray. Unlike water, it will add moisture while also helping it to avoid sticking.

- *Freezing Dough:*
  I mention freezing extra 1 cup balls of dough. I'm usually asked how I freeze it and how long it lasts in the freezer. I wrap it in plastic wrap, then put that in a ziplock bag. I've thawed dough out 6 months later and used it. Haven't died yet. Wooot!

Asian

Forget "everybody was Kung Fu fighting", as far as I'm concerned, everybody should be making this mix. I came up with this mix, while trying to make my low point Bahn Mi chicken sliders. Though I used ground chicken breast for this recipe, you can definitely use extra lean ground turkey.

Serving Info:
YIELDS: 4 cups
Servings: 8
Serving Size: 1/2 cup
Points: 1 serving = 0 points
      2-5 servings = 1 point

Ingredients:
- 1lb Ground Chicken Breast (or xtra lean ground turkey)
- 1 Tbsp Asian "fish sauce"
  It's Pretty much, bottled anchovy water. YUM!
- 1-1/2 tsp ground black pepper
- 1 tsp ground ginger
- 3-4 medium garlic cloves, minced
- 1-1/2 tsp sesame oil
- 1 Tbsp soy sauce, reduced sodium
- 1/4 tsp baking soda dissolved in 1 tsp water **(TRUST ME!!)**
- 1 tsp lime juice
- 1 Tbsp fat free Greek yogurt
- 1/4 cup green onion, thinly chopped (not the white part)
- 1 Tbsp chicken flavored bouillon (granules)

Directions:
- Combine all ingredients in a mixing bowl, until well combined. Allow to sit for 30 minutes, covered.
- Cook as desired.

Bratwurst

Guten Morgen, friends! I originally came up with this seasoning blend for my Bratwurst sliders. It took multiple attempts to finally get the seasoning right. Yes, of course the texture of ground turkey isn't the same as ground pork, but... it tastes great, and cuts hundreds of calories.

Serving Info:
YIELDS: 4 cups
Servings: 8
Serving Size: 1/2 cup
Points: 0 points, total.

Ingredients:
- 1 pound extra lean ground turkey
- 2 Tbsp plain fat free Greek yogurt
- 1 Tbsp beef flavored granules
  (in the soup aisle, or in the mexican food aisle, like the "Knorr" brand)
- 1/2 tsp ground cumin
- 1 tsp onion powder
- 1 tsp garlic powder
- 1/2 tsp smoked paprika
- 3/4 tsp dried mustard
- 1/2 tsp dried sage (might be in the spices as rubbed sage)
- 1/2 tsp dried marjoram
- 1/2 tsp black pepper
- 1/4 tsp baking soda dissolved in 1 tsp water **(TRUST ME!!)**
- 3/4 tsp nutmeg
- 1/2 tsp salt
- 3/4 tsp caraway seed
- 1 tsp worcestershire sauce
- 1/2 cup diced onion (**OPTIONAL**, for bulk, if desired)

Directions:
- Combine all ingredients in a mixing bowl, until well combined. Allow to sit for 30 minutes, covered.
- Cook as desired.

Breakfast Sausage

Low Point, Low Calorie Breakfast Sausage

Chorizo

Low calorie, virtually fat free, delicious Chorizo

There are a lot of different low point breakfast sausage recipes out there, that call for ground turkey.... this is mine. Mine's a little more on the maple-side of things, because I like that kind of sausage. In this recipe, the sugar free pancake syrup is completely optional. You can replace it with some maple extract, from the baking aisle, if you can't have artificial sweeteners. Also, I HIGHLY recommend using the cayenne pepper. Even if you only use a tiny little 1/8 tsp of it, it makes a huge difference.

Serving Info:
YIELDS: 4 cups
Servings: 8
Serving Size: 1/2 cup
Points: 0 points, total.

Ingredients:
- 1 lb extra lean ground turkey
- 1/2 tsp salt
- 1/2 tsp fresh ground pepper
- 1 tsp dried sage
- 1 tsp dried thyme
- 1 tsp fennel seed (ground fennel seed is best)
- 1 tsp onion powder
- 1 tsp dried marjoram
- 2 tsp brown sugar
- 1 tsp beef flavored granules (like Knorr brand)
- 1/4 tsp baking soda dissolved in 1 tsp water **(TRUST ME!!)**
- 1/2 tsp smoked paprika
- 3 Tbsp plain fat free Greek yogurt
- 1 Tbsp sugar free pancake syrup
- 1/8-1/4 tsp cayenne pepper to taste
- 1/4 tsp liquid smoke, hickory (OPTIONAL)

Directions:
- Combine all ingredients in a mixing bowl, until well combined. Allow to sit for 30 minutes, covered.
- Cook as desired.

Traditional Chorizo is a heavily seasoned, extremely fatty and greasy mixture of ground pork that's loaded with "Pimenton", a type of smoked paprika. If you go to a mexican restaurant and order Chorizo, you'll usually need a good pair of wading pants to get through all of the grease on your plate. My version is really good, has a lot of the traditional flavor, but cuts out 99% of the fat, while still retaining moisture. Mine is ultra low in points, so feel free to add more smoked paprika if you want, but adjust your points accordingly, as always.

Serving Info:
YIELDS: 4 cups
Servings: 8
Serving Size: 1/2 cup
Points: 1 serving for 0 points
      2-5 servings for = 1 point

Ingredients:
- 1 lb extra lean ground turkey
- 1 Tbsp plain fat free Greek yogurt
- 3 tsp minced garlic (3 med. cloves)
- 1 Tbsp chili powder
- 2 tsp paprika
- 1/2 tsp smoked paprika
- 3/4 tsp salt
- 1/2 tsp fresh ground pepper
- 1 tsp dried oregano
- 1/4 or 1/2 tsp cayenne pepper or chipotle powder *(to taste)*
- 1/2 tsp ground cumin
- 1/2 tsp ground coriander
- 1/4 tsp ground cinnamon
- 1/4 tsp baking soda dissolved in 1 tsp water **(TRUST ME!!)**
- 1 Tbsp beef flavored granules (like Knorr brand)
- 2 Tbsp apple cider vinegar

Directions:
- Combine all ingredients in a mixing bowl, until well combined. Allow to sit for 30 minutes, covered.
- Cook as desired.

Cuban

Italian Sausage

This is tied with Kafta for the most flavorful of all of these mixes. It tastes so insanely good. It has strong notes of typical latin flavors, like cumin and oregano... but then you get slapped with little pops of olive, lime and even the exotic hint of cinnamon. It sounds so weird, but it tastes SO GOOD!

Serving Info:
YIELDS: 4 cups
Servings: 8
Serving Size: 1/2 cup
Points: 1-3 servings = 0 points
         4-8 servings = 1 point

Ingredients:
- 1lb extra lean ground turkey
- 3 tsp beef flavored granules (bouillon)
- 1/2 tsp onion powder
- 1/2 tsp garlic powder
- 1-1/2 tsp worcestershire sauce
- 1-1/2 tsp ground cumin
- 1/2 tsp dried oregano
- 1/4 tsp baking soda dissolved in 1 tsp water **(TRUST ME!!)**
- 1/2 tsp salt
- 1/4 tsp pepper
- 6 green olives, stuffed with pimientos, chopped (don't get the HUGE olives, you want 6 for 1 point)
- 1 small red bell pepper, finely diced (around 1/2 cup)
- 1 small green bell pepper, finely diced (around 1/2 cup)
- 2 medium garlic cloves, minced
- 1/4 tsp ground cinnamon
- 1 Tbsp lime juice
- 1/4 cup fresh chopped cilantro

Directions:
- Mix everything together in a large mixing bowl, until well combined. Allow to sit for 30 minutes, covered. Cook until browned.

When I was trying to lose my weight, when I dove into WW, one thing that I REALLY wanted was Italian sausage, but let's face it... I'm the Ebenezer Scrooge of Points, so I couldn't make myself use my points on pork sausage. I tried tons of different versions of this recipe, before finally coming up with this baby.

Serving Info:
YIELDS: 4 cups
Servings: 8
Serving Size: 1/2 cup
Points: 0, period.

Ingredients:
- 1 lb extra lean ground turkey
- 1 tsp ground fennel seed *(you can use whole seed, but I prefer ground)*
- 1 tsp garlic powder
- 1 tsp onion powder
- 3 Tbsp plain fat free Greek yogurt
- 1 tsp dried italian seasoning
- 1/2 tsp dried basil
- 1 Tbsp dried parsley
- 1/4 tsp baking soda dissolved in 1 tsp water **(TRUST ME!!)**
- 1/4 tsp salt
- 1/4 tsp fresh ground pepper
- 3/4 tsp paprika
- 2 Tbsp red wine vinegar
- 1 Tbsp beef or chicken granules (bouillon)
- red pepper flakes to taste (OPTIONAL)

Directions:
- Combine all ingredients in a mixing bowl, until well combined. Allow to sit for 30 minutes, covered.
- Cook as desired.

Jerk Seasoning

No, you don't need to be a meanie-head to make this. "Jerk" is a traditional Jamaican seasoning, normally used on chicken. It typically calls for chopped scotch bonnet peppers, which are hotter than satan's kidney stones. I decided to tone it down a little, by using Habanero peppers, which are easier to find in grocery stores. This mix has it all. Exotic spices, a good deal of heat, a little sweet, and a little acidity from lime juice and zest.

Serving Info:
YIELDS: 4 cups
Servings: 8
Serving Size: 1/2 cup
Points: 1-3 servings = 0 points
4-8 servings = 1 point

Ingredients:
- 1lb extra lean ground turkey
- 1 medium garlic clove, finely chopped
- 1-1/2 tsp fresh ginger, finely chopped
- 3 Tbsp green onion, thinly sliced
- 2 medium cloves garlic, minced
- 2 tsp lime juice
- 1 tsp lime zest, minced
- 2 tsp soy sauce, reduced sodium
- 1 Tbsp fat free plain Greek yogurt
- 1/4 tsp baking soda dissolved in 1 tsp water **(TRUST ME!!)**
- 1 tsp fresh thyme, finely chopped
- 2 tsp brown sugar
- 1/2 tsp ground allspice
- 1/4 tsp ground cinnamon
- 1/4 tsp black pepper
- 1/4 tsp nutmeg
- 1/2 tsp cayenne pepper
- 2 habanero peppers, deseeded, finely diced **(use gloves!!)**
- 2 tsp chicken flavored bouillon

Directions:
- Combine all ingredients in a mixing bowl, until well combined. Allow to rest for a minimum of 30 minutes.
- Cook as desired.

Lebanese Kafta

Kafta is Lebanese a ground meat mixture, usually ground beef or lamb, mixed with a ton of fresh parsley, onion, and seasonings. This is a hybrid of my father's traditional recipe and my own "savory ground turkey". It has a deep, savory, beefy flavor and you won't believe that this is ground turkey.

Serving Info:
YIELDS: 4 cups
Servings: 8
Serving Size: 1/2 cup
Points: 0 points, total.

Ingredients:
- 1lb extra lean ground turkey
- 1 Tbsp beef flavored bouillon
- 1 tsp onion powder
- 1 tsp garlic powder
- 1/2 tsp smoked paprika
- 1/2 tsp ground cumin
- 2 tsp worcestershire sauce
- 1 Tbsp fat free plain Greek yogurt
- 1/4 tsp salt
- 1/4 tsp black pepper
- 3/4 tsp ground allspice
- 3/4 tsp ground cinnamon
- 1/4 tsp baking soda dissolved in 1 tsp water **(TRUST ME!!)**
- 1/2 cup fresh parsley, finely chopped, loosely packed
- 3/4 cup onion, finely diced/chopped
- 3-4 garlic medium cloves garlic, minced

Directions:
- Combine all ingredients in a mixing bowl, until well combined. Allow to rest for a minimum of 30 minutes.
- Cook as desired.

Linguica

A smoky and spicy Portuguese sausage mix

Linguica is a super fatty, smoked and very spicy Portuguese sausage. My version is a low fat, calorie and point seasoning blend that gets its smokiness from smoked paprika and a touch of liquid smoke. The heat comes from black pepper and red pepper flakes, which you can adjust to your own tastes. Still... this is SUPPOSED to be a bit spicy.

Serving Info:
YIELDS: 4 cups
Servings: 8
Serving Size: 1/2 cup
Points: 0 points, total.

Ingredients:
- 1lb extra lean ground turkey
- 1 Tbsp chicken (or beef) flavored granules (bouillon)
- 1-3/4 tsp salt
- 3/4 tsp black pepper
- 1/8 to 1/2 tsp red pepper flakes **(TO TASTE)**
- 1/4 tsp baking soda dissolved in 1 tsp water **(TRUST ME!!)**
- 1 tsp liquid smoke (I used Hickory flavored)
- 2 tsp smoked paprika
- 1 tsp paprika
- 3/4 tsp dried oregano
- 1 Tbsp red wine vinegar
- 1 tsp 0 point sugar substitute of choice (swerve, splenda, stevia, monkfruit, etc)

Directions:
- Combine all ingredients in a mixing bowl, until well combined. Allow to rest for a minimum of 30 minutes.
- Cook as desired.

Savory Mix

A versatile mix that gives a deep, beefy flavor

I use this recipe whenever I need a standard, beefy flavor for a dish. What's the one complaint that you hear about ground turkey from EVERYONE? "It tastes bland...It's dry... It has no flavor". Well, of course it doesn't, so OPEN YOUR SPICE CABINET AND FIX THAT! A lot of thought went into this mix. Think that ground turkey has no flavor? Add beef bouillon, smoked paprika, worcestershire and a touch of cumin. Now you have ground turkey that's saturated with beefy, smoky, earthy flavors.

Serving Info:
YIELDS: 4 cups
Servings: 8
Serving Size: 1/2 cup
Points: 0 points, total.

Ingredients:
- 1lb extra lean ground turkey
- 2 Tbsp plain fat free Greek yogurt
- 3 tsp beef flavored granules
- 1 tsp onion powder
- 1 tsp garlic powder
- 1/2 tsp smoked paprika
- 1/2 tsp ground cumin
- 1/4 tsp baking soda dissolved in 1 tsp water **(TRUST ME!!)**
- 1 tsp low sodium soy sauce
- 2 tsp worcestershire sauce
- 1/4 tsp black pepper
- 1/4 tsp salt

Directions:
- Combine all ingredients in a mixing bowl, until well combined. Allow to rest for a minimum of 30 minutes.
- Cook as desired.

Note:
- This recipe works great as a stand in for ground beef for most recipes, such as burgers, shepherd's pie, sloppy joes, meatloaf and much more.

Things You'll Need:

Chicken & Beef Flavored Granules

Add Instant Deep Flavor
Wish that ground turkey tasted more like beef or chicken? IT CAN! There are many different brands of bouillon at your local grocery store, but they are not all created equal. Some are lower or higher in points, sodium and calories than others. Most Walmarts carry the Knorr brand, which I use in anything that has ground turkey. While most brands will turn to 1 point at 2 or 3 teaspoons, Knorr stays at 0 points until you use 3-1/2 teaspoons. At the majority of supermarkets, you most likely won't find it in the soup aisle, which is where you'd THINK to find it. 99% of the time it'll be in the aisle with the Mexican or Latin foods, even at Walmart. Scan any brand of granulated bouillon that you find, to make sure you get a brand that stays at 0 points for 1 Tablespoon. If you can't find one, get what you can, but adjust the points of the recipes accordingly.

Greek Yogurt (or tofu for dietary restrictions)

Replace The Missing Fat
As stated earlier, one of the biggest excuses that people use for not using ground turkey is "it's dry and has no fat!"... (insert crying emoji). Yes, that's true, but we can do something about it. What does fat add to raw, ground meat? Why... white, creamy moisture, of course. What's one thing we ALL have in our fridges that's white, creamy, moist and 0 points? Greek Yogurt. Add 2 to 3 tablespoons of fat free Greek yogurt into raw, LEAN ground meat, and it'll go a long way to replace the fat and moisture that's missing.

Do you follow a dairy free, or Kosher diet and can't have Yogurt (dairy) mixed with raw meat (kosher)? There's an easy fix. Go to the store, to the refrigerated aisle, usually nearby where the wonton wrappers and vegan items are, and you'll find tofu. Buy the "soft" (also called silken) tofu and use it in place of the yogurt. You can also use silken tofu in place of Greek yogurt (in the batter) for ALL of my cupcake and cake recipes.

Meatballs

Make ANY of these mixes into meatballs
With a 1lb batch of the meat mixes, use a measuring spoon to scoop out 1 Tbsp rounds of meat. When rolled they make perfect snack sized meatballs. You can get around 30 out of 1 pound, or 15 2 Tbsp sized meatballs. I've had good luck baking them at 425 for 15 minutes.

Baking Soda

What'chu talkin 'bout, Willis??
I wish I could explain the science behind it, but this is a legit game changer. I was browsing an old French cooking site one night, and came upon a technique for making ground meat awesome. For every 1lb of ground meat, mix in 1/4 tsp of baking soda dissolved with 1 tsp of water, then allow the meat to rest for 30 minutes before cooking. It completely changes the texture of the meat. It retains a TON of it's own moisture. You know how when you normally cook ground turkey, it's swimming in a pool of it's own liquids? Who wants grey meat! Doing this locks in so much liquid, that the meat ends up more juicy AND it browns in the pan sooooo much better. It's a flippin' Vatican-worthy miracle imho. Ground turkey ends up having a texture closer to cooked ground pork, which makes these seasonings REALLY sing. Give it a try, you won't regret it. **NOTE: Though this works amazing with ground turkey, I would not recommend it with ground chicken. The baking soda makes chicken have a slightly tough exterior, though it gives ground turkey a great texture and mouth feel.**

Cuban Picadillo Turkey Meatballs

Dips & Spreads

Artichoke & Spinach ... pg 28
Black Bean ... pg 29
Cheddar Cheese, Beer & Bacon ... pg 30
Chik Fil A ... pg 31
Cocktail Sauce ... pg 32
Creamy Chimichurri ... pg 33
French Onion ... pg 34
Guacamole ... pg 35
Herbed "Cream Cheese" Spread ... pg 36
Hummus (regular and chocolate) ... pg 37
Ketchup ... pg 38
Roasted Red Pepper & Balsamic ... pg 39
Smoked Salmon ... pg 40
Sweet and Sour (regular and Thai sweet chili) ... pg 41
Tartar Sauce ... pg 42
Thai Peanut Dip ... pg 43

All of the Greek yogurt based Dips will "tighten up" a bit more, as they rest in the fridge. If they get too thick, simply stir in a little water to thin them out to your desired consistency.

Also: If you have allergies to dairy, you can substitute Silken Tofu in place of the Greek yogurt. The taste will be sliiiiiightly different, but it will still work.

Artichoke Spinach

Creamy and Savory Artichoke Spinach Dip & Spread

There are a million recipes out there for "low point" artichoke spinach dip, however, I want to be different. Where most people use low fat mayonnaise mixed with Greek... I had an idea for how to "hack" the mayo out of the recipe. I'm only using Greek yogurt... but I'm blending egg yolks and a little cornstarch into the Greek. I read about that in an old French cookbook I found. This adds 0 point fat to the Greek and the cornstarch helps bind the yogurt while it's baking. Like I always say, out-smart your food and think outside the box.

Ingredients:

- (2) 1lb bags frozen, chopped spinach
- (2) 14oz cans whole artichoke hearts, in water
- 1/2 cup diced onion
- 2 medium garlic cloves, crushed
- 2 cups plain fat free Greek yogurt
- 2 egg yolks
- 1-1/2 tsp cornstarch
- 1/2 cup reduced fat parmesan cheese topping (like the Kraft brand, used to sprinkle on pizzas)
- 1 tsp onion powder
- 1/2 tsp black pepper
- 1-1/4 tsp salt
- 1 tsp worcestershire sauce
- 1/4 cup water
- 3/4 cup reduced fat shredded mozzarella cheese

Serving Info.:

Yields: 7 cups
Servings: 28
Serving Size: 1/4 cups

Freestyle Points:

1 serving = 0 points
2-3 servings = 1 point
4-6 servings = 2 points
7-8 servings = 3 points

Directions:

1. Place a few layers of paper towels onto a large pan. Empty the frozen spinach bags onto the pan and allow to thaw. Use additional paper towels to soak off as much water as you can. Drain the water from the Artichokes, then place ALL of the ingredients into a food processor. Process the mixture until it all blends together.
2. Preheat your oven to 375 degrees. Spray 2 quart casserole dish with cooking spray, then spoon all of the spinach mixture into the casserole. Smooth the top. Cover and bake for 40 minutes at 375 degrees. Remove the lid, then bake for an additional 15 minutes. Done.

NOTES:

- This recipe makes a LARGE amount of dip, perfect for a good sized gathering. As you can tell by looking at the ingredient measurements, you can EASILY halve the recipe without needing a PHD in Mathematics. However, if you halve the recipe, reduce the baking time.
- If you feel that your finished dip is too thick for your personal taste, once it's finished baking, simply stir in some hot water to thin it to your desired consistency.
- Don't have a food processor? Use a knife to chop the bajeezus out of it all, then mix it together.

Black Bean Puree

This is so INSANELY great that you'll lap it up like a thirsty dog

Comparing this to a can of blended black beans is like comparing a Formula One race car to a 76 Ford Pinto. Years ago, my wife surprised me by having a cooking show come to our house. The Chef helped my wife prepare a Latin dinner to surprise me when I got home. The most memorable part of that meal for me (of the food), was the black bean puree. I had NEVER had anything like it before and asked him to show me how to make it. This is my WW-erized version of his dish, which was served in place of regular beans. I'm presenting it here as a dip.

Ingredients:

- 1/2 cup diced onion
- 1/2 cup diced poblano pepper, seeds removed
- 1/2 cup diced red bell pepper
- 1 medium garlic clove
- 1/2 cup chopped cilantro, packed
- 45oz canned black beans, rinsed and drained.
  (1 30oz can and 1 15oz can, oooooor 3 15oz cans lol)
- 1-1/2 tsp ground cumin
- 1/2 tsp salt
- 1/4 tsp black pepper
- 1 Tbsp red wine vinegar
- 1/2 cup chicken broth
- 1/2 tsp garlic powder

Serving Info.:

Yields: 3-1/2 cups
Servings: 14
Serving Size: 1/4 cups

Points Value:

0 points, period

Directions:

1. Use a colander to rinse and drain the black beans. Rinse off that disgusting black goop from inside the cans, till the water runs clean. Let the beans drain, then set aside.
2. In a medium sized pot, use cooking spray to cook the onion, garlic, and both the poblano and red peppers, over medium heat. Add the salt and pepper, cook until softened.
3. Add the vinegar, chicken broth, garlic powder, salt, pepper and cumin. Stir to combine. Allow the mixture to come to a simmer, then add the black beans and cilantro. Allow to cook down for 5 minutes, stirring occasionally.
4. Carefully pour or scoop the hot bean mixture into a food processor, then process on high speed until smooth.
5. Taste, then season with additional salt & cumin, if needed. Garnish with cilantro, diced tomatoes and a small amount of fat free feta cheese, enough to stay 0 points.

Notes:

- You can use a green bell pepper instead of a Poblano. A poblano is pretty much the same as a regular bell pepper, but a darker green, and with a slight smokiness when cooked. It's not spicy.
- If you don't have a food processor, use an immersion blender in the pot, though.
- I call this a dip, but you can use it in place of refried beans as a side dish. Trust me... it's good.

Cheddar Cheese & Beer

A Creamy, Cheesy Dip, with Beer and Crumbled Bacon

My buddy, **@ncbluehog** on Connect, was the inspiration for this dip. He's an uber cool, motorcycle ridin' macho man cook. He helped give me feedback with my Bratwurst recipe, which got me thinking that most macho dudes would LOVE to have a low point and calorie dip like this for football parties, poker parties… or in place of a glass of water, in Wisconsin.

Ingredients:

- 3/4 cup Campbell's Healthy Request, Condensed Cheddar Cheese Soup. (just the goop)
- 1/2 cup light beer
- 3 slices fat free sharp cheddar cheese singles
- 1/4 cup water
- 1/4 tsp ground mustard
- 1/2 tsp salt
- 2-1/2 tsp cornstarch, dissolved in a little water
- 1/2 cup fat free plain Greek yogurt
- 1 slice turkey bacon, cooked, finely chopped
- Pinch of cayenne pepper or dash of hot sauce

Serving Info.:

Yields: 2 cups
Serving Size: 1/4 cup
Servings: 8

Point Values:

1 Serving = 1 point
2 servings = 2 points
3 servings = 3 points

Directions:

1. Heat the cheddar cheese soup, beer, cheese slices, water, ground mustard and salt in a small pot over medium heat. Stir till all of the ingredients melt together and become smooth.
2. Bring to a low boil, then stir in the dissolved cornstarch. The sauce will immediately begin to thicken. Cook for 2-3 minutes, stirring constantly. It should be very thick now. Remove the sauce from heat and pour into a bowl. Cover with plastic wrap and let cool for 30-40 minutes.
3. Whisk in the Greek yogurt until smooth. Season with additional salt if desired. I also highly recommend adding a pinch of cayenne pepper, or a dash of hot sauce.
4. Cook bacon until it's suuuuper crispy. Finely dice/crush it into small bits, then sprinkle on top of the dip. Garnish with thinly sliced green onion or chives.

Note:

- The sauce/dip continues to thicken as it cools.
- If you cannot find fat free cheese singles, you can use any low point American or Cheddar singles, such as Velveeta, but adjust your points accordingly.
- If you want even more cheese flavored punch added to it for no additional points, you can use a 0 point amount of Macaroni and Cheese powder, Molly McButter Cheese Flavored sprinkles (in the spice aisle at Walmart), or easier to find… go to the aisle where they sell popcorn. There are tons of flavored popcorn sprinkles, such as Nacho Cheese flavored. Scan the cheese flavored popcorn sprinkles, then use a 0 point amount in the dip.

Chick Fil A Copycat

A Delicious Mix of Honey Mustard, BBQ and Mayonnaise

Everybody in the Western Hemisphere, with a functioning brain stem, loves Chik Fil A. Or at least everyone loves their sweet, tangy and vinegary dipping sauce. Unfortunately, the real thing has 1 billion points and calories per serving... roughly. The cool thing is that their sauce is just a mix of bbq sauce, honey mustard, and mayo, so the trick was just cutting the calories, fat and sugar, to make a healthier and lighter version.

Ingredients:

- 1/2 cup tomato sauce (scan to ensure 0 points)
- 1/2 tsp worcestershire sauce
- 1/4 tsp garlic powder
- 1/4 tsp onion powder
- 3/4 tsp chili powder
- 1/4 tsp black pepper
- 1/2 tsp smoked paprika
- 2 Tbsp apple cider vinegar
- 1 Tbsp 0 point natural sweetener o' choice (stevia, monkfruit, truvia, swerve, etc)
- 1 Tbsp dijon mustard
- 5 Tbsp yellow mustard
- 5 Tbsp sugar free syrup (pancake syrup)
- 1 Tbsp honey
- 2 Tbsp lemon juice
- 1/2 tsp dried mustard
- 1/8 tsp ground turmeric
- 1 cup fat free Greek yogurt
- 1/4 cup low fat mayonnaise

Serving Info.:

Yields: 2-1/2 cups
Servings: 10
Serving Size: 1/4 cups

Points Value:

1-2 servings = 1 point
3 servings = 2 points
4 servings = 3 points

Directions:

1. First, we're making the BBQ sauce part of the sauce. In a medium pan, heat and stir together the tomato sauce, worcestershire, garlic, onion and chili powders, black pepper, paprika, vinegar and sweetener. Mix till well combined, then turn off the heat.
2. Now, the Honey Mustard part. Add the dijon, yellow mustard, dried mustard, syrup, honey, lemon juice and turmeric. Whisk till combined. Then, add the yogurt and mayonnaise. Whisk till smooth and combined. Serve immediately or refrigerate to let the flavors meld.

NOTES:

- If you want to use low point, store bought bbq sauce and honey mustard sauces, look up "copycat" recipes for the famous sauce, then just sub your low point condiments into the recipes.
- If you can't have dairy, you can substitute the yogurt for semi firm tofu mixed with water, to thin it to the same consistency as Greek. Check connect for my post in #dairyfreeyogurthack

Creamy Chimichurri

A Spicy Argentinian Dip with Cilantro and Parsley

Ingredients:

- 2 cups fresh parsley, chopped, packed
- 2 cups fresh cilantro, chopped, packed
- 3 Tbsp capers, drained
- 4 medium cloves garlic
- 3 Tbsp red wine vinegar
- 2 Tbsp lemon juice
- 1-1/2 tsp salt
- 1/4 to 1/2 tsp red pepper flakes, to taste
- 1/4 tsp black pepper
- 2 Tbsp + 1-1/2 tsp extra virgin olive oil
- 8 second spray, olive oil cooking spray
- 1-1/4 cups plain fat free Greek yogurt

Servings:
Yield: 2 cups
Servings: 8
Serving Size: 1/4 cup

Points:
1 serving = 1
2 servings = 3
3 servings = 4

Chimichurri is one of those sauces that once you have it, you'll never forget it. Think of it like an Italian Pesto. A Pesto that left its family and ran away to South America to join a violent street gang. Where Pesto is loaded with tons of fresh basil and parmesan, chimichurri is loaded with cilantro, parsley, lemon juice, vinegar and a good amount of heat from red pepper flakes. I'm making it a low point dip by stretching out the servings with the addition of Greek yogurt. This makes it have more volume, a creamier taste, drastically reduces the amount of oil in it, and helps curb some of the red pepper kick. Enjoy, Gringos!

Directions:

1. Place the chopped, packed, parsley, and cilantro, as well as the capers, garlic, red wine vinegar, lemon juice, salt, pepper, and red pepper flakes into a food processor. Spray the olive oil cooking spray into the ingredients.
2. Process the mixture on high, until broken down.
3. Add the Greek yogurt and olive oil, then process again.
4. Add more water to achieve your desired consistency, if the dip is too thick. If it's too thin, add a little more yogurt, then add more salt and pepper if needed.

NOTES:

- I'd recommend starting with 1/4 tsp of red pepper flakes, then adding more if you'd like more kick. I used 3/4 tsp in my batch and really liked it. However, it seems to have melted off the roof of my wife's mouth... so add more if needed.
- Chimichurri Sauce/Dip is AWESOME on grilled meats and vegetables. It enhances the flavor of most any savory dish that you put it on and adds a bright, citrusy, herby, tangy punch.
- Remember, this is Pesto's tough cousin who went to live abroad. Treat it accordingly. Avoid eye contact.

Cocktail Sauce

I'll preface this recipe by stating, as fact, that I have HATED cocktail sauce for most of my adult life. I've just never really liked the store bought, jarred goop. A while back, a friend mentioned that she'd like me to look into low point cocktail sauce. I blew it off, because I hate cocktail sauce and I'd have to taste my batch. A few days ago, I looked into it, because I wanted to try making ketchup, then saw that a lot of simple cocktail sauce recipes call for ketchup, so BOOM... 2 dips for 1. When I finally tasted this, I completely and utterly am in love now. It is amazing, absolutely awesome and I'd use it as sunscreen if it offered any SPF rating.

Ingredients:

- 2-1/4 cup batch of my Ketchup, recipe in this section.
- 3 Tbsp store bought "prepared" horseradish sauce (scan it, you want 3 Tbsp for 1 point)
- 1 tsp black pepper
- 3 Tbsp lemon juice
- 1/2 tsp hot sauce of choice, or more to taste

Serving Info.:

Yields: 2-1/2 cups
Servings: 10
Serving Size: 1/4 cup

Points Value:

1 serving = 0 points
2-4 servings = 1 point
5-8 servings = 2 points

Directions:

1. Add all of the ingredients into a mixing bowl. Whisk until combined.
2. Done.

Notes:

- You can add up to 1 more Tablespoon of the prepared horseradish before the points would need to be adjusted.
- Add more hot sauce if desired. Most all recipes call for Tabasco sauce, however, my wife's Latina, so we have Chalula in this house. lol
- You CAN use other brands of sugar free, low point Ketchups as a base for this cocktail sauce, however... I know I'm biased when I say this... the depth of flavor will be nowhere near what it would be using mine. *pats himself on the back* ...Just sayin.
- This dip/sauce is typically only really served with seafood, but I'm sure you can look online to find other applications for it.

French Onion Dip

Using the Flux Capacitor to bring a 50's classic into the 20th century.

This dip was a direct result of going to a get-together, potluck kinda thing yesterday. My wife made one of the onion dip packets from the store, along with regular sour cream. The amount of points and calories in that blew my freaking mind, soooo... here we are. This recipe calls for caramelizing diced sweet onions with beef broth and seasonings, then mixing them together with fat free Greek yogurt and just a touch of light mayonnaise for creaminess. You won't want to buy those high calorie, high point, store bought dried packets again.

Ingredients:

- 3 cups Vidalia onions, diced (1-1/2 large onions)
- 0 point butter flavored cooking spray
- 1 medium garlic clove, minced
- 1/2 cup beef broth, reduced sodium/fat
- 1 Tbsp white vinegar
- 1 tsp salt
- 1/4 tsp black pepper (use white pepper if'ya want)
- 2 tsp onion powder
- 1-1/2 cups plain fat free Greek yogurt
- 2 Tbsp light mayonnaise

Serving Info.:

Yields: 2 cups
Serving Size: 1/4 cup
Servings: 8

Point Values:

1 Serving = 0 points
2-3 servings = 1 point
4-6 servings = 2 points

Directions:

1. Cook the onions and garlic in a large pan over medium heat, covered, for 10 minutes. Coat with butter flavored cooking spray, but keep it at 0 points worth. Stir the onions occasionally, to ensure that they don't burn. You want them to be softened, like the 2nd picture.
2. Add the beef broth, vinegar, salt, pepper and onion powder. Lower the heat to medium-low and cook, uncovered, for 7-8 minutes. You want almost all of the liquid to evaporate.
3. Remove the caramelized onions from the heat and allow them to cool. Once cooled, add them to a bowl with the yogurt and mayo, then whisk to combine. Season with additional salt and pepper if required. Done.

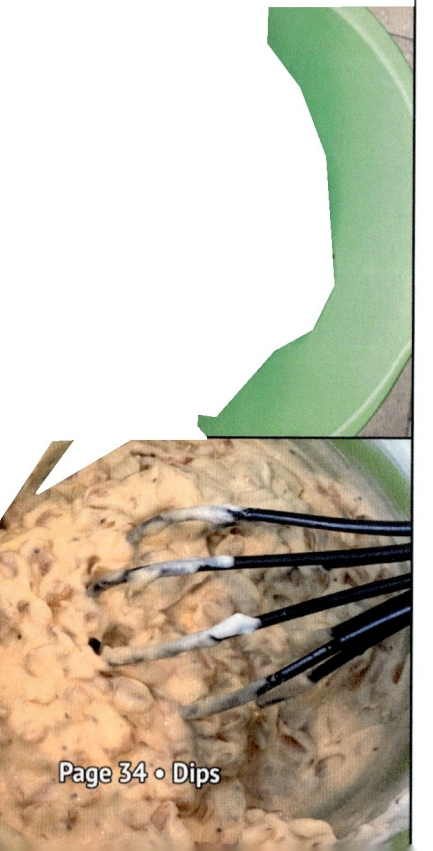

Note:

- Most recipes for french onion dip call for white pepper. I personally don't care if you see little black flecks of pepper in a dip or sauce, but that's because I like pepper. Feel free to buy white pepper if you want. I'm on a budget, so until they start carrying white pepper at the 99 cent store, black's good enough lol.
- If you'd like a smokier flavor to your dip, you can add 1/2 tsp of smoked paprika, it'll give an additional little reddish tint to your dip and add a slight smokiness.
- Have a beef with France and don't want to make this dip because of 'mmmmmURICA!? Well, just call it Freedom Onion dip. It'll go great with your Freedom Fries, apple pie and sweet tea.

¡ Holy Guacamole !
AWESOME FREAKIN' GUACAMOLE, Cut with Roasted Zucchini

A friend of mine mentioned to me that some Mexican restaurants actually cut their Guacamole with zucchini when avocado prices go through the roof.... which led me to start scouring the internet for recipes. Unable to really find anything, I decided to try and modify the highest rated Guacamole recipe from a popular television food network. By mixing an equal amount of avocado with roasted zucchini, we can stretch the heck out of the points and servings. It's actually "smack yo' abuelita" good.

Ingredients:

- 15oz zucchini (around 3 medium) rough chopped
- 1 tsp salt
- 3/4 tsp cumin
- 2-3 medium cloves garlic (to taste)
- 3/4 cup finely diced onion
- 3/4 cup roma tomatoes, seeds removed, diced
- 15oz avocado flesh (around 3 medium)
- 2 Tbsp lime juice
- 1/4 cup fresh cilantro, finely chopped

Serving Info.:

Yields: 5-1/2 cups
Serving Size: 1/4 cup
Servings: 22

Point Values:

1 Serving = 1 point
2 servings = 2 points
3 servings = 3 points

Directions:

1. Preheat your oven to 375 degrees and line a baking pan with foil. Lightly spray the pan with cooking spray, then set aside.
2. Quarter and slice the zucchini into 1/4 wedges, spray with cooking spray, then roast for 18 minutes at 375 degrees. Do not season the zucchini. Remove from oven and place into a food processor with the salt, cumin and garlic. Process until smooth, set aside.
3. Slice and remove the seeds from your tomato, then dice the tomato and onion. Set aside.
4. Scoop the flesh out of your avocado skins and place into a medium mixing bowl. Use a potato masher (or a large fork) to mash the avocado, while keeping them chunky.
5. Mix the tomatoes, onions, lime juice and cilantro into the avocado, till well combined.
6. Pour the zucchini puree into the avocado mash and mix. Cover with plastic wrap and store in the fridge for 1 hour, allowing the flavors to meld.
7. Remove from the fridge, taste, and add more salt, pepper, cumin, lime juice or cilantro, if needed.

Note:

- This recipe makes a good amount of Guacamole, feel free to halve the recipe if desired. Most of my dips are made in a quantity that would allow them to be used for a party.
- This Guacamole is slightly creamier than regular Guacamole, due to the puree. It thickens slightly as it sets in the fridge.

Herbed "Cream Cheese"

A Healthy Mix of Cheese, Strained Yogurt and Fresh Herbs

This EXTREMELY versatile mixture can be customized to use pretty much any cheese or herb mixture that you'd like. By straining greek yogurt overnight, we force liquid out of it, which makes the yogurt more dense, ultimately making it take on the texture of cream cheese. By mixing our "cream cheese" with herbs and a nominal amount of real cheese, we can make an awesome, creamy and delicious spread with a fraction of the fat and calories.

Ingredients:

- 34oz nonfat plain Greek yogurt (use Fage!)
- 1 medium garlic clove, chopped
- 1 tsp salt
- 3/4 cup fresh parsley, finely chopped
- 1/4 cup fresh chives, finely chopped
- 1/2 tsp lemon zest, minced
- 3 oz goat cheese (or 8 points of any other cheese)

Serving Info.:

Yields: 3-1/4 cups
Serving Size: 1/4 cup
Servings: 13

Point Values:

1-2 Servings = 1 point
3-4 servings = 2 points
5 servings = 3 points

Directions:

1. Strain greek yogurt (I HIGHLY recommend using FAGE brand for this) for a minimum of 12 hours, as directed in the "Cream Cheese Hack" recipe, Foundations section, pg 13. The longer you strain the mixture the better. At 20 hours, my yogurt had removed 3/4 cup of liquid.
2. Add the strained Greek yogurt, garlic, salt, parsley, chives, lemon zest and goat cheese to a food processor. Process until well combined. Garnish with additional fresh chives or other herbs.
3. If you'd like to serve it as shown in the bottom left of the page... line a ramekin with plastic wrap and scoop some of the cheese mixture in, filling up the ramekin. Cover with plastic wrap and place in the freezer for 15-20 minutes. Remove from the freezer, place the ramekin upside down onto a serving platter, then remove the ramekin and plastic wrap. Top with fresh herbs or any other toppings of your choosing. Done.

Notes:

- Don't like goat cheese? Not a problem. Use up to 8 points of ANY type of cheese that you want. Baby Bell, reduced fat cheddar, toss in some sundried tomatoes (not in oil), shallots, experiment and play around with this. It's highly, highly, highly customizable. Just use mine as a template.
- Mix the strained cream cheese with a bunch of chopped green onions, cooked, drained and cooled taco meat, then form it into a big ball wrapped in plastic wrap and let it sit in the fridge. When it firms up, roll it in a bunch of chopped up fat free cheddar cheese for a great taco cheese ball. Think outside the box. Play around with seasonings and fillings.

Traditionally, Hummus is made with garbanzo beans, garlic, lemon juice, tahini (crushed sesame seed paste), and lots and lots and looooooots of extra virgin olive oil. It's usually so high in points and calories that the popular skinny cooking sites, and even the manufacturers, have their serving sizes at a mere 2 tablespoons. Anyone who has ever had hummus knows... 2 Tablespoons is NOT a realistic serving size. I also recently decided to take a crack at chocolate hummus. Chocolate hummus is a sweet dip that can be used for sliced fruit, dessert spreads, frosting pastries, or as an evil way to trick your kids into eating a bunch of pureed beans.

LOW POINT HUMMUS

YIELDS: 4 cups
Servings: 16
Serving Size: 1/4 cup
Points: 1-2 servings = 1 point

Ingredients:

- 29-30oz canned garbanzo beans/chickpeas, drained, reserve liquid
- 2 Tbsp tahini (sesame paste)
- 1/4 cup lemon juice
- 3-4 fresh garlic cloves (to taste)
- 2 Tbsp reserved garbanzo bean juice
- 3 Tbsp water
- 1/3 cup fat free yogurt (or greek)
- 1 tsp extra virgin olive oil
- 2 tsp ground cumin
- 1 tsp salt
- 1/4 tsp sesame oil *(OPTIONAL, though RECOMMENDED!!)*

Directions:

1. Drain the garbanzo beans, reserve the liquid, and rinse off the beans.
2. Add the garbanzo beans, tahini, lemon juice, garlic, garbanzo bean juice, water, yogurt, oils, cumin, and salt to a large blender or food processor and process until pureed and smooth.
3. If the mixture is too thick, add more reserved garbanzo bean juice, 1 Tablespoon at a time, until it takes on a very smooth, creamy, and easily spreadable consistency. Season with more salt and pepper, if necessary.
4. Garnish with a dusting of paprika and minced parsley. Spray the top of the hummus with a quick touch of olive oil cooking spray.

CHOCOLATE "DESSERT" HUMMUS

YIELDS: 2-1/2 cups
Servings: 10
Serving Size: 1/4 cup

POINTS: 1 serving = 0 points
2-3 servings = 1 point
4-6 servings = 2 points

Ingredients:

- 30oz canned garbanzo beans/chickpeas, drained and thoroughly rinsed
- 6 Tbsp unsweetened vanilla almond milk
- 4 Tbsp unsweetened cocoa powder
- 8 tsp sugar free instant chocolate pudding mix
- pinch of salt
- 1 tsp caramel extract (or vanilla if you can't find it)
- 1-1/2 Tbsp sugar free maple syrup (pancake syrup)
- 1/4 cup 0 point sweetener (I used Monkfruit extract)
- 1/8 tsp ground cinnamon (OPTIONAL)
- 2 tsp powdered peanut butter (OPTIONAL)

Directions:

1. Add ALL of the ingredients into a food processor and puree on high for 1-2 minutes, or until mixture is completely smooth and creamy. Add a little bit more almond milk, if necessary.

NOTES:
- SCAN THE CHOCOLATE PUDDING. Walmart's brand is lower in points than the Jello brand. Jello's ***chocolate fudge*** flavor, is lower in points than their regular chocolate pudding.
- You can remove the peanut butter for allergy restrictions.
- I used monkfruit extract as my sweetener but you can also use swerve, splenda, stevia or truvia.
- You can leave out the cinnamon, or for an interesting twist, keep the cinnamon, but also add additional cayenne chili powder for a mexican hot chocolate spiced hummus.

Dips • Page 37

Awesome Ketchup

Fast, DELICIOUS, No Sugar Added, with Amazing Depth of Flavor

Alright, let me get this out of the way in the first sentence, YES... I am fully aware that G. Hughes has sugar free condiments! But, realize that not everyone has it at their stores and HOMEMADE sauce beats bottled sauce. This baby has depth of flavor that most store bought, bottled ketchups have inappropriate dreams about. It's like comparing the flavor of powdered lemonade in a tin jar to grandma's homemade lemonade. This also was a must-make for me, because I needed it for my low point cocktail sauce.

Ingredients:

- 1-3/4 cup tomato sauce (scan to ensure 0 points)
- 1/4 cup tomato paste
- 2 Tbsp apple cider vinegar
- 1/2 tsp worcestershire sauce
- 1/2 tsp salt
- 1/4 tsp black pepper
- 1 Tbsp Natural 0 point sweetener of choice (Stevia, Monkfruit, Truvia, Swerve, etc)
- 1/2 tsp dry mustard
- 1/2 tsp onion powder
- 1/2 tsp garlic powder
- 1/4 tsp celery salt
- 1/8 tsp ground allspice

Serving Info.:

Yields: 2-1/4 cups
Servings: 9
Serving Size: 1/4 cup

Points Value:

1-2 servings = 0 points
3-6 servings = 1 point
7-9 servings = 2 points

Directions:

1. Add all of the ingredients into a mixing bowl. Whisk until combined. Done.
2. Take 10 minutes, to ponder the fact that I actually have a recipe with only 1 real step. Then let it dawn on you that I'm only mentioning this as #2 so that I can have a #2 in the directions.
3. See #2.

Notes:

- You can use 1 Tbsp of regular sugar if you wish, it will still be a VERY low point ketchup, but adjust your points accordingly.
- If you are on a sodium restrictive diet, you can leave out the salt, celery salt, and worcestershire sauce, though it WILL make the sauce sweeter. You can counter that by adding some more savory seasonings. Try adding more onion powder instead of celery salt, heck... you can even add some savory dried/ground mushroom powder, for a big Umami 1-2 punch.

Roasted Pepper and Balsamic

A Sweet Red Pepper Sauce with a touch of Balsamic Vinegar

This sweet and savory dip is a nice change of pace from dairy based dips. The natural sweetness of the red peppers, along with the tiny bits of burnt char, savoriness of the roasted red onion and the sharpness of the garlic, make this a versatile condiment. Use it as a spread in sandwiches, or dip your favorite veggie in it.

Ingredients:

- 4 large red bell peppers, sliced into large pieces, seeds removed. (around 2 lbs)
- 1 medium red onion, sliced in half
- 2 medium garlic cloves
- 1 tsp dried basil
- 1 Tbsp + 1 tsp balsamic vinegar
- 1 Tbsp water
- 1/4 tsp smoked paprika
- 1/2 tsp salt
- 1/4 tsp pepper
- 1/4 cup plain fat free Greek yogurt
- red pepper flakes, to taste (I used 1/4 tsp)

Serving Info.:

Yields: 2 cups
Serving Size: 1/4 cup
Servings: 8

Point Values:

1 Serving = 1 point
2 servings = 2 points
3 servings = 3 points

Directions:

1. Place one of your oven racks to the 2nd position from the top. Turn on your Broiler.
2. Line a large baking pan with aluminum foil, coat with olive oil cooking spray.
3. Place the sliced red onion and peppers on the pan. Place both of the garlic cloves under a chunk of bell pepper, covering them like a red vegetarian blanket.
4. Coat the vegetables with cooking spray. Broil for 8 minutes, then rotate the pan. Cook for an additional 5-8 minutes or until the peppers are charred. Remove from the oven.
5. Place ALL of the ingredients into a food processor, and run on high speed, until the puree is broken down and smooth. Thin with additional water if desired.
6. Season with additional salt, pepper, or red pepper flakes, to taste.

Note:

- If you'd prefer to not use your oven's broiler, you can roast the vegetables at 425 degrees for 35-45 minutes, until charred. You can also grill the onions, peppers, and wrap the garlic in a few layers of foil, with some olive oil cooking spray. Place them on the grill also.
- A lot of folks that are allergic to tomato have been able to have my red pepper marinara sauce without side effects, even though both are in the "nightshade" family. It would stand to reason that this dip would be the same.
- I keep the skin on the peppers, because I like the little flecks of black and the smokiness.

Smoked Salmon

I absolutely LOVE a good smoked salmon dip. It's my favorite type of dip, other than Hummus of course... but I'm ethnically obligated to like Hummus. This recipe is a heavily modified combination of the recipe from 2 different chefs, both ridiculously famous. I decided to meld their two recipes into a Terminator 1000 dip of salmon destruction. I then WW-ified it with my own dastardly and diabolical point-cutting shenanigans. I bet half of you are going to have a heart attack that I'm using actual mayonnaise in a recipe... for the first time, ever. lol

Ingredients:

- 8oz smoked salmon (2 4oz packages)
- 1-1/2 cups plain fat free Greek yogurt, strained overnight (at least 12 hours).
- 1/2 cup low fat mayonnaise (*GASP!!!*)
- 1-1/2 tsp prepared horseradish sauce
- 2 Tbsp lemon juice
- 1/4 cup diced red onion
- 1/8 tsp paprika
- 2 Tbsp finely chopped fresh dill
- 2 Tbsp finely chopped fresh chives
- 1/4 cup diced celery
- 1/4 tsp worcestershire sauce
- 1/4 tsp salt
- 1/4 tsp pepper
- 1/4 to 1/2 tsp hot sauce, to taste (optional)

Serving Info.:

Yields: 3 cups
Serving Size: 1/4 cup
Servings: 12

Point Values:

1 Serving = 0 points
1-3 servings = 1 point
4-6 servings = 2 points

Directions:

1. The night before you plan to make this, put the 32oz of fat free Greek yogurt into a colander lined with cheesecloth or paper coffee filters. Cover with plastic wrap and let sit for at least 12 hours. (Mine lost 3/4 cup of liquid in 12 hours). ALSO... Mix the lemon juice, paprika and red onions, then store in the fridge overnight in an airtight container.
2. Place the strained Greek yogurt, mayo, horseradish, red onion/lemon juice mixture, dill, chives, celery, worcestershire sauce, salt, pepper and hot sauce in the food processor. Add 4 oz of chopped smoked salmon, then process until broken down and well combined.
3. Add the remaining 4oz of smoked salmon, chopped, and pulse the food processor a few times to break down the salmon, but leaving chunks. Cover, put into the fridge, then allow to rest for 1 hour. Taste, add more salt, pepper and hot sauce, if desired.

Note:

- If you want your dip to be chunkier, add the celery in step 3, rather than 2. You can also add even more red onion and celery if desired, though you may need to increase the seasoning.
- Soaking the red onions overnight in the lemon juice is essential for the pink color. The acidic lemon juice sucks the coloring from the red onions. Adding the paprika enhances it.

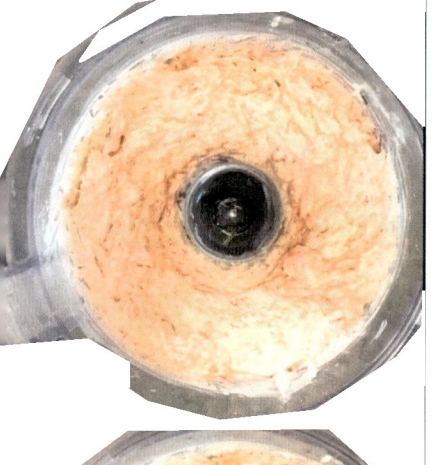

Thai Sweet & Sour Sauce

Two Delicious Variations of one Asian Culinary Classic

This recipe takes a traditional asian sweet and sour sauce and gives you two different dips. One is the standard sweet and sour (bottom middle sauce), but then I realized that with just the addition of a few ingredients, it can be turned into a Thai Sweet Chili sauce (top left sauce).

Ingredients:

- 1-1/8 cup water (1 cup, plus 2 Tbsp)
- 1 cup rice vinegar or rice wine vinegar
- 1 cup 0 point Natural sweetener
- (stevia, monkfruit, truvia, swerve, etc)
- 2 Tbsp tomato sauce or puree
- 1 Tbsp garlic, minced
- 1 Tbsp fresh ginger root, minced
- 2 Tbsp cornstarch

Thai Sweet Chili Sauce Variation:

- only use 1 cup water, remove the extra 2 Tbsp
- add 1 Tbsp low sodium soy sauce
- add 1 Tbsp sugar free peach preserve/jelly/jam
- add 1 Tbsp red pepper flakes

Serving Info.:

Yields: 2 cups
Serving Size: 1/4 cup
Servings: 8

Point Values:

1 Serving = 0 points
2-3 servings = 1 point
4-6 servings = 2 points

Directions: (base sauce directions)

1. Place the water, vinegar, sweetener, tomato sauce, garlic, ginger and cornstarch into a small pot (around 1.5 quarts), whisk until everything is well combined and the cornstarch is dissolved.
2. Bring the mixture up to a rolling boil and allow to cook for 5-7 minutes, stirring occasionally. Continue until the sauce has the thickness of warm maple syrup. Remove from heat, set aside. Allow the sauce to cool to room temperature. Come back and stir the sauce occasionally, while cooling, so that it doesn't develop a slightly thick layer on top. Done.
3. To make the Thai Sweet Chili variation, perform the listed changes to step 1. Reduce the water, while adding the soy sauce, peach preserves and red pepper flakes to the recipe.

Note:

- Rice vinegar and rice wine vinegar are not with the "normal" vinegars, at the grocery store. They are found in the aisle with the asian foods, usually near the soy sauce, sesame oil, teriyaki sauce... stuff like that. However, if you don't want to spend the extra $$, use regular distilled white vinegar. It won't taste exactly the same, but it's still very good.
- You can add the sugar free peach preserves to the regular sweet & sour sauce as well as the spicy variation, if you want. It's 0 points, so won't change the point value.
- If you would like the dip a little thicker, you can add up to an extra 1-1/2 tsp of cornstarch, without changing the point values for the recipe.

Dips • Page 41

Tartar Sauce

A Simple Dill Pickle Based Tartar Sauce for Seafood

Ok, as ALL OF YOU KNOW, from Connect... for the longest time, I have been a huge advocate for swapping out mayo in pretty much everything, for Greek yogurt... because I'm the Ebenezer Scrooge of points. I made my tartar sauce with Greek yogurt for months, but never really loved it. So... I bit the bullet and swapped a little of the Greek for some low fat mayo. I DO acknowledge now, that in very few (to me anyways) instances, there are some dips or dishes that you just haaaave to have a touch of mayo in. Tartar sauce is one of them. I've purposely kept this at 0 points for the first serving to allow you some wiggle room to modify it for your own tastes.

Ingredients:

- 1-1/2 cups fat free Greek yogurt
- 1/4 cup low fat mayonnaise
- 4 Tbsp dill pickle relish
- 2 Tbsp onion, finely diced
- 1/2 tsp sweetener of choice (stevia, splenda, truvia, monkfruit, swerve, etc.)
- 1/2 tsp fresh dill, finely chopped
- 1/4 tsp salt
- 1/4 tsp pepper
- 2 tsp lemon juice
- 1/2 tsp worcestershire sauce
- 1 Tbsp water or almond milk
- 1/4 tsp hot sauce (optional)

Serving Info.:

Yields: 2 cups
Servings: 8
Serving Size: 1/4 cup

Points Value:

1 serving = 0 points
2-5 servings = 1 point
6- 8 servings = 2 points

Directions:

1. Add all of the ingredients into a mixing bowl. Whisk until combined. Done.
2. Take 10 minutes, to ponder the fact that I actually have a recipe with only 1 actual step. Then let it dawn on you that I'm only mentioning this, so that I can have a #2 in the directions.
3. See #2.

Notes:

- None of the grocery stores around me have Sugar Free sweet relish, which is why I made my tartar sauce with dill relish and sweetener. You lucky east coasters... with your snazzy Kroger stores. *grumbles*
- The flavor of this tartar sauce develops more as it rests in the fridge. However, don't be shy about adding more seasoning to it, if desired.
- I used 0 point sweetener instead of 1/2 tsp of real sugar... because it's my recipe... so pffft. Feel free to use real sugar if you'd like, but adjust the points.

Thai Peanut Dip

Creamy Peanut Butter, Coconut and Curry Dip

This dip is my low point, low calorie, low fat take on an asian classic. Anyone who has ever gone out for Thai food knows what I'm talkin' about with this dip. It's a very traditional dip/sauce, that's a luxuriously thick and creamy dip, made with loads of peanut butter, ultra fatty coconut milk, red curry and other assorted asian awesomeness. My version uses powdered peanut butter, low calorie coconut almond or soy milk, combined with additional coconut extract.

Ingredients:

- 1-1/2 cup water
- 1 tsp asian chili sauce (like sriracha)
- 1 tsp asian "fish sauce"
- 1 Tbsp reduced sodium soy sauce
- 2 tsp lime juice
- 1/4 to 1/2 tsp red curry paste (to taste)
- 3/4 tsp coconut extract (from the baking aisle. **HIGHLY RECOMMENDED**)
- 10 Tbsp Powdered Peanut Butter *(that's 1/2 cup + 2 Tbsp)*
- 1/2 cup Coconut Milk Beverage, unsweetened
 ("*So Delicious!*" "*Silk*" and other brands of Almond Milk flavored coconut beverages)
- 3 Tbsp 0 point natural sweetener of choice *(stevia, truvia, monkfruit, etc.)*
- 2 Tbsp + 1 tsp cornstarch (dissolve with 2 Tbsp water)
- 1/4 tsp salt
- 3 peanuts, crushed as garnish (yes.... 3 single peanuts)

Serving Info.:

Yields: 2 cups
Servings: 8
Serving Size: 1/4 cups

Points Value:

1 serving = 1 point
2 servings = 2 points
3 servings = 3 points

Directions:

1. Combine the water, chili sauce, fish sauce, soy sauce, lime juice, curry paste, and coconut extract n a medium sized pot. Stir to combine and begin heating over medium heat.
2. In a separate mixing bowl, whisk together the powdered peanut butter, coconut milk beverage, sweetener, salt and dissolved cornstarch. Then pour into the pot with the curry water. Heat to a simmer, stirring continuously, until the sauce comes to a low boil. It will begin to thicken rapidly, so lower the heat slightly and continue stirring for 3-4 minutes.
3. Remove from heat and pour the mixture into a large bowl or dish to cool for 20 minutes. It will thicken as it cools. But don't ignore it. It will start to develop a firm film on top as it cools, so...
4. Stir the mixture **EVERY 5 MINUTES** to avoid having the top of the dip become a thick solid film. Stirring it every 5 minutes will break up that top film and have it melt back into the hot dip. After doing this 4 times, the top no longer develops that layer. That's just the cornstarch trying to continue thickening and meeting the cool air. It stops after you stir it a few times.
5. Crush the 3 peanuts in a plastic baggy, then sprinkle on top of the sauce as garnish, once plated.

Note: If you cannot find "So Delicious" or "Silk" brand coconut beverage, most grocery stores carry Coconut ALMOND MILK blends, near the almond milk. Use whatever type you can find, as long as it scans for no more than 2 points per cup.

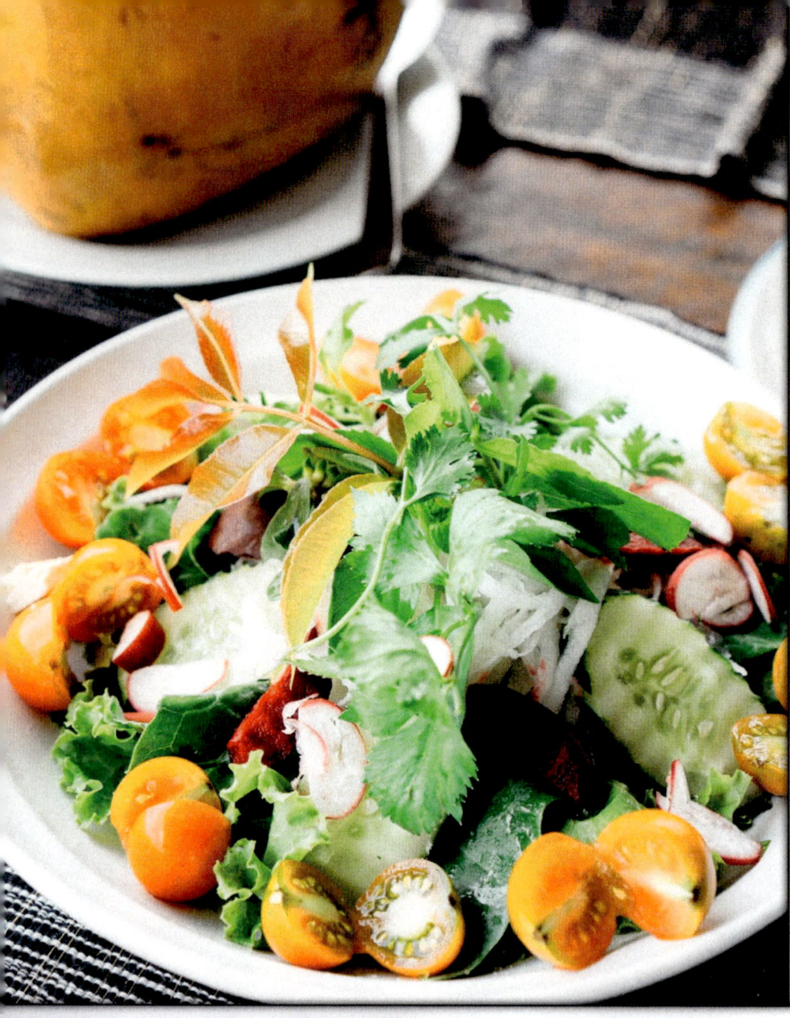

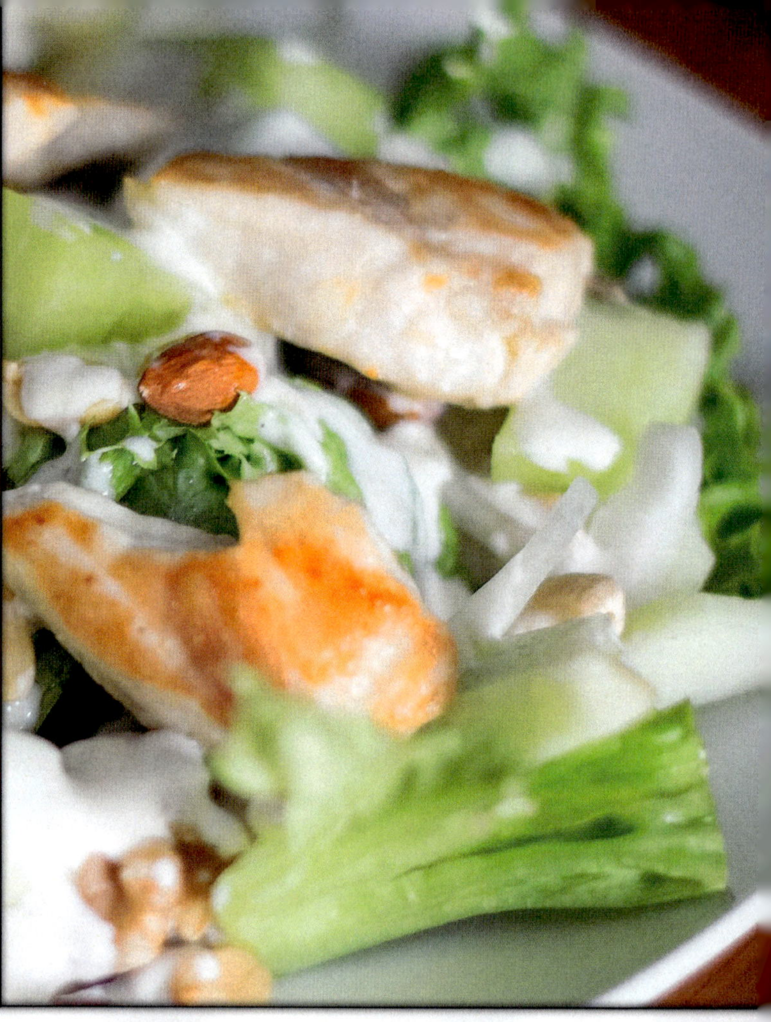

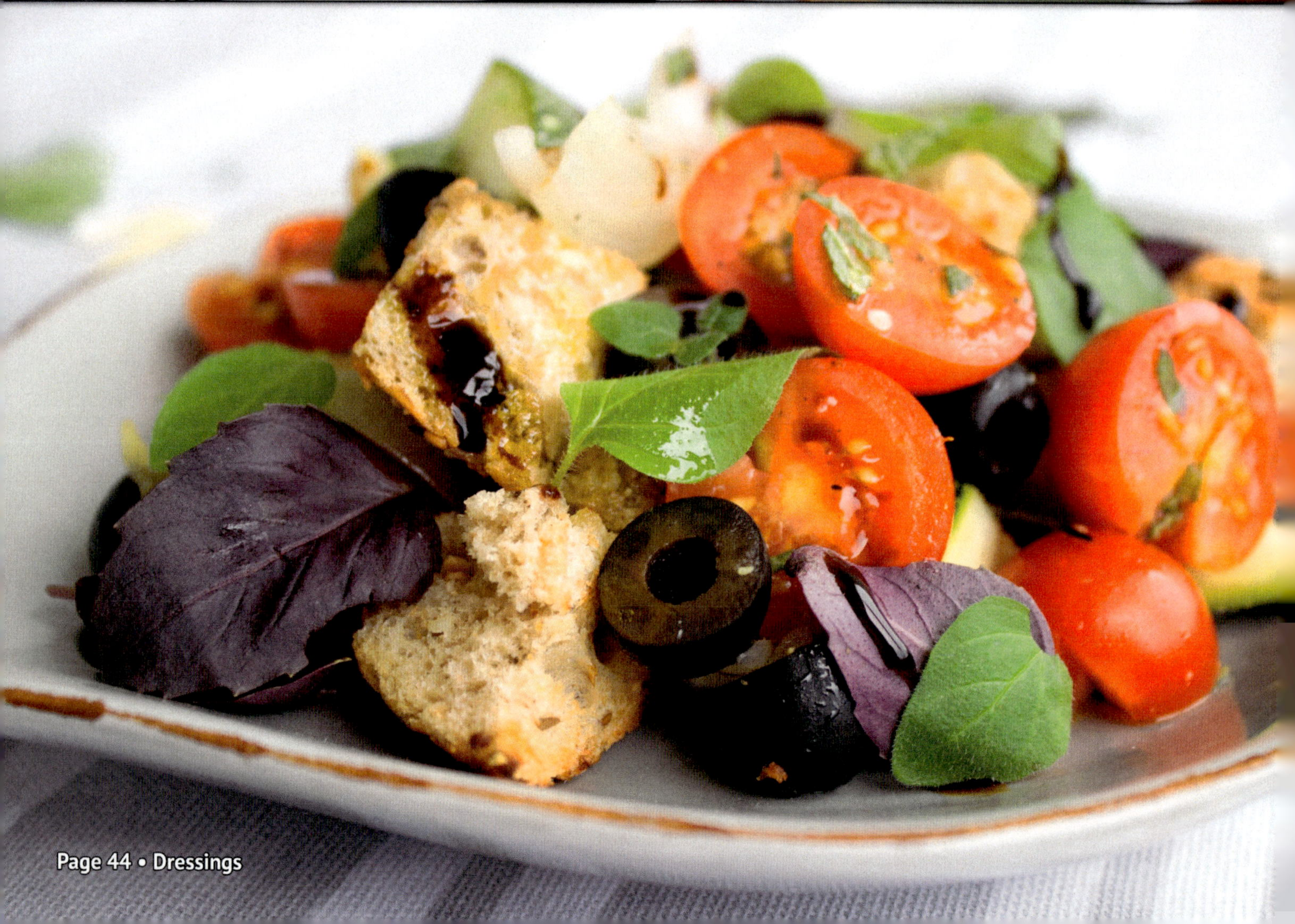

Salad Dressings

Apple Vinaigrette ... pg 46
Blue Cheese ... pg 46
Carrot Ginger ... pg 47
Catalina ... pg 47
Caesar ... pg 48
Creamy Chipotle ... pg 49
Creamy Cilantro ... pg 49
Creamy Roasted Garlic & Onion ... pg 50
Creamy Greek Feta & Dill ... pg 50
French ... pg 51
Italian ... pg 51
Peppercorn Parmesan ... pg 52
Russian ... pg 52
Sesame Ginger ... pg 53
Thousand Island ... pg 53

All of the Greek yogurt based Dressings will "tighten up" a bit more as they rest in the fridge. If they get too thick, simply stir in a little water to thin them out to your desired consistency.

Also: If you have allergies to dairy, you can substitute Silken Tofu in place of the Greek yogurt. The taste will be sliiiiiightly different, but it will still work.

Apple Vinaigrette

A light and crisp vinaigrette that gets it's creamy apple flavor from blended Fuji apples, honey and dijon mustard.

Serving Info.:
Yield: 2 cups
Servings: (8) 1/4 cup

Points:
1 serving = 1 point
2 servings = 3 points
3 servings = 4 points

Ingredients:
- 1-1/2 cups water
- 4-1/2 tsp cornstarch
- 1/4 cup apple cider vinegar
- 1/4 cup white wine vinegar
- 1 medium garlic clove
- 1 Tbsp dijon mustard
- 2 Tbsp honey
- 2 tsp sugar
- 2 Tbsp plain fat free Greek Yogurt
- 1/4 cup Fuji apples, peeled, finely diced, packed

Directions:
1. Stir the water and cornstarch together in a small pot. Bring to a rolling boil and allow to simmer for 3 minutes. Remove from heat and **cool to room temperature**.
2. Use a regular or immersion blender to process the vinegars, garlic, mustard, honey, sugar, yogurt and diced apples together until fairly smooth.
3. Stir the cooled and thickened water into the dressing until well combined. Allow to sit in the fridge for 1 hour, to set.

- You can use 0 point sweetener instead of sugar if you'd prefer. Adjust the points accordingly.
- You can use a different variety of apple other than Fuji, if you prefer.

Blue Cheese

This was a special request from my WW friends in Elizabethtown, Kentucky. This blue cheese dressing is creamy, delicious, and ultra pungent... Have breath mints handy.

Serving Info.:
Yield: 2 cups
Servings: (8) 1/4 cup

Points:
1 serving = 1 point
2 servings = 3 points
3 servings = 4 points

Ingredients:
- 1-1/4 cup fat free plain Greek Yogurt
- 6 Tbsp unsweetened plain almond milk
- 1 Tbsp + 1 tsp white wine vinegar
- 1 medium garlic clove
- 1/2 tsp salt
- 1/4 tsp black pepper
- 9 Tbsp (1/2 cup + 1 Tbsp) Blue cheese crumbles

Directions:
1. Use a blender or immersion blender to process all of the ingredients together until just combined. Allow to sit in the fridge for at least 1 hour, for flavors to meld.
2. Buy mouthwash

- If you like it chunkier, blend half of the cheese into the dressing, then stir in the other half of the blue cheese crumbles.
- It has a very strong taste at first, but after a few hours, the flavors mellow and it becomes a much better dressing.
- Using reduced fat or fat free blue cheese isn't worth it. I've tried making this dressing with regular, reduced fat and fat free blue cheese. It is NOT worth it to get the reduced fat stuff. Buy the regular, the taste is sooooooo much better. Trust me.

Carrot Ginger

This dressing has some serious zing to it. This is actually the first dressing that anyone ever requested for me to try. **@andmatsmom** actually asked if I could make a lower point and calorie version of Benihana's Sesame Carrot & Ginger salad dressing. So here'ya go, lady. Domo arigato, Mrs. Roboto.

Serving Info.:
Yield: 2 cups
Servings: (8) 1/4 cup

Points:
1-2 servings = 1 point
3 servings = 2 points
4 servings = 3 points

Ingredients:
- 3/4 cup water
- 1-1/2 tsp cornstarch
- 1/2 lb bagged shredded carrots, chopped
- 1/4 cup fresh ginger root, peeled, minced
- 1/4 cup shallots, peeled and diced
- 1/4 cup rice vinegar *(asian food section at the store)*
- 5-6 Tbsp low sodium soy sauce, to taste
- 1 Tbsp sesame oil *(asian food section at the store)*
- 1/4 tsp salt

Directions:
1. In a small pot, stir together the water and cornstarch till dissolved. Bring to a rolling boil and simmer for 3 minutes. Remove from heat, **cool to room temperature.**
2. Use an immersion or regular blender to process the shredded and chopped carrots, shallots, ginger, vinegar, soy sauce, sesame oil and salt until mostly smooth. NOT pureed.
3. Stir in the cooled and thickened water. Allow to set in the fridge for 1 hour.

- Start off with 5 Tbsp of soy sauce in the dressing. Once you've finished it, try a taste and see if you'd like to add the extra 1 Tbsp. You might think 5 Tbsp tastes great, but think 6 Tbsp is too salty. Better safe than sorry.
- There IS gluten free soy sauce at the grocery store, it's called "Tamari" soy sauce.

Catalina

I'll be the first to admit that prior to this recipe, I had no idea what the heck Catalina dressing was. Now, however, I am totally in love with it. It's sweet, tangy, creamy and has a slight pepperiness to it that is just awesome.

Serving Info.:
Yield: 2-1/4 cups
Servings: (9) 1/4 cup

Points:
1 servings = 0 points
2-3 servings = 1 point
4-5 servings = 2 points

Ingredients:
- 1 cup water
- 2-1/2 tsp cornstarch
- 1/2 cup canned tomato sauce *(the 0 point kind)*
- 3-1/2 Tbsp red wine vinegar
- 1/2 cup onion, diced
- 1 tsp paprika
- 1 tsp worcestershire sauce
- 2 tsp vegetable or canola oil
- 1/4 cup sweetener of choice (swerve, monkfruit, stevia, etc)
- 1/2 tsp salt
- 1/4 tsp pepper

Directions:
1. Heat the water and cornstarch in a small pot. Bring to a rolling boil and allow to simmer for 3 minutes. Remove from heat and **cool to room temperature**.
2. Use an immersion blender or regular blender, to process the tomato sauce, vinegar, diced onion, paprika, worcestershire, oil, sweetener, salt and pepper until the onions are mostly broken down.
3. Stir in the cooled and thickened water. Allow to set in the fridge for 1 hour. Done

- You can use regular sugar instead of sweetener, but your points will increase to 2 points per serving. The dressing will also gain 200 calories and 50g carbs.

Hail Caesar!

All hail Caesar, Emperor of...

Typically, a Caesar dressing is a ton of olive oil, whisked with raw egg yolks and other ingredients, giving the real thing a pretty short self life. We're blowing both of those issues out of the water. We're cooking the egg yolks in water, that we're about to thicken to the consistency of oil. We'll still be using olive oil in the dressing, but just enough to give a taste of it.

Serving Info.:
Yields: 3 cups
Servings 12
Size: 1/4 cup

Point Values:
1 serving = 1 point
2 servings = 2 points
3 servings = 4 points

Ingredients:
- 1-1/4 cup water
- 2 tsp cornstarch
- 3 egg yolks**
- 2 Tbsp olive oil
- 1 cup plain fat free Greek yogurt
- 1/4 cup lemon juice
- 3 Tbsp dijon mustard
- 3 anchovy fillets, oil drained**
- 2 tsp worcestershire sauce
- 1/4 cup reduced fat Parmesan topping
- 1/2 tsp pepper
- 1/8 tsp cayenne pepper

Directions:

1. In a small pot, stir together the water and cornstarch with the 3 egg yolks till mixed well. Heat on low-medium heat, stirring with a rubber spatula to scrape clean the sides and bottom of the pot. The sauce will begin to thicken and reach a low simmer. Reduce the heat till just simmering. Stir on low heat for 2-3 minutes. It's ok if there is some slight curdling in the liquid. Remove from heat, allow to cool to room temp.

2. Pour the cooled egg yolk mixture into a wire strainer over a bowl. Use a rubber spatula to move the liquid back and forth along the mesh, to push the liquid through, while catching any pieces of cooked egg yolk. Any pieces that get through will be broken into tiny particles.

3. Pour the strained, cooked egg mixture into a tall container if using an immersion blender, or use a regular blender, to blend together the liquid, olive oil, yogurt, lemon juice, mustard, anchovy fillets, worcestershire, Parmesan topping, black pepper and cayenne pepper until smooth. Pour into a container and put into the refrigerator for 1 hour before serving.

Notes:
- You can use 2 teaspoons of worcestershire sauce instead of the anchovy fillets. The taste will be different, but it will still be close.
- If you're vegan, you can also leave out the egg yolks, though it will also change the taste. Leave out the egg yolks, thicken the water with 2 additonal teaspoons of cornstarch and then allow it to cool. Skip the straining step, and proceed to step 3.
- For an awesome full-tilt 2 point caesar salad, use a slice of Sara Lee 45 calorie 1 point bread (or other 1 point per slice bread) to bake your own croutons with cooking spray. Then slice up some grilled chicken. Boom... grilled chicken caesar salad WITH croutons for 2 points.
- If you're impatient, forget straining out the lil egg bits. Just throw the whole danged thing into a blender, or puree it with an immersion blender. Boom, done.

Creamy Ch[ipotle]

Whoever suggested that I try making this, you suck! You could have said, "Hey Daniel in case you didn't know, Chipotle peppers are actually smoked Jalapeno's." My face is melting and I can feel the fluid in my eyes simmering because of you. With that said, this is a popular dressing... because people are crazy.

Serving Info.:
Yield: 2-1/4 cups
Servings: (9) 1/4 cup

Points:
1-2 servings = 1 point
3-4 servings = 2 point

Ingredients:
- 1-3/4 cups plain fat free greek yogurt
- 3 Tbsp reduced fat light mayonnaise
- 1/2 cup unsweetened almond milk
- 3 Tbsp lime juice
- 2 pieces, canned chipotle peppers in adobo sauce
- 1 medium clove garlic
- 2 Tbsp fresh cilantro leaves, packed
- 1-1/2 tsp chili powder
- 1/2 tsp McCormick chipotle chili pepper powder **
- 1 tsp paprika
- 1/4 tsp cumin
- 1/2 tsp salt
- 1/4 tsp pepper

Directions:
1. Use either an immersion blender, or a regular blender, to blend all of the ingredients together until smooth. Pour the dressing into an airtight container or serving vessel and allow to refrigerate for 1 hour.

- Chipotle chili powder is highly recommended, though it's optional. It really gives an intense smoky chipotle flavor.
- If you can't find chipotle chili powder at your local grocery stores, you can use another type of smoked chili powder, such as Ancho chili powder. It has a milder smoky flavor than Chipotle.

Creamy Cilan[tro]

This one was requested quite a bit back when I was asking folks for salad dressing ideas. This is my ww-ified version of the El Pollo Loco creamy cilantro dressing that they give you when you order a tostada. My version is loaded with fresh cilantro, garlic, lime juice and more. It's a very fresh, vibrant dressing.

Serving Info.:
Yield: 2 cups
Servings: (8) 1/4 cup

Points:
1 serving = 0 points
2-3 servings = 1 point
4-6 servings = 2 points

Ingredients:
- 2 cups fresh cilantro, chopped, loosely packed
- 2 medium cloves garlic
- 2 Tbsp light mayonnaise
- 1-1/2 cups fat free Greek yogurt
- 3 tsp lime juice
- 1/4 cup unsweeteened plain almond milk
- 1 tsp salt
- 1/4 tsp black pepper
- 2 tsp 0 point natural sweetener o' choice. Or you can use sugar, but adjust your points accordingly.

Directions:
1. Place all of the ingredients into a food processor and pulse until combined. Then run on high speed for around 20 seconds.
2. Store in an air tight container, in the fridge, for around 1 hour. Done.

- Ooooooooonce again, for all of the artificial sweetener police, feel free to replace it with regular sugar. Remember to adjust your points accordingly however. Easy peasy.

Creamy Garlic & Onion

A delicious and savory dressing with roasted garlic and onions, blended with greek yogurt and reduced fat mayo.

Serving Info.:
Yield: 2-1/4 cups
Servings: (9) 1/4 cup

Points:
1-4 servings = 1 point
5-7 servings = 2 points

Ingredients:
- 1 medium onion, peeled and sliced in half
- 5 medium cloves of fresh garlic, peeled
- olive oil cooking spray
- 1 cup fat free Greek yogurt
- 2 Tbsp reduced fat light mayonnaise
- 1/3 cup plain unsweetened almond milk
- 2 tsp worcestershire sauce
- 3 Tbsp white wine vinegar
- 1/2 tsp dry mustard
- 1/2 tsp onion powder
- 1/2 tsp garlic powder
- 1 tsp salt
- 1/4 tsp pepper

Directions:

1. Preheat oven to 425 and line a pan with aluminum foil. Place the sliced onion in the pan and coat with cooking spray. Make a small pouch with foil and place garlic cloves inside. Spray garlic with cooking spray, to coat, then close the pouch. Roast for 30 minutes, then remove from oven.
2. Use an immersion blender, or a regular blender, to process all of the ingredients together until smooth. Done.

Dill and

A yummie Greek salad dressing that will have you in the mood to roast a whole lamb in your front yard, then paint your garage door like the Greek flag. Opa!

Serving Info.:
Yield: 2 cups
Servings: (8) 1/4 cup

Points:
1-2 servings = 1 point
3 servings = 2 points
4 servings = 3 points

Ingredients:
- 1 cup fat free Greek yogurt
- 1/2 cup almond milk
- 3 Tbsp lemon juice
- 2 medium garlic cloves, chopped
- 1/4 cup cucumber, <u>peeled</u> and diced
- 1/2 cup reduced fat feta cheese crumbles**
- 3 Tbsp fresh dill
- 1/2 tsp salt
- 1/4 tsp pepper

Directions:

1. Place all of the ingredients into a large mixing bowl or into a blender. Use either an immersion blender or a regular blender, to blend the ingredients together. Don't completely puree them, you want to leave a little texture.
2. If the mixture is too thick for your personal taste, add a bit more almond milk or some water, until you get your desired consistency.. Set aside in the fridge, to set for 1 hour.

- Different brands of reduced fat feta can be different points. Some brands are 4 points for 1/2 cup, some are 5. For purposes of this recipe, I used the higher value of 5.
- You give me a salad dressing… aaaany salad dressing… and I tell you how'a the root word of'a that dressing… is'a Greek.
- If you nick yourself while peeling the cucumber, try'a some windex… and there you go.

I absolutely loathed, hated and gnashed my teeth, full-on Old Testament style, at French dressing prior to this recipe. I have always hated the canned orange goop. THIS IS NOT THAT DRESSING!!! This is fantastic! Sweet, savory, peppery... mmmm.

Serving Info.:
Yield: 2-1/4 cups
Servings: (9) 1/4 cup

Points:
1-2 servings = 0 points
3-6 servings = 1 point
7-9 servings = 2 points

Ingredients:
- 1 cup water
- 3-1/2 tsp cornstarch
- 1/2 cup tomato sauce (0 points, scan it to make sure)
- 3 Tbsp plain fat free Greek yogurt
- 5 Tbsp apple cider vinegar
- 1/2 tsp worcestershire sauce
- 1/4 cup diced onion
- 2-1/2 tsp paprika
- 1/2 tsp onion powder
- 3/4 tsp dry, ground mustard
- 1/4 cup 0 point natural sweetener o' choice**
- 1/2 tsp salt
- 1/4 tsp black pepper

Directions:
1. Heat the water and cornstarch in a small pot until boiling. Cook at a rolling boil for 2-3 minutes. Remove from heat and pour into a dish. Cool to room temperature.
2. Use an immersion or regular blender to process the tomato sauce, yogurt, vinegar, worcestershire, raw onion, paprika, onion powder, mustard powder, sweetener, salt and pepper until smooth.
3. Pour in the cooled, thickened water. Stir till well mixed. Allow the dressing to sit in the fridge for 1 hour. Done

Note:
- Use REGULAR sugar if you want. It will take the points up to 1 serving for 1 point, 2 servings for 3 points.
- You can use a hand whisk to mix it all together too.

This is my knockoff of the Olive Garden Italian dressing. This is one of the first that people asked for, it's also the one that I've gotten the most lip about. Yes, Olive Garden sells their own... But some of us like to cook our own stuff. lol

Serving Info.:
Yield: 2-1/4 cups
Servings: (9) 1/4 cup

Points:
1 serving = 1 point
2 servings = 3 points
3 servings = 4 points

Ingredients:
- 1-1/2 cups water
- 1 egg yolk
- 5 tsp cornstarch
- 2/3 cup white wine vinegar
- 1 Tbsp lemon juice
- 1 tsp worcestershire sauce
- 2 tsp olive oil (robust, if possible)
- 1/4 cup reduced fat parmesan grated topping (like Kraft)**
- 1/2 tsp salt
- 1/4 tsp pepper
- 2 tsp sugar
- 1 garlic clove, medium
- 1/2 tsp dried oregano
- 1/2 tsp dried basil
- 1/2 tsp dried parsley
- 1/8 to 1/4 tsp crushed red pepper flakes (to taste)
- 2 Tbsp plain fat free Greek yogurt

Directions:
1. Bring the water, egg yolk and cornstarch to a low boil for 3 minutes. Remove from heat, cool to room temperature.
2. When the liquid has cooled, use a blender or immersion blender to process ALL of the ingredients together until combined. Just pulse it a few times, you don't want it liquified. Set in the fridge for 1 hour to set.

Peppercorn and Parmesan

Russian

This creamy dressing has a smoky and subtle heat from loads of black pepper, combined with the savoriness of parmesan cheese, worcestershire sauce and garlic powder.

Serving Info.:
Yield: 2 cups
Servings: (8) 1/4 cup

Points:
1 serving = 1 point
2 servings = 2 points
3 servings = 3 points

Ingredients:
- 1-1/2 cup fat free Greek yogurt
- 2 Tbsp light mayonnaise
- 6 Tbsp unsweetened almond milk
- 2 Tbsp lemon juice
- 1/2 tsp garlic powder
- 1/2 tsp onion powder
- 3/4 tsp salt
- 1-1/2 to 2 tsp coarse or fresh ground black pepper
- 3 Tbsp reduced fat parmesan topping (like Kraft)
- 1/2 tsp worcestershire sauce

Directions:
1 Whisk all of the ingredients together, in a mixing bowl, until smooth. Done.

Notes:
- This dressing has a subtle, smoky heat that builds up. I'd start with 1-1/2 tsp of pepper, then add more if you think it needs it.
- Feel free to use real parmesan cheese if you wish, but make sure to adjust your points accordingly.

Russian dressing is similar to French, but where French is seasoned with a slight mustard flavor, Russian has hot sauce, paprika and a good amount of horseradish.

Serving Info.:
Yield: 1-3/4 cups
Servings: (7) 1/4 cup

Points:
0 points, total.

Ingredients:
- 1-1/4 cup fat free Greek yogurt
- 1/4 cup tomato sauce
- 3 Tbsp finely minced onion
- 3 tsp prepared horseradish (jarred, 0 point total)
- 1-1/2 to 2 tsp hot sause of choice
- 1 tsp worcestershire sauce
- 1/2 tsp paprika
- 2 Tbsp unsweetened almond milk
- 1 tsp salt
- 1/4 tsp black pepper

Directions:
1 Whisk all of the ingredients together to combine. Done.

Notes:
- In the grocery store, different brands of "prepared" horseradish can have different points. Most are 0 points, but some have points. Scan to ensure that you aren't buying a brand that gains points at 3 tsp.
- Use whichever brand of hot sauce that you like. Some recipes call for Tobasco, some call for Mike's Red Hot... use whichever brands you like.

This is a hiiiiiiiighly modified version of a classic Japanese dressing. It's sweet, savory and a little spicy... just like me. 🤪

Serving Info.:
Yield: 1-1/2 cups
Servings: (6) 1/4 cup

Points:
1 serving = 1 point
2 servings = 2 points
3 servings = 3 points

Ingredients:
- 1/2 cup fat free Greek yogurt
- 1/2 cup rice wine vinegar
- 1/4 cup low sodium soy sauce
- 3 Tbsp sugar free syrup (pancake syrup)
- 2 tsp powdered peanut butter
- 1 tsp fresh ginger, peeled, minced
- 2 medium cloves garlic, crushed, minced
- 1-1/2 tsp sesame oil
- 1/2 tsp curry powder
- 1 tsp asian chili sauce
- 1/8 tsp pepper (optional)
- 2-3/4 tsp sesame seeds

Directions:
1 Whisk all of the ingredients together, in a mixing bowl, until smooth. Done.

Notes:
- In place of the sugar free syrup, you can use regular syrup as a straight 1 to 1 substitute, but adjust your points.
- You can use 1 Tbsp of honey in place of the syrup, for a more traditional flavor. However you will lose 1 serving and gain a few points. Adjust accordingly.
- If you don't have fresh ginger, you can use 1/2 tsp ground ginger.
- If you don't want to buy rice wine vinegar, you can use white vinegar. It'll still taste good, just slightly different.

If we're being honest here, the only reason I made this, was so that I could put it on burgers, not salads. Now I can finally make an In-n-Out "Double Double Animal" at home!!!

Serving Info.:
Yield: 2-1/2 cups
Servings: (10) 1/4 cup

Points:
1 serving = 0 points
2-4 servings = 1 point
5-8 servings = 2 points

Ingredients:
- 1-1/2 cups plain fat free Greek yogurt
- 2 Tbsp light mayonnaise
- 3 Tbsp almond milk**
- 1/4 cup tomato sauce
- 3/4 tsp salt
- 1/4 tsp pepper
- 1/2 cup finely diced onion
- 2 tsp lemon juice
- 1 tsp paprika
- 1/4 cup no sugar added sweet relish (see notes)**

Directions:
1 Whisk all of the ingredients together to combine. Done.

Notes:
- If you don't want to use almond milk, you can use any liquid you want, that's 0 points for 3 Tbsp.
- If you can't find 0 point sweet relish at your local grocery store, you can easily work around it. Simply use 1/4 cup of dill pickle relish instead, then add 1 to 2 teaspoons of 0 point natural sweetener to the dressing (depending on how sweet you want it). Use real sugar if you want, but adjust your points accordingly.

Page 54 • Appetizers

Appetizers

Arancini al Ragu ... pg 56-57
Bolitas de Tamales ... pg 58-59
Breaded Calamari ... pg 60-61
Chicken Croquettes ... pg 62-63
Chicken Satay Skewers ... pg 64-65
Chorizo Stuffed Sweet Peppers ... pg 66-67
Crab Mac n Cheese with Gnocchi ... pg 68-69
Cuban Meatballs Picadillo ... pg 70-71
Focaccia Bread ... pg 72-73
Garlic Mushrooms ... pg 74-75
Kafta Kababs ... pg 76-77
Mussels in Saffron Cream Sauce ... pg 78-79
Onion Rings ... pg 80-81
Pineapple Jerk Skewers ... pg 82-83
Portuguese Clams ... pg 84-85
Rotolo il Lasagne ... pg 86-87
Salmon Cakes ... pg 88-89
Sausage Stuffed Mushrooms ... pg 90-91
Scallops with Lemon Cream Sauce ... pg 92-93
Shrimp Cocktail ... pg 94-95

Arancini al Ra...

Italian Sausage, Onions, Garlic and Rice, Breaded and Baked till Crispy

For those of you who've never had it, Arancini is traditionally a ball of risotto, with a meat filling in the center, that is breaded and deep fried. I decided to lighten it up and make it easier to prepare. Mine is regular rice, mixed with my low calorie italian sausage, onions, garlic, spices and my marinara sauce. It's all mixed together, formed into a ball, then breaded and baked.

Servings Info.:
Yield: 21 (1/4 cup balls)
Servings: 21
Serving Size: 1 ball

Point Values:
1 point per serving

Ingredients:

Meat Filling
- 1 pound batch of my 0 point italian sausage. Recipe can be found in my Low Point Cooking Guide on my website.
- 3/4 cup diced onion
- 2 medium garlic cloves, minced
- 1 tsp salt
- 1/4 tsp black pepper
- 1/4 cup tomato sauce (scan it, make sure it's 0 points)
- 4oz fat free feta cheese, crumbled and chopped
- 2 cups cooked rice
- 1/3 cup instant mashed potato flakes
- 2 egg yolks
- 1/2 cup green peas

Breading:
- 1-3/4 cups rice krispies (measured, then crushed down)
- 1-1/2 tsp regular breadcrumbs
- 2 tsp panko bread crumbs
- 1/2 tsp garlic powder
- 1/2 tsp onion powder
- 1-1/2 tsp all purpose flour
- 1-1/2 tsp corn flour ("maseca" brand instant masa mix)

Egg Wash:
- 2 large eggs
- 2 tsp dijon mustard
- 1/2 tsp water
- 1-1/2 tsp self rising flour
- 1-1/2 tsp cornstarch

Directions:

1. **(A)** Mix together a batch of my ground turkey italian sausage recipe. Mix the onions and garlic to the meat and cook over med-high heat, until browned. Use a kitchen spoon to break up the meat while it's cooking. **(B)** When the meat is browned, add the salt, pepper, tomato sauce and feta cheese to the meat and mix till combined. Use a rubber spatula to push down and scrape the cheese in the pan. You want to try to break it all up into tiny bits. **(C)** Spoon the meat mixture into a large mixing bowl, then add the cooked rice and mashed potato flakes, then mix to combine, followed by the egg yolks. **(D)** Finally, add the green peas and fold them into the meat. Cover and set aside.

2. To make the breading, place the rice krispies cereal into a large ziplock bag. Use a rolling pin to crush the cereal until it resembles breadcrumbs.

3. Pour the crushed rice krispies into a bowl, along with the breadcrumbs, panko, garlic and onion powders, all purpose flour and corn flour. Stir to combine.

4. For the egg wash, in a small dish, mix together the dijon mustard, water, cornstarch and self rising flour till smooth. In a larger bowl, whisk the 2 eggs together, then whisk in the flour/dijon mixture till smooth. Set aside.

5. **(A)** Use a 1/4 cup measuring scoop, to scoop an even 1/4 cup of the meat and rice mixture into your palm, then form into a rounded ball. **(B)** Place each of the formed Arancini into a casserole dish until they are all ready to be breaded. **(C)** Coat the Arancini, one at a time, in the egg mixture. Allow extra egg wash to drip off of the ball. **(D)** Place the coated Arancini into the large bowl of breading and gently move the bowl around, to roll the ball around in the breading. When it's mostly coated, use your hand to gently roll the ball around till it's uniformly coated. **(E)** Line a baking pan with foil and coat with cooking spray. Place all of the Arancini onto the pan, then grab a can of olive oil cooking spray (the 0 point kind) and coat all of the Arancini balls from every angle. Seriously, coat these babies like they're being baptized in the Jordan river. Bake at 425 degrees for 30 minutes, or until golden brown. Place onto a platter and garnish with fresh chopped parsley.

NOTES:
A) There is enough breading left over when all of the meat mixture is used up, so that you will be able to "double bread" 3 of the balls with a second layer of egg wash and breading.
B) If you don't want to use peas, you can replace them with 1/2 cup of some other vegetable, but that mass is required for the servings and points per serving.
C) These are pretty danged low in points. There is room for a few more points of ingredients to be used in the recipe, while still allowing the first few servings to be 1 point each. You can definitely add a little bit of mozzarella reduced fat or fat free cheese to the mixture, if you'd like. I try to keep all of my recipes as low in points as possible, to allow you the freedom to customize them and keep them low.

Appetizers • Page 57

Bolitas de Tamales

Chorizo Stuffed "Tamale Balls" with ~~

These amazingly versatile appetizers utilize one of my "foundation" recipes, my Low Point Masa, found in the FREE cooking guide download on my website, as well as the low point and calorie ground turkey chorizo recipe and roasted tomatillo sauce, also found in the same book/download. You can use this recipe as a base, from which you can make Tamale balls filled with whatever filling you'd like. Chicken, Pork, Shrimp... using my low point Mole' sauce, red enchilada sauce, the options are endless. Well... kinda.

Yield: 16 Tamale Balls
Servings: 1 Ball
Points: 1 Ball = 2 points
2 Balls = 3 points

Chorizo Tamale Balls with Roasted Tomatillo Sauce

Ingredients:

Tomatillo Sauce:
- 2-1/2 lbs. Tomatillos, husks and stems removed
- 1 medium onion, rough chopped
- 2 medium green bell peppers, rough chopped, seeds removed
- 3 medium cloves garlic
- 4 good sized poblano peppers, chopped, seeds removed (they aren't spicy)
- 1/2 bunch fresh cilantro, around 1 handful
- 1/2 tsp salt
- 1 whole Jalapeno pepper *(OPTIONAL!)*

Low Point & Calorie Chorizo:
- 1 batch of my Low Point Chorizo recipe on pg. 21

Low Point Masa:
- 1 batch of my Low Point Masa, recipe on pg. 14

Directions:

1. Preheat your oven to 375 degrees.
2. Line a large sheet pan with foil and spray with olive oil cooking spray. Place all of the vegetables (NOT THE CILANTRO) on the tray and spray them liberally with the cooking spray, then sprinkle lightly with salt and pepper.
3. Cook the vegetables at 375 degrees for 45 minutes, or until the tops of the vegetables are starting to blacken, then turn on the oven's "Broiler" function. Place the tray on the top rack under the broiler. Watch so that the vegetables don't burn to a crisp. You want to develop some black char across the tops of some of them.
4. Remove the tray from the oven and spoon all of the roasted veggies into a food processor or large blender. Make sure to also pour all of the juices in as well, along with the fresh cilantro and 1/4 tsp salt.
5. Process the vegetables on high for up to 1 minute. It should give you a thick green salsa.

6. **(A)** Take your (2) 1 cup balls of prepared Masa dough, and **(B)** section each into 8 relatively equal portions, JUST like when you section 2 ingredient dough. **(C)** Roll each 1/8 cup section into a ball, in your palm, then **(D)** flatten it into a thick tortilla shape. **(E)** Place 1 Tablespoon of the prepared and cooked chorizo into the center of each round of masa. **(F)** Carefully roll it into a ball, in your palm, then set the tamale balls, seam side down, onto a cutting board or plate. Set aside.

7. Fill a large pot, (that has steamer inserts) with enough to steam for a good 15 minutes, without actually touching the bottom insert tier, if using one.

8. (a) Place your formed Tamale Balls into the lower and upper steamer inserts. Then place into the pot with the boiling water.

9. Cover, then steam for 16 minutes. Remove from heat. Top with roasted tomatillo sauce and garnish with fresh chopped cilantro and a small amount of crumbled fat free Feta cheese.

NOTES:

- You can easily HALF this recipe if you don't want to make a big batch. OR, If you would like larger, main course-sized Tamale balls... Rather than sectioning the 1 cup Masa balls into 1/8's, section them into 1/4's. They will end up being 3 points per, but they are much more filling and end up being the size of a baseball.
- If you would like to NOT use the yogurt in this recipe due to dairy allergies, replace it with tofu that's blended with water. In Connect, you can search for #dairyfreeyogurthack, for my post on it. Blend 1/2 cup of water with a 16oz package of semi-firm tofu, to use as a viable replacement for Greek yogurt in recipes. Thin with a little water if needed.
- If you would like an even MORE chewie tamale or tortilla, from your Masa, you can substitute 1/4 cup of the corn flour with 1/4 cup of all purpose flour. I personally love the texture that way... but I'm a full-on Gringo.
- You can definitely substitute the Red Enchilada sauce (pg. 60) or the Low Point Mexican Mole' sauce (pg. 57), from my cooking guide, in place of the Roasted Tomatillo sauce.

Appetizers • Page 59

Breaded Calamari

Breaded & Baked, Crispy Calamari Rings with Italian Seasoning

These low calorie, low point rings are breaded with my new breading recipe, that I first used on my onion rings appetizer. They are dipped in egg wash, lightly coated with the rice krispies breading, then hosed off with 0 point cooking spray and baked. These rings are "Smack'yo Momma" good. Minus the time it takes to bread the rings individually, this is a pretty quick dish to throw together. You can prep them ahead of time, and keep them in the fridge, on a pan, ready to go into the oven.

Servings Info.:

Yield: 4 cups of rings
Servings: 4
Serving Size: 1 cup

Point Values:

1 serving = 1 point
2 servings = 2 points
3 servings = 3 points

Ingredients:

- 2 lbs fresh or frozen, cleaned Calamari rings

Breading:
- 1-1/4 cup rice krispies, crushed. (crushes to 1/2 cup)
- 2 tsp corn flour
- 1-1/2 tsp cornmeal
- 2 tsp panko breadcrumbs
- 1-1/2 tsp regular plain breadcrumbs
- 1/2 tsp onion powder
- 1/2 tsp garlic powder
- 1 tsp dried italian seasoning
- 1/4 tsp black pepper
- 1/2 tsp salt

Egg Wash:
- 2 large eggs
- 1 tsp dijon mustard
- 1-1/2 tsp self rising flour
- 1-1/2 tsp cornstarch

Garnish:
- fresh chopped flat leaf (italian) parsley
- 1/2 tsp reduced fat grated parmesan style topping
  lemon wedges

Not every grocery store is going to have squid rings. I HIGHLY suggest finding a nearby asian grocery store. They have INSANE seafood departments. My local asian store had frozen AND whole squid. No thanks, I'm not brave enough for whole, slimy squid, so I bought a bag of frozen rings.If your store has whole squid, they'll cut and clean if for you.

Directions:

1. Whether you purchased frozen or fresh rings, rinse them off and drain them. Place the rings on a large platter or pan lined with 2-3 layers of paper towels. Use additional paper towels to dry the the rings as much as possible. We want to remove as much moisture as possible so the egg wash sticks.

2. In a small dish, mix together the flour, cornstarch and dijon mustard till smooth. In a medium sized bowl, whisk together the eggs, then add the mustard/flour mixture and whisk till smooth and thick. Place the rice krispies in a gallon sized ziplock bag. Use a pan, or rolling pin, to crush the cereal until it's the texture of plain breadcrumbs. Pour them into a large bowl and add the corn flour, cornmeal, panko and regular breadcrumbs, garlic powder, onion powder, italian seasoning, salt and pepper. Stir to combine.

3. **(A)** Pour the egg mixture into a large bowl with the dried calamari rings. **(B)** Mix to coat all of the rings with egg wash. **(C)** Place the rings, 1 at a time, into the bowl with the breading and gently use a fork to push breading around the ring, till coated. **(D)** Use the fork to gently lift the ring out of the breading. Gently shake it to remove excess breading. **(E)** place rings onto large baking pans, lined with foil and coated with cooking spray. Generously spray all of the rings with a good coat of cooking spray. **(F)** Bake the rings for 10 minutes at 425 degrees.

4. Remove the pans from the oven. Use 2 forks to quickly, yet gently, flip each ring over. Spray with cooking spray, then place back in the oven and bake for another 8-10 minutes, till golden brown. Garnish with chopped parsley or basil and serve immediately.

NOTES:

A) A lot of people think that eating Calamari is like chewing rubber bands. If you get THICK Calamari rings... that may be an issue. The thicker the rings, the more chew that they have. If you are able to get smaller, thinner rings, they will naturally be more tender. Think of it like trying to chew a big thick cut of steak, versus a thin sliced piece. Thinner Calamari cooks to be more crisp and tender than thicker pieces.

B) The actual serving size and points per serving, will vary each time that you make this. It is completely dependant on how many rings you make out of this recipe. There are a total of 4 ingredient points in this recipe from the breading. Count out how many rings you end up making, and then create a quick "throw away" recipe in the WW recipe builder. Add 4 points of ingredients, and for the number of servings, enter how many rings you made, then save it. You can then scroll up and down to see exactly how many rings you get, per serving, out of those 4 points.

C) These rings are great served hot. However, take note... These ARE NOT DEEP FRIED. Like any breaded and baked dish, it will be crispy for a while, but will eventually lose it's crispiness. Mine stayed crispy for 10 minutes or so. After that, they STILL tasted really good, but the breading was no longer crispy. If you have an air fryer, these will be even more awesome.

Chicken Croquettes

Cooked, Seasoned Chicken Breast, Shredded, then Breaded & Baked

These were a special request from **@rbberens** on Connect and **mrsbatsycooks** on instagram. I'd never had one before, so I thought "sure, why not." Chicken Croquettes are traditionally minced/finely shredded up chicken that's lightly seasoned, breaded, then deep fried into either balls or short cylinder shapes. I decided to go with that idea, but switch it up a little bit by seasoning the bajeezus out of the chicken. I made this appetizer at the same time that I was working on a meat seasoning recipe for spicy Linguica. So.... I figured what the heck, let's use it. You can definitely forego the Linguica seasonings in these.

Servings Info.:
Yield: 20 croquettes
Servings: 20
Serving Size: 1 croquette

Point Values:
1 serving = 0 points
2-5 servings = 1 point
6-9 servings = 2 points

Ingredients:

Spicy Chicken Linguica Mixture
- 2 pounds chicken breast, diced, strips, or ground**
- 1 Tbsp chicken flavored bouillon *(like Knorr brand)*
- 1 tsp salt
- 1 tsp liquid smoke *(I used hickory flavored liquid smoke)*
- 2 tsp smoked paprika
- 1 tsp paprika
- 3/4 tsp black pepper
- 1/8 to 1/4 tsp red pepper flakes *(or more, to taste)*
- 3/4 tsp dried oregano
- 1 Tbsp red wine vinegar
- 1 tsp 0 point sweetener o' choice *(splenda, swerve, stevia, etc)*
- 3/4 cup fat free plain Greek yogurt
- 1 large egg

Breading:
- 1-1/4 cup rice krispies cereal
- 1-1/2 tsp all purpose flour
- 1-1/2 tsp corn meal
- 1-1/2 tsp regular bread crumbs
- 2 tsp panko breadcrumbs
- 1/2 tsp onion powder
- 1/2 tsp garlic powder
- salt and pepper

Egg Wash:
- 2 large eggs
- 1-1/2 tsp self rising flour
- 1-1/2 tsp cornstarch

Directions:

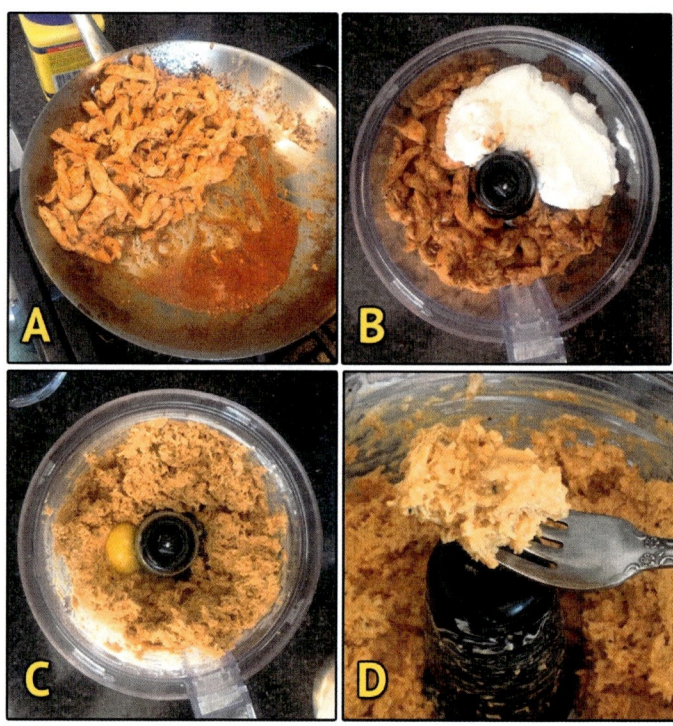

1. In a large mixing bowl, combine the chicken, bouillon, salt, liquid smoke, smoked paprika, paprika, red pepper flakes, black pepper, oregano, vinegar and sweetener. **(A)** Cook in a large pan until cooked through. Prop the pan handle up, to allow the liquids to drain to one side of the pan. We don't want the liquid added into the processor. **(B)** Move the meat to a food processor, add the Greek yogurt and pulse a few times to shred the chicken (don't puree it). **(C)** Add the egg into the food processor and process until all of the yogurt and egg are mixed throughout the meat. But do not OVER process it, you want it to still have finely shredded texture, as shown in **(D)**.

croquette out of the breading and tap it to remove excess crumbs. **(2F)** Use the forks to transfer the croquettes to a baking pan, lined with tinfoil and sprayed with cooking spray. **PREHEAT YOUR OVEN TO 425 DREGREES.**

3. **(3A)** Once your oven reaches temperature, spray the croquettes with a healthy coating of cooking spray. Bake for 12 minutes at 425 degrees. **(3B)** Remove from oven and flip the croquettes. Spray again with cooking spray, then return to the oven and bake for an additional 10-12 minutes or until the croquettes are golden brown. Serve hot, with a dipping sauce. Garnish with fresh basil and sprinkle with a pinch of reduced fat, grated parmesan topping (like Kraft).

NOTES:
A) It's going into the food processor, so it doesn't matter if you use ground chicken breast, chicken breast strips, or diced chicken.
B) You don't need to season the chicken with the linguica mixture that I did. Season it however you'd like. The picture below, shows the coloring of the chicken with the linguica seasoning. Seasoned normally, the interior would be white.
C) These can be prepared in advance. Bread the croquettes, then place them in a covered container in the fridge. The next day, put them on a baking pan, then once thawed, coat with cooking spray. Bake as directed.
D) These are crispy when right out of the oven. However, like most breaded and baked things… they only stay "crispy" for about 15-20 minutes after coming out of the oven. Then they start to lose their crispness. They still taste great though.
E) Don't have a food processor? Use a knife and just start chopping the cooked chicken until minced.

2. **(2A)** Use a measuring spoon to scoop out 2 even Tablespoons of the shredded chicken into your palm. Roll it into a ball. **(2B)** Place the ball onto a cutting board, then use your palm to roll it into a cylinder shape, around 3/4" thick. **(2C)** Place the shaped meat onto a large plate or platter, to help organize your work space. **(2D)** Use a whisk, or an immersion blender, to combine the egg wash ingredients until smooth. Dredge the croquettes, one at a time, in the egg wash. **(2E)** Place the croquette into the breading mixture. Use 2 forks to gently toss breading onto the meat on all sides. Use the forks to gently lift the *(cont.)*

Chicken Satay is pretty much the most popular appetizer in all of Thai cuisine. Traditionally, it's long strips of chicken thighs, pounded thin and marinated for a looooooooong time with a mixture of oil, tons of turmeric or curry powder and other spices, depending on which region's recipe you're following. In this case, I'm using chicken breast and instead of mixing all of the spices with oil for the marinade, I'm using a low calorie coconut milk beverage. Because not everyone has a grill, my recipe calls for using your oven's broiler. Also, because not everyone has access to lemongrass, I'm using lemon juice. I'm accomodating like that.

Servings Info.:
Yield: 42 skewers**
Servings: 42**
Serving Size: 1 skewer

Point Values:
1-20 servings = 0 points
21+ servings = 1 point

Ingredients:
- 2 pounds boneless, skinless chicken breast (thin cut breasts or pre cut "fajita" strips work too)

Marinade:
- 2 Tbsp lemon juice
- 4 medium garlic cloves
- 1/2 pound shallots, peeled, chopped**
- 1-1/2 tsp ground turmeric
- 1 tsp ground coriander
- 1 tsp chili powder
- 1-1/2 tsp salt
- 1-1/2 Tbsp 0 point natural sweetener of choice (stevia, truvia, monkfruit, etc)
- 1/4 cup Coconut Milk Beverage, unsweetened** (located near the almond milk in your grocery store. You might find the brands "So Delicious" or a blend of almond milk or soy milk and coconut milk. As long as it scans as being 1 point per 1/4 cup)

Additional:
- Wooden Skewers
- 0 point cooking spray

**Chicken Note:
Though my instructions show me slicing up THICK chicken breasts, you can purchase 2 pounds of thin cut chicken breasts, or even 2 pounds of "fajita" sliced chicken breasts. You won't have as much control over the size of the strips, but you'll be able to skip over a few of these first steps.

Directions:

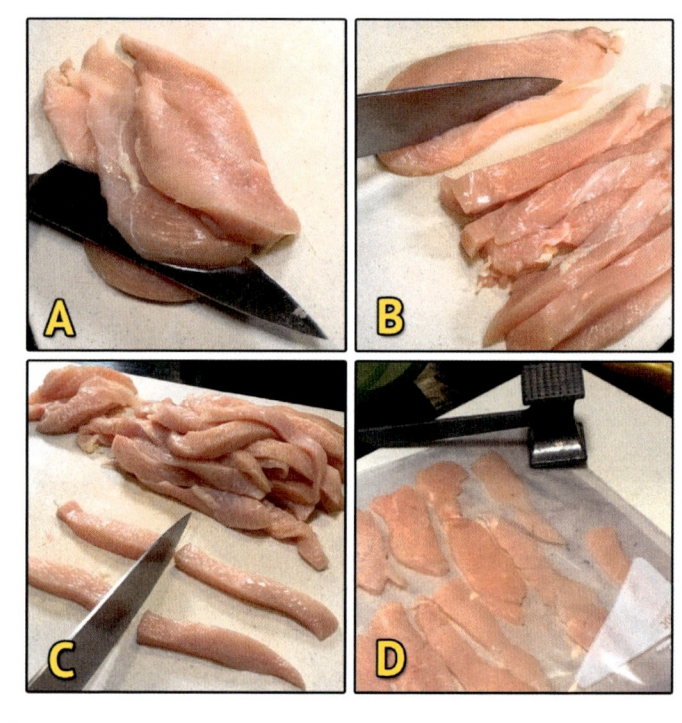

1. **(A)** My grocery store had THICK chicken breasts on sale, so that's what I used. I wanted the strips to be just shy of 1/2 inch thick, so I had to slice the chicken breast, horizontally, in 1/3's. **(B)** Slice all of your breast cutlets into long strips, there will be a LOT of them. **(C)** These are appetizers, so cut all of the really long strips in half. Hey... you're entertaining, so the more skewers you can get out of that 2 pounds of chicken the better. **(D)** Place a handful of the sliced chicken strips between 2 separate gallon sized plastic bags and using a mallet, play whack-a-mole with them. You don't want to tear them apart, just flatten them a little bit. If you need to let out more aggression, might I suggest using **Talk Space** in the app?

4. **(A)** Carefully skewer each chicken strip and place onto the foil lined pans. **(B)** Turn on your oven's BROILER to High. Once the flame has turned on the broiler, spray the chicken with cooking spray, then place it into the oven. **(C)** After about 7-8 minutes, the chicken on the top rack should start getting some burnt char, that's what you want. Swap the pans, moving the top pan to the bottom rack and the bottom pan up to the top so that it starts to get charred. It should take 5-6 minutes this time. Keep an eye on it. **(D)** When the tops of both pans of chicken have a little bit of black char on them, remove from the oven. **Serve with my low point & calorie Thai Peanut Dip, recipe found in the "Dips & Spreads" section.** Garnish by squeezing a lime over the skewers, then sprinkle with fresh chopped cilantro or sliced green onion. Done.

NOTES:
A) I was able to get 42 thin sliced chicken strips from the 2 lbs of chicken, HOWEVER, you may get less. Adjust your points per serving accordingly. To help with that, know that there is only 1 single ingredient point in this marinade.
B) If you want to add a little bit more yellow coloring and flavor, add a little 0 points-worth of yellow curry powder.
C) Keep an eye on your skewers when they are under the broiler, once they start to char, they can burn quickly.
D) If time heals all wounds, why don't belly buttons fill in?

2. **(A)** Put all of your marinade ingredients together for a cool picture. **(B)** Place all of the listed marinade ingredients into a food processor or blender and **(C)** process until smooth. In a large mixing bowl, **(D)** coat all of the chicken with the marinade. Cover with plastic wrap, allow to marinate for AT LEAST 12 hours.

3. The next day.... Soak your wooden skewers in a pan of water for 30 minutes. Line 2 baking sheet pans with foil, then spray with cooking spray. Position 1 of your oven racks onto the 2nd position from the top, then preheat your oven to 450 degrees.

Appetizers • Page 65

These... are... amaaaazing! There's a lot of prep involved, but it's so incredibly worth it. When I was looking through pictures of Spanish Tapas, I saw these and fell in love, I had to try them. For folks not familiar with mini peppers... they aren't hot, they are little teeny bell peppers, which you can find in the produce aisle. I veer away from traditional Spanish recipes by using my low point and calorie Chorizo recipe. I also use fat free Feta cheese instead of mexican cheese, because it's lower in points, and instead of mayo for the dip, we're using fat free Greek Yogurt mixed with Mexican hot sauce (like Chalula).

Servings Info.:

Yield: 33 peppers**
Servings: 33**
Serving Size: 1 Pepper

Point Values:

1-8 servings = 0 points
9-24 servings = 1 point

Ingredients:

- (1) 32oz bag multi colored mini peppers
- 1 pound batch of my Low Point ground turkey Chorizo.
- *(recipe can be found in the "Meat Seasonings" section.)*
- 1/4 cup fat free feta cheese crumbles *(in the meat)*
- 1/2 cup finely diced onion *(in the meat)*
- 2 Tbsp fat free feta cheese crumbles *(for garnish)*
- thin sliced green onion *(for garnish)*

Mexican Hot Sauce Dip:
- 1 cup plain fat free Greek yogurt
- 1/2 tsp ground cumin
- 1/2 tsp salt
- 1-1/2 Tbsp of Mexican Hot Sauce *(like Cholula or Tapatio)*

Directions:

1. First... the filling. You'll be making a batch of my ground turkey chorizo, but with 2 changes. Season the meat according to the regular recipe, but in addition, mix 1/4 cup of feta cheese crumbles and 1/2 cup diced onion. Mix until well combined, then cover with plastic wrap and set aside.

2. Though I purchased a large bag of mini peppers at the store, you may have to buy multiple smaller bags, depending on what your local store carries. Remember, these aren't spicy, they are little bell peppers.

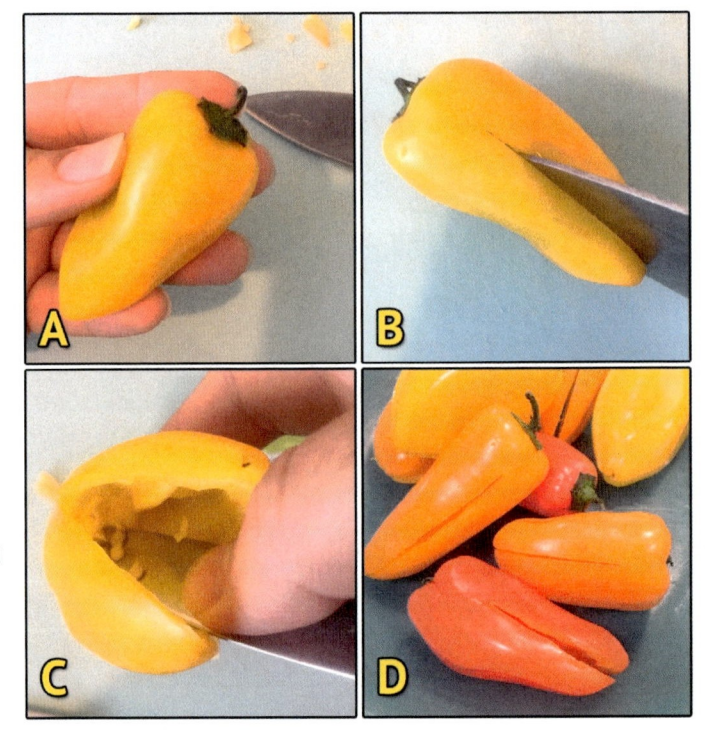

3. (A) Take all of your peppers out and then wash and dry them. You are NOT allowed to get E-Coli when cooking my food... this isn't Chipotle. (B) Use a sharp knife to carefully slice 3/4 of the way through each pepper. (C) Use a butter knife, thin spoon, or any preferred kitchen tool, to scoop the seeds out of every pepper. You don't have to get all of the vein out also, though you can if you want. This is the time consuming step. (D) When you are done, you can move on to the next step, or store the peppers in a ziplock bag overnight, but put a paper towel inside the bag.

4. Take your Chorizo mixture and use a Tablespoon measuring spoon to scoop out an even 1 tablespoon of meat. Use your fingers to pinch the back ends of the pepper, to open it wide enough to stuff the meat inside. Press the 2 halves of the pepper together to squish the filling and make as small of a seam as possible. Then preheat your oven to 425 degrees, placing 1 of your oven racks at the top position, right under your broiler.

NOTES:
A) You can make an Italian version of these peppers by using my 0 point Italian Sausage recipe instead of the Chorizo. Instead of garnishing with feta cheese crumbles and green onion, use parmesan cheese and chopped basil. Serve with my 0 point marina sauce as a dip.
B) The 14-15 minute cook time doesn't sound like a lot, but it DOES cook the meat all the way through because of the high heat. Also, 1 tablespoon of meat filling per pepper doesn't sound like a lot, but it's perfect. Trust me.
C) Your actual points per serving, will vary by how many peppers you make. My chorizo filling made 33 peppers.

5. Line a large sheet pan with foil, then spray with cooking spray. Place all of your peppers on the tray, then coat the ever-livin bajeezus out of them with cooking spray. Pretend you're applying spray-tan. **(A)** Bake for 10 minutes at 425 degrees, on the top rack. **(B)** When they have baked for 10 minutes, turn on your oven's BROILER to High. Broil the peppers on the top rack for 2 minutes, then carefully rotate the pan and BROIL for an additional 1-2 minutes, until they are lightly charred. Remove from oven. You're aaaaalmost done.

6. Now, let's make the dip, it's ridiculously easy. In a bowl, mix together all of the sauce ingredients till well combined. Add more hot sauce if desired. Eat.

Appetizers • Page 67

Cheese

...Gnocchi and a Creamy Cheddar Cheese Sauce

This Mac n Cheese is a direct byproduct of the infamous Lobster Fiasco of 2019 that **@andmatsmom** thrust upon me. She attempted to murder me by sending 2 extremely angry, extremely live and extremely vicious LIVE lobsters to me in the mail. Though battling those vile sea predators will likely require years of therapy, I am consoling myself with Crab Mac n Cheese. Glorious, glorious crab mac n cheese. She sent me a whole box of fresh seafood and I wanted to take full advantage of it to make some snazzy dishes, with ingredients that I'd never buy on my own, namely a bunch of fresh lump crab meat. For those of you who don't want to pony up the Benjamins for crab, you can definitely use chopped up shrimp for this recipe too.

Servings Info.:
Yield: 3 cups
Servings: 4
Serving Size: 3/4 cup

Point Values:
1 serving = 3 points
2 servings = 7 points
3 servings = 10 points

Ingredients:

Pre Made:
- For this recipe you will need a 1/2 cup dough ball of my Ricotta Gnocchi, rolled out, cut, prepared and cooked, as detailed in my Low Point Pasta Guide, on my website: www.theguiltfreegourmet.net, in the "Cooking Guides" area.

Cheese Sauce:
- 1/2 cup Campbell's Healthy Request, Condensed Cheddar Cheese Soup. (you want 1/2 cup of the goop, from the can)
- 1/2 cup unsweetened almond milk
- 1/2 cup chicken broth
- 3 slices fat free cheese slices (or 2 points total cheese)
- 1/8 tsp dried mustard
- 4 tsp cornstarch, dissolved with 1 Tbsp water
- 1-1/2 tsp Kernel's Seasons popcorn seasoning white cheddar or nacho cheese flavored popcorn sprinkles.

Ingredients:
- 1/2 pound lump crab meat
- 2/3 cup onion diced
- 2/3 cup red bell pepper diced
- 2/3 cup celery diced
- 1 medium clove garlic, minced
- 1/2 tsp old bay seasoning
- 1/2 tsp salt
- 1/4 tsp pepper
- olive oil cooking spray, 0 point
- 4 tsp panko breadcrumbs, for topping

Directions:

1. **(A)** First, make the sauce. Add the condensed soup, almond milk, broth, cheese slices, dried mustard and cheese flavored popcorn seasoning (optional) to a sauce pot and bring to a low boil. **(B)** Pour in the dissolved cornstarch mixture, stir and allow to cook at a low boil for 2-3 minutes. Remove from heat, set aside. **(C)** Cook the onions, red peppers, celery, garlic, old bay, salt and pepper in a large pan, using cooking spray, **(D)** for 4-5 minutes, till slightly softened. If the mixture is a little dry, hit it with more spray while it cooks.

NOTES:
A) If you don't want to make the ricotta gnocchi, you CAN use storebought pasta of your choosing, but adjust your points per serving accordingly.
B) I use the cheese flavored popcorn seasonings, which can be found at pretty much ANY major grocery store, for an added cheese boost for the sauce. It is optional and not required. You can also use Molly McButter Cheese flavored sprinkles if you'd like, just scan them to make sure you only use 0 points of whatever seasoning you choose. They can be found next to the popcorn in all major grocery stores, as well as target, walmart, etc.
C) Chopped up shrimp would make a great substitute for crab in this dish.
D) Though teeeeeeeechnically a side dish... this is my book and I can put it where I want, so neener neener. Besides... a good Mac n Cheese transcends all barriers.

2. **(A)** While your veggies are cooking, heat up a small pot of water to a boil. Drop your premade Ricotta Gnocchi into the boiling water for 1 minute, to reheat them. Drain and set aside. **(B)** Crank up the heat on your veggies and add the lump crab meat, gently fold in to combine. **(C)** Pour the gnocchi into the pan and gently fold into the veggie & crab mixture. **(D)** Pour in the cheese sauce and gently fold in.

3. Preheat your oven to 375 degrees. **(A)** Spray (4) 1 cup ramekins with cooking spray and fill with 3/4 cup of the pasta. Top serving with 1 tsp of panko bread crumbs, spray with cooking spray, then **(B)** bake for 15-20 minutes, or until the breadcrumbs are golden and toasted. Done. **(C)** You can also bake it all in a 1 quart casserole dish, if desired.

Appetizers • Page

Cuban Beef Picadillo is traditionally made with ground beef, seasoned with cumin, garlic, oregano, cilantro, lime juice.... even olives and cinnamon. Sofrito sauce is a basic cuban tomato sauce that's made with diced onions, green bell peppers, coriander, paprika and more. My version uses ground turkey and a skinnied down sofrito, that doesn't rely on gobs of olive oil.

Servings Info.:
Yield: 32 (1/4 cup meatballs)
Servings: 32
Serving Size: 1 meatball

Point Values:
1-3 servings = 0 points
4-9 servings = 1 point
10-15 servings = 2 points

Ingredients:

Picadillo-Spiced Meatballs
- 2 pounds xtra lean ground turkey
- 1 tsp onion powder
- 1-1/2 tsp garlic powder
- 2 Tbsp chicken flavored granules (bouillon)
- 2 tsp worcestershire sauce
- 3 tsp ground cumin
- 1/2 tsp pepper
- 1 tsp dried oregano
- 12 pimiento-stuffed olives, drained and chopped. (med. sized)
- 1/2 cup finely diced red bell pepper
- 1/2 cup finely diced green bell pepper
- 2 medium garlic cloves, minced
- 1/4 cup chopped cilantro
- 1/2 tsp ground cinnamon
- 2 Tbsp lime juice
- 1/2 tsp baking soda dissolved in 1 tsp water **(TRUST ME!!)**
- 1 egg yolk

Sofrito Sauce:
- 30oz tomato sauce (make sure you buy a 0 point can)
- 1 cup each, diced onion and green bell pepper
- 3 Tbsp white wine
- 1/2 cup chicken broth
- 2 tsp smoked paprika
- 1/4 tsp salt
- 1/4 tsp pepper
- 1/2 tsp ground cumin
- 1 tsp dried oregano
- 3 medium garlic cloves, minced
- 1/4 cup chopped cilantro
- 1/4 tsp ground cinnamon
- 1 tsp lime juice

Directions:

1. **(A)** Mix ALL of the meatball ingredients together in a large mixing bowl. Cover and allow to rest 30 minutes. **(B)** Use a Tablespoon measuring spoon to scoop out 2 even Tablespoons into your palm, then roll into a ball. **(C)** Line a baking pan with foil and spray with cooking spray. Place the meatballs on the pan and preheat your oven to 400 degrees. **(D)** Bake the meatballs at 400 degrees for 20 minutes. Remove from heat and set aside.

Big Ballin' Tip:
If the stickiness of the meat mixture is making it hard to roll them into "nice" balls, rub your palms with a little bit of water.

2. **(A)** Dice the onions, garlic and bell peppers for the Sofrito sauce. **(B)** Heat a large pan over medium heat, then use olive oil cooking spray to cook the onions for 5 minutes, until they begin to soften, then add the bell peppers.
(C) Coat the bell peppers and onions with a bit more olive oil cooking spray, then continue cooking until the bell peppers begin to sweat. **(D)** Add the garlic, chicken broth and white wine. Simmer for 2-3 minutes.

3. **(A)** Add the tomato sauce, smoked paprika, salt and pepper, paprika, cumin, dried oregano, cinnamon and lime juice. Stir to combine. **(B)** Stir in the chopped cilantro.
(C) Add the meatballs and pan juices, cover the pan with a lid. Simmer for 10 minutes. **(D)** Garnish with a little bit of crumbled fat free feta and cilantro. Get your grub on.

NOTES:
A) This sounds like a big batch of meatballs, but this recipe has been created as if it was being used for a dinner party, or for entertaining. Feel free to halve the recipe.
B) This makes a lot of meatballs. They are very delicious and extremely low in points and calories, perfect for meal prep throughout the week. Awesome, low point and calorie, yet hearty snacks are totally doable with these.
C) Unlike what you normally expect with ground turkey meatballs, the addition of the baking soda REALLY makes the meat retain a TON of moisture. They end up having a texture and mouth-feel like juicy ground pork.
D) You can use this same method to make any type of meatballs from any of my seasoning mixes. For instance: Use my "Asian" ground turkey recipe to make Asian-spiced meatballs, then mix them with a batch of my sweet & sour dip. Boom.
E) Traditional Sofrito calls for "sweet paprika". I used smoked paprika, because I figured it'd be easier for folks to get.

Appetizers • Page 71

Focaccia

A Hearty, Rustic, Italian-Style, Herbed Bread

I'm pretty sure that if ANYTHING that I ever make will possibly get me sainthood, it'll be this bread. Now, I know that you Italian purists are going to rant about this not being a traditional recipe, like your Sicilian grandma used to make for your mafia uncles... but who cares. This bread is light and airy, with just the right amount of tooth to it. This large loaf makes 24 respectably sized pieces of bread, at 1 point per slice. It's time consuming, but worth it.

Servings Info.:
Yield: 1 loaf
Servings: 24
Serving Size: 1 slice

Point Values:
1 point per slice
(assuming 24 slices per loaf)

Ingredients:

- 2-1/4 tsp active dry yeast
- 3 tsp granulated sugar. (Yes, you HAVE to use real sugar)
- 1/4 cup of aaalmost hot water. (around 100 degrees)
- 1-2/3 cups all purpose flour
- 1-1/2 tsp dried thyme
- 2 medium garlic cloves, smashed and minced
- 1/2 tsp onion powder
- 1/2 tsp garlic powder
- 1/2 tsp salt
- 1/8 tsp black pepper
- 1/2 tsp baking powder (just roll with it, no whining)
- Additional water, for mixing (I used 7-8 Tablespoons)
- olive oil cooking spray

Directions:

1. Place the active dry yeast and 1 teaspoon of sugar, into a tall container, along with 1/4 cup of almost hot water, around 100 degrees (any hotter than 110 degrees and you'll kill the yeast). Stir the water gently to mix the ingredients, then allow to sit, untouched, for 10 minutes. It will foam up, a LOT.

2. Put the flour, 2 remaining teaspoons of sugar, thyme, garlic, onion & garlic powders, salt, pepper and baking powder, into a mixing bowl. After the yeast has risen for 10 minutes (pictured in step 1b), pour it into the flour, along with an 8 second blast of olive oil cooking spray.

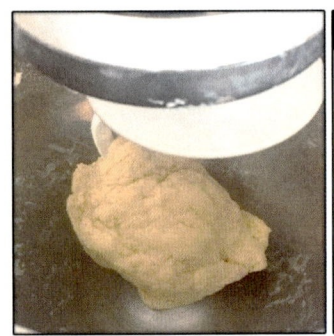

3. Begin to mix the dough. At this point it will be dry and will need more liquid. Add the "additional water" to help bring the dough together into a workable ball. It took my batch 7 Tablespoons, though yours may require a little more or less. Mix the dough for 2-3 additional minutes. If it is a little tacky, spray it with cooking spray to make it easier to handle without sticking to your hands. Also, in the next step, rather than dusting your dough and cutting board with flour, which adds points... spray your work surface, lightly, with cooking spray.

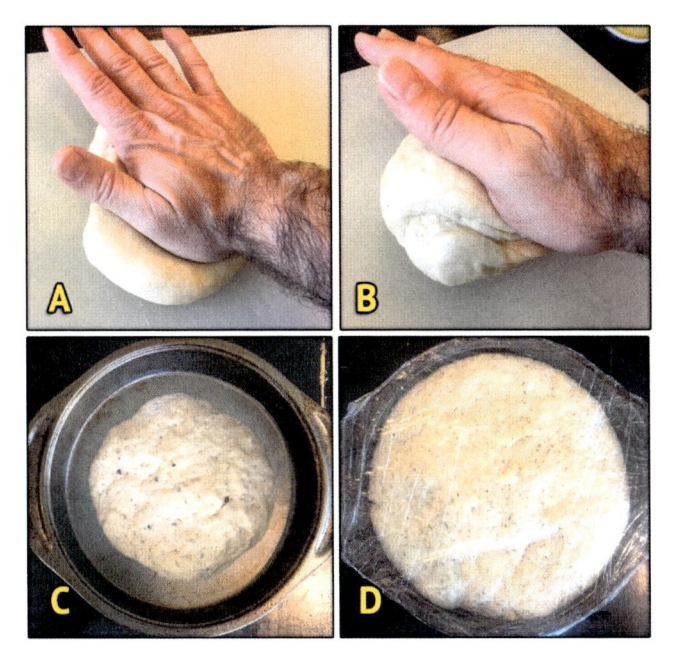

4. (A) Push down on the dough with your palm, then (B) fold the dough over and push down again. Repeat the folding process 30 times, then roll the dough back into a large ball. (C) Spray a 9" pie pan with cooking spray, then use your hands to push the dough down into the pan, stretching it to fill 3/4 of the pan. Spray the top of the dough with olive oil cooking spray, cover the pan tightly with plastic wrap and (D) walk away for 1.5 hours. The dough will expand and fill the entire pan.

5. Heat your oven to 400 degrees, then go wash your hands 🤣. Remove the plastic wrap and poke down into the dough with your finger. Spray the top of the dough with olive oil cooking spray, sprinkle with coarse salt, then bake at 400 degrees for 20 minutes, or until lightly browned.

5. Place your hot bread loaf onto a cutting board. Use a knife to carefully slice the loaf into 4 equal sections. Using the center lines as guides, cut all the way across the loaf, making slices that are just over a 1/2 inch wide. Cutting the bread in this manner will give you 24 slices. The recipe has 24 points of ingredients, Boom.

NOTES:
A) You don't need to season yours like I did, with dried thyme, garlic and onion powders, etc. Season it however you want. Use fresh herbs, if you'd like. At restaurants, you typically see Focaccia bread prepared with chopped fresh rosemary, both inside the bread and placed on top, prior to baking.
B) If you are allergic to Gluten, Bob's Red Mill has a celiac friendly All Purpose Flour. It already has stabilizers and is available at most major grocery stores, as well as Walmart, Target, etc.
C) Trust me on the baking powder. This isn't a traditional recipe, but I don't care about tradition, I care about points, calories and texture. I've made a ton of different variations of this bread and adding this little bit of baking powder, combined with the yeast, had the best results.

Appetizers

I absolutely love mushrooms, but my wife can't stand them, therefore, I never cook them. As you can imagine, I was ecstatic when I saw a traditional Spanish Tapas dish that revolved around them... they're aaaaaaall mine, baby! This recipe makes an insanely delicious serving bowl full of savory mushrooms. Loaded with tons of earthy, smoky flavor from Smoked Paprika, a touch of acidic lemony brightness, the crispy pop of fresh parsley and garnished with Parmesan... This dish is big on flavor, yet comes together easily.

Servings Info.:

Yield: 4 cups
Servings: 8
Serving Size: 1/2 cup

Point Values:

1-3 servings = 0 points
4-8 servings = 1 point

Ingredients:

- (3) 8oz packages, fresh whole mushrooms, any type.
- 4-5 medium cloves garlic, finely diced
- 1/4 cup fresh parsley, finely chopped
- olive oil cooking spray, 8 second spray
- 2 tsp smoked paprika
- 1/2 tsp salt
- 1/4 tsp pepper
- 1 Tbsp lemon juice
- 2 Tbsp chicken broth
- 1/2 tsp reduced fat Parmesan grated topping (like Kraft)

Directions:

1. For this recipe, we're going to need to have a spice that a lot of you don't have on hand, though it's pretty common to find in grocery stores nowadays. Smoked Paprika. You CAN use regular paprika, but the flavor will be dramatically different. Smoked Paprika has an aroma and flavor that I can only describe... as powdered bacon bits. When you take your first smell of it, it blows your mind. It adds a great, earthy, smoky flavor to dishes. Unfortunately though, it has 1 point at 1 tsp. You'll use it a lot in my recipes, so, if you bite the bullet and purchase it, it'll definitely be worth the investment of $6.

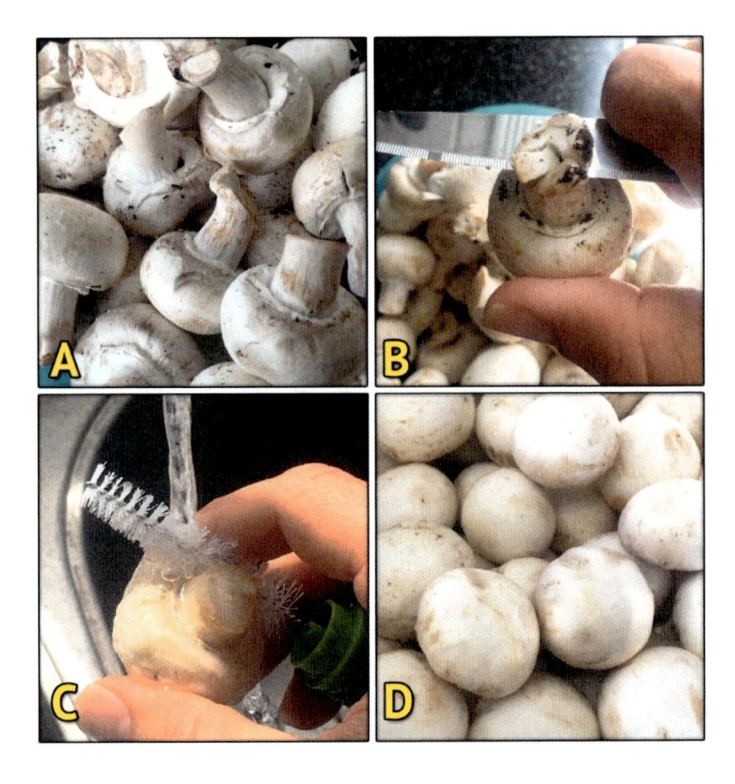

2. (A) Whole mushrooms are covered in dirt when you take them out of the package. First thing that we're going to do is clean them off. (B) Use kitchen scissors or a knife to snip off the very bottom of the stem. (C) Under running water, gently rinse the dirt off of the mushrooms. Use a small brush if desired, but be gentle, the skin is delicate. (D) Set the cleaned mushrooms into a large bowl that has a few layers of paper towels on the bottom. Set aside.

NOTES:

A) This dish gets its uniquely smoky flavor from the Smoked Paprika, which is a key component of the recipe. However, if you do not have access to it, you can definitely substitute regular Paprika in its place, though the flavor will be different, it'll still taste good.
B) I chose to use regular white button mushrooms when I made this recipe because I figured more people would have access to them, versus saying you needed to go buy cremini or baby bella mushrooms. Plus, it sounds less stuck-up-foodie to not demand that you buy a specific type. Use whatever small, whole mushrooms that you like.
C) If you'd like, you can substitute the parsley with basil.
D) You can use REAL reduced fat Parmigiano cheese in place of the grated style topping, if you'd like. It's the same points. I have a toddler that likes spaghetti... I am NOT going to spend $$ on real Parmigiano for a 5 year old. We have the fake stuff. Use what'cha have.
E) Though it's ok in California and Colorado... I would highly recommend not using any "funny" mushrooms for this appetizer. The last thing that you want, is to have your dinner guests all sitting around, giggling and eating your cheetos. Stick to the legal 'shrooms mis amigos.

3. (A) Finely chop the garlic and parsley, then set aside. (B) Heat a large pan over medium high heat. Spray for 8 seconds with olive oil cooking spray, creating a nice, thick layer of 0 point spray. Add the Mushrooms to the pan and lightly spray the top of the mushrooms with cooking spray. (C) Cover and cook for 5 minutes, moving the pan around to stir the covered mushrooms. (D) After 5 minutes, remove the lid and get ready for the fun stuff.

4. Add the smoked paprika, salt, pepper, garlic and parsley to the pan, use a rubber spatula to gently mix the ingredients together. It will be pretty dry. Continue stirring and cooking for another 2-3 minutes, until all of the dry ingredients are distributed pretty evenly, though still thick. Add the lemon juice and chicken broth, stir to create a thick gravy-like sauce from all of the dry ingredients on the bottom of the pan. Cook for another 2 minutes, stirring and allowing the sauce to slighty reduce.

5. Pour or spoon the mushrooms into a large serving bowl and garnish with the Parmesan cheese topping.

Kafta Kabab

Appetizer Sized Roasted Skewers of Lebanese Spiced Ground Turkey

Kafta is a deliciously flavorful ground/minced mixture of meat, herbs, seasonings and onions that is common across all of the Middle East, India and Africa. In Lebanon, which is where my father was raised, it's called Kafta. Traditionally made of ground lamb or beef, mixed with onions, parsley and spices, my recipe is heavily modified to taste amazing with ground turkey.

You would typically find a dish like this is ANY kabab house, made out of beef or lamb. Mine will stand toe to toe with them, and at a fraction of the fat and calories, but with ALL of the full, beefy flavor. Trust me. This mix actually TASTES like beef. It will blow your mind. Your guests won't even know that it's turkey.

Servings Info.:
Yield: 11 skewers
Servings: 11
Serving Size: 1

Point Values:
0 Points, period.

Ingredients:

Ground Turkey Kafta Mixture:
- 1lb batch of my ground turkey Kafta. Recipe on pg 29

Additional:
- 11 Wooden Skewers

Optional:
- Belly Dancer Outfit
- Blu Ray disk of either Lawrence of Arabia, Prince of Persia, or Aladdin. (the original, not the freaky Live Action one)

Directions:

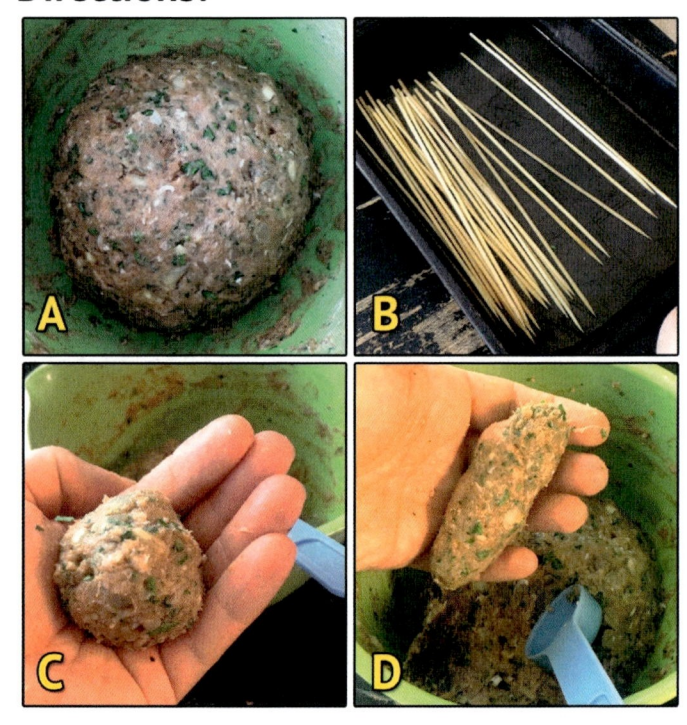

1. **(A)** In a large mixing bowl, combine all of the listed ingredients for the Turkey Kafta. Cover with plastic wrap and let it rest, in the fridge, for at least 30 minutes. **(B)** Fill a large pan or container with water and place your wooden skewers in, allowing them to have a relaxing spa day, for at least 30 minutes. Meanwhile, prepare a baking pan with cooking spray and preheat your oven to 425 degrees. **(C)** When the meat has had a chance to rest, use a measuring spoon to scoop out 3 even Tablespoons of meat, into your palm, then form it into a ball. If the meat starts sticking to your palms, rinse your hands with a little water. **(D)** After you've formed a ball, gently use your palms to squeeze and shape it into a thick cigar shape.

NOTES:
A) I purposely made this recipe using an oven instead of a grill, to accomodate folks who don't own a grill.
B) Adding that small bit of dissolved baking soda to the meat, then letting it rest, is freaking INSANE. There is some magical foodie-voodoo magic that happens, because it makes these end up with the cooked texture and mouth-feel of ground beef/pork, rather than turkey.
C) I would highly recommend serving these with some roasted Roma Tomatoes. When you preheat the oven to 425 and allow the meat to rest… Put a few of the tomatoes into a 9" pie pan, coat them with cooking spray, season with salt and pepper, then put them into the oven. Put them in about 20 minutes before you plan to cook the meat. When the kababs are finished, take the meat out, then turn on your broiler to char the top of the tomatoes.
D) These would also go awesome with a batch of my low point hummus.
E) This recipe definitely works as a main course also, just use more meat when forming the skewers.

2. **(A)** When you have formed one of the balls of meat into a long cigar shape, gently remove one of the wooden skewers from its water bath… I say gently, because they're pretty calm and relaxed right now after their bath… and shove the skewer, mercilessly through the meat. Ignore the terror filled cries from the skewers. Repeat your Vlad the Impaler-ish style stabby spree, until all of the meat is run through and stops twitching. **(B)** Lay each skewer down on the pan, leaving enough space between them, for the wooden skewers that will be facing the opposite way. Then spray them all with a good dose of 0 point cooking spray (olive oil spray is preferred). **(C)** Place the tray into your preheated oven. Bake the kafta kababs for 14 minutes at 425 degrees. **(D)** Remove from the oven and quickly turn each of the kababs over. Lightly spray with cooking spray, then place the tray back into the oven for an additional 6-10 minutes, or until the meat is nicely browned. Don't worry about it drying out. The baking soda trick, combined with all of the moisture we added into these, will keep them moist and delicious.

3. Pop on a DVD of Lawrence of Arabia or Prince of Persia, then start chowing down. You can follow up your meal with some belly dancing fitpoints, if desired.

Appetizers • Page 77

First thing's first... I know not everyone can get saffron. The notes will have suggestions for not using it. Ok, with that out of the way, OMG THIS IS DELICIOUS!!!! Prior to this dish, I had never made mussels before. Want to know how easy it is? I watched a 5 minute Youtube video to learn how to do it. It's that simple. This dish is so rich, flavorful and elegant, that it is sure to be a huge eye poppin' crowd pleaser for parties or entertaining. First, I'll show how to make them with fresh mussels, followed by steps for using frozen mussels... because I'm cool like that.😎

Servings Info.:

Yield: 2 pounds
Servings: 4-6
Serving Size: 1/2 lb.+

Point Values:**

0 points, period.

Ingredients:

- 2 pounds mussels (fresh is preferable)
- 1 tsp reduced fat parmesan topping sprinkles (like Kraft)
- fresh chopped basil or parsley for garnish

Broth Ingredients:
- 8 second spray, butter flavored cooking spray
- 1 medium shallot, finely diced (around 1/4 cup)
- 3 medium garlic cloves, diced
- 8oz bottled clam juice
- 1 Tbsp lemon juice
- 1 Tbsp white wine vinegar
- 2 Tbsp unsweetened plain almond milk
- 1 tsp salt
- 1/4 tsp black pepper
- 3 tsp Molly Mcbutter butter sprinkles (OPTIONAL)
- 1-1/2 tsp cornstarch
- 1/2 tsp loosely packed saffron threads**

Directions:

Just a reminder. I'm going to first, be going over how to make this recipe using FRESH mussels, followed by instructions for making them with Frozen ones.

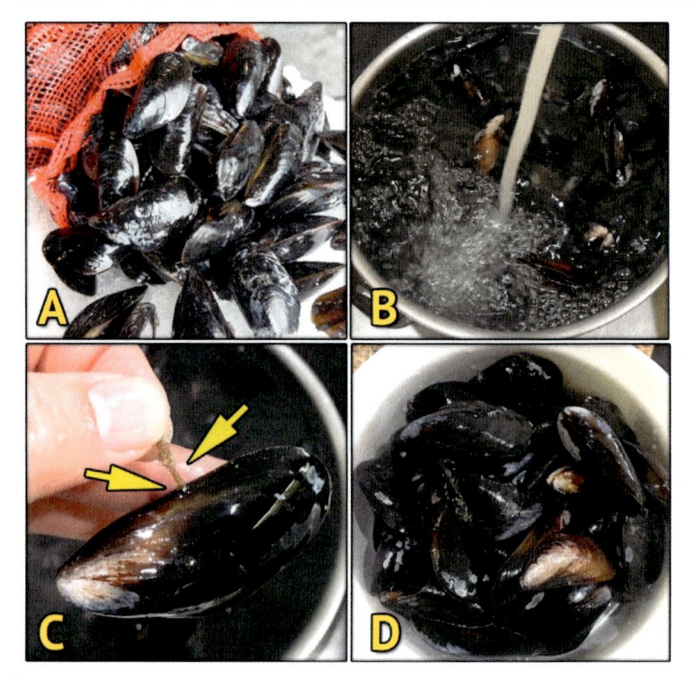

1. (A) Go to the store and buy 2 pounds of fresh mussels. (B) Place them into a large bowl and cover with cool water. Allow them to soak for at least 1 hour. (C) Most all of the mussels have a little fiberous strand, kind of like seaweed, that they use to attach themselves to things in the ocean. It takes a lil effort, but you can either pull it off with your fingers, or use a pair of scissors to snip it off. (D) Put the mussels back into a bowl while you get the sauce ready.

2. In a small bowl, combine the clam juice, lemon juice, vinegar, almond milk, salt, pepper, cornstarch, butter sprinkles (if using) and the saffron threads. Stir together, then let sit for 10 minutes.

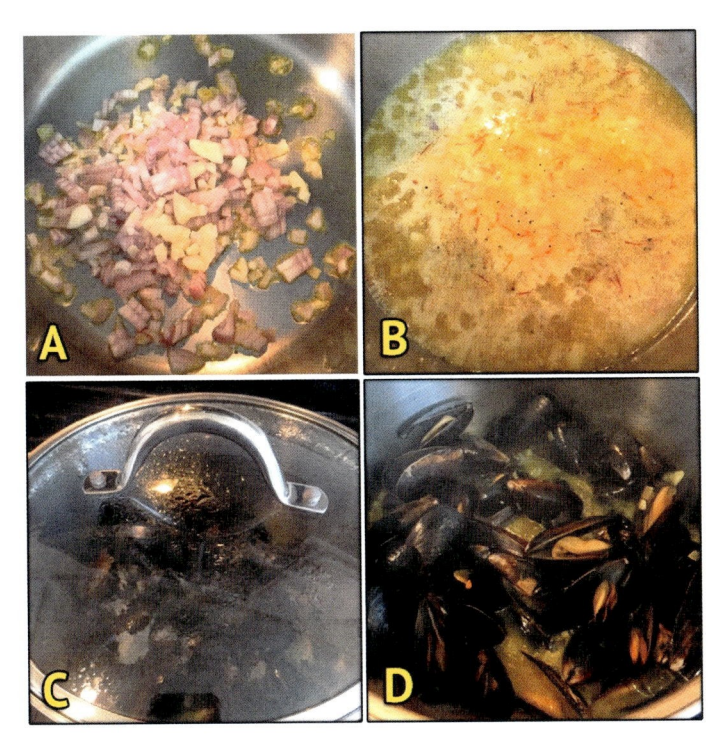

3. (A) In a large pot, sautee the diced shallots and garlic over medium heat, with an 8 second spray of butter flavored cooking spray. Cook until the garlic is fragrant and the shallots are slightly softened. (B) Pour in the Saffron infused liquid, bring to a boil and simmer for 2-3 minutes. (C) Take the mussels out of their water and place them into the pot. Cover and cook on medium heat for 6-7 minutes. (D) Scoop the mussels out into a large serving bowl and pour sauce over the mussels. Sprinkle with the parmesan cheese and garnish with fresh chopped basil or parsley.

Using Frozen Mussels:

Not everyone has access to fresh mussels, so in typical me-fashion, here's how I'd recommend using frozen mussels for this recipe. You can find frozen mussels at your grocery store, in the seafood section, or in the frozen food aisle.

Though those bags say NOT to thaw them out prior to cooking, screw that! These bags have SO MANY bits of tiny shells in them, so yeah... don't thaw them out... but I recommend opening the bag and putting the frozen block o' mussels into a colander. Rinse the frozen mussels off in your sink so that you dissolve all of the chunks of ice. There are TONS of tiny shards of shell trapped in that ice. Now, you'll have gotten rid of 99% of the shell shards. Put the mussels into your pot with the simmering sauce, cover the pot, and cook for 10 minutes. There still might be some little bits of shell, but there will be a lot less. So if you use frozen mussels, skip step #1 of the recipe instructions.

NOTES:
A) Saffron can be found in the spice aisle of most grocery stores, along with the "fancy" spices. It's also at trader joes. Saffron IS pricey (except for at trader joes). If you can't toss money at a random spice, don't worry. Your sauce will still taste great if you replace the saffron with pretty much any other spice. Add some old bay, or some extra garlic and onion powder... maybe a little chicken bouillon... get creative. Heck, want to mimic a little bacon flavor? Add some smoked paprika. Seriously, the Saffron is a big part of Saffron sauce, but you can definitely customize this to whatever you'd like. I encourage you to mess around with the recipe.
B) The purpose of the almond milk and cornstarch is to help mimic a little bit of heavy cream in the sauce. But that's just me. This entire huge platter is 0 points as-is, so feel free to add some I can't believe it's not butter Light, a little bit of whole milk, a splash of white wine... I make my stuff ridiculously low point for a reason, it allows you a LOT of room to put your own personal touch on it, while still staying low calorie and low point.
C) If you can find fresh mussels, USE THEM. It's a little bit more work... but it's worth it to not have all the tiny little shell shards in your dish. As far as price goes, the frozen mussels are almost the same exact price as fresh ones.
D) The saffron sits in the sauce for 10 minutes, to hydrate and pull as much flavor out of it as possible, prior to putting it in the pan.

Yup, I went there. Though not speciiiiifically mentioned in the Good Book... real, crispy, gloriously low point, baked onion rings are something worthy of a choir of Angels. This recipe has gone through a few variations and will no doubt continue to be tweaked. Please tag me in Connect with thoughts for tweaking it. I decided on crushed rice krispies because they are lower in points than crushed bran flakes and have an identical texture to regular breadcrumbs. People with Gluten allergies can use gluten free rice cereal, or can make their own bread crumbs with gluten free bread as well.

Servings Info.:
Yield: 1 full sheet pan o' rings
Servings: 4
Serving Size: 1/4 tray

Point Values:**
1 serving = 1 points
2 servings = 2 points

Ingredients:
- 2 large onions, sliced into 1/2" thick rings

Breading:
- 1-1/4 cup crispy rice cereal (like rice krispies). Place it in a ziplock bag and crush it. You'll end up with around 2/3 cup.
- 1-1/2 tsp plain breadcrumbs
- 2 tsp panko breadcrumbs
- 1/4 tsp salt
- 1/4 tsp black pepper
- 1/4 tsp garlic powder
- 1/4 tsp onion powder
- 1/2 tsp italian seasoning

Egg Wash:
- 2 large eggs
- 1-1/2 tsp self rising flour
- 1-1/2 tsp cornstarch
- 1 tsp dijon mustard
- 1/2 tsp water

Directions:
1. Preheat oven to 425 degrees. Line a large 11"x22" baking sheet with tin foil, spray with cooking oil, set aside.

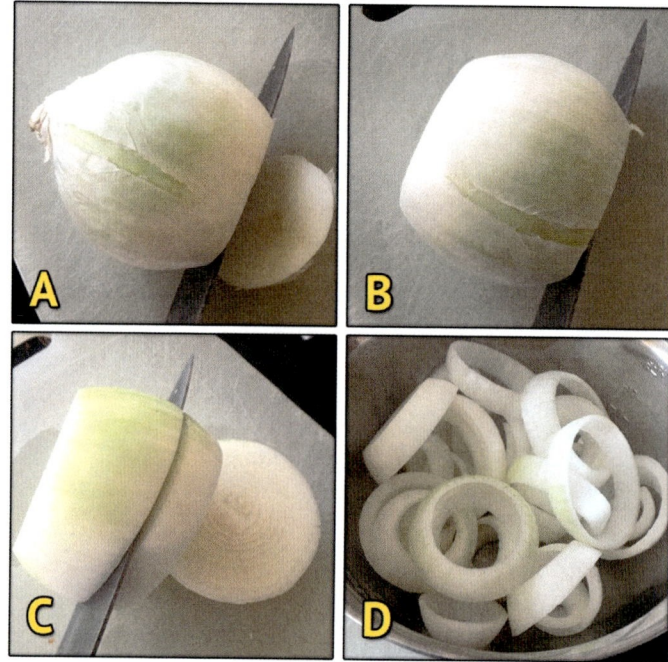

2. Slice the ends off of each side of the onions, then peel off the first layer. Slice each onion into roughly 1/2" thick cross sections. Use your fingers to push the rings apart, separating them into a large bowl. Cover with a damp paper towel, it'll catch all of the fumes that normally make you look like you just watched the end of "Steel Magnolias" and "Old Yeller."

3. For the egg wash, mix the flour, cornstarch dijon mustard and water until smooth. Then whisk the eggs in a medium bowl and add the mustard/flour mix. Whisk till smooth. Mix together the breading ingredients in a separate bowl, set aside.

4. (A) Dredge the onion rings, one at a time, into the thickened egg wash. (B) Place the ring into the bowl with the breading and gently shake the bowl around, to lightly coat the rings, one at a time. (C) Remove the rings with a fork, to minimize contact with your fingers. It's much less messy this way. (D) Place the rings onto the large baking sheet pan. I was able to get 20 good sized onion rings to squeeze onto my pan. Coat your onion rings with a healthy dose of cooking spray. Seriously... pretend that you're a cast member on Jersey Shore, applying spray-on bronzer.

5. (A) Bake the saturated onion rings at 425 degrees for 15 minutes, then remove from oven and (B) flip the rings with a fork. Return to the oven and bake for an additional 5-10 minutes at 425, depending on how crispy you want them. I was happy with mine at 5.

6. Remove from the oven, and flip them back over. Trust me, the original side will look prettier. It spent less time cooking against the tin foil, so it will have more of a golden brown coloring than the side that was originally on the bottom.

NOTES:

A) The amount of onion rings per serving will vary, depending on how many rings YOU make from your onions and are able to cram onto your baking pan. When I made it, I got 20 good sized rings crammed onto my pan, therefore, I counted it as 2 separate 10 ring portions. There is only 4 points in this recipe, so the points per serving is completely dependent on how many servings YOU choose to have from your tray. 2 servings, 3 servings (the first serving would be 1 point), it's entirely up to you. But this is 4 points in total.

B) As stated before, I chose to use crispy rice cereal, rather than bran flakes, which others suggested, because an equal amount of flakes is more points than rice cereal. You may definitely swap out some of the crushed rice cereal with some crushed flakes if you wish, which would add a bit of "Panko breadcrumbs" texture, but make sure to adjust your points accordingly.

C) Most major supermarkets offer a Gluten Free rice cereal, REMEMBER... Kellogg's Rice Krispies IS NOT GLUTEN FREE.

D) I add a small amount of actual breadcrumbs to this recipe, in addition to the rice cereal, to add an extra bit of 0 point bulk to the breading. You can always crush up some dried low point, Gluten Free bread, if you need to make your own bread crumbs.

E) This recipe, though good, is a work in progress. As always, I do not take offense, and actually welcome any and all feedback and thoughts of yours, for how my recipes can be tweaked or improved. AS LONG AS THE POINTS PER SERVING DON'T GO UP! If you have a thought or suggestion, please tag me, @dhallakx7, in Connect. If I don't respond to your tag in a few days, tag me again in that post. Your comment got buried in my notifications.

I have to admit that prior to attempting this recipe, I've never eaten "Jerk" anything before, in my life. No, eating food that's been PREPARED BY a Jerk, doesn't count... I looked it up and the internet never lies. Jerk seasoning is a popular seasoning mix in the Caribbean, but is most famously associated with Jamaica. The most famous dish, of course, being Jerk chicken. "Jerk" is a very exotic flavor blend, containing allspice, cinnamon, nutmeg, brown sugar and a ton of heat from hot peppers. In this appetizer, I wanted to try to make a single bite, fun take on a Cuban/Caribbean dish. In WW, plaintains are a lot of points, where bananas are 0 points. So, I set out to make a crispy, baked and breaded banana slice to take the place of fried plantains. This dish has a nice balance of spicy, sweet, citrusy, and texture combinations.

Servings Info.:
Yield: 30
Servings: 30
Serving Size: 1 skewer

Point Values:
1 serving = 0 points
2-4 servings = 1 point
5-8 servings = 2 points

Ingredients:

Caribbean Jerk Meatballs
- 1 pound batch of my "Jerk" seasoned ground turkey. Recipe found in Meat Seasoning section, as well as in the Low Point Meat Seasoning Guide at:
www.theguiltfreegourmet.net > Cooking Guides

Breaded Banana Bites:
- (30) 3/4" slices of banana
- 1-3/4 cups rice krispies cereal, measured, then crushed.
- 1-1/2 tsp bread crumbs
- 2 tsp panko breadcrumbs
- 1-1/2 tsp self rising flour
- 1/2 tsp ground cinnamon
- 2 large eggs, whipped, for egg wash

Sauce/Glaze:
- 3/4 cup water
- 1/4 cup sugar free maple syrup (pancake syrup)
- 1 Tbsp 0 point natural sweetener of choice (Stevia, Monkfruit, Truvia, etc)
- 2 tsp rum extract (in the spice aisle, by the vanilla extract)
- 1 Tbsp lime juice
- 1/8 tsp cayenne pepper
- 1-1/2 tsp cornstarch dissolved in a little water

Additional Ingredients:
- 30 bite sized chunks of fresh pineapple
- Additional fresh thyme for garnish, finely chopped

Directions:

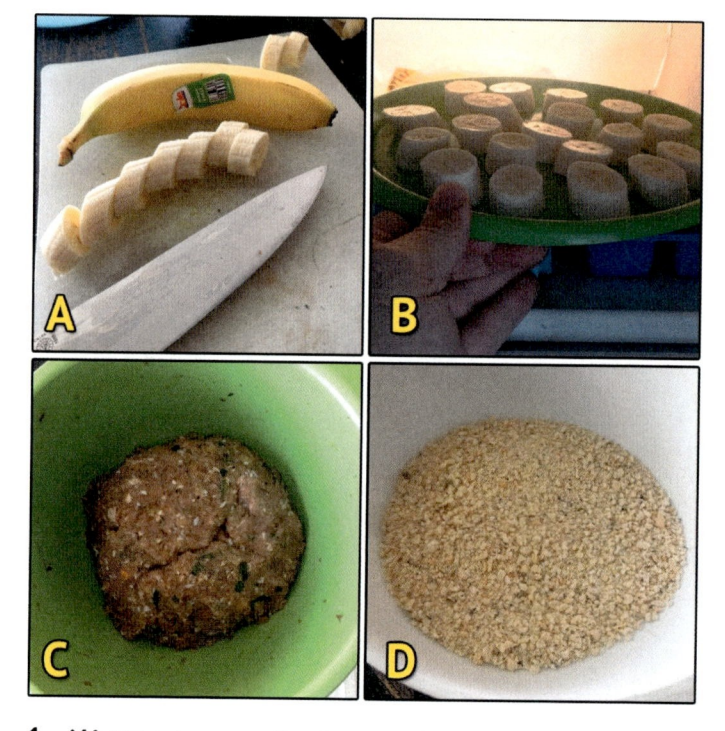

1. **(A)** It'll take you a few bananas, but make 30 slices, roughly around 3/4 inch thick and set onto freezer-safe plates, spritzed with cooking spray. **(B)** Place the bananas into the freezer while you prepare the other ingredients. **(C)** Mix a 1lb batch of the "Jerk" seasoned ground turkey, from my recipe that can be found in my meat seasoning guide at **www.theguiltfreegourmet.net**. Cover with plastic wrap and allow to sit for 30 minutes. **(D)** While the meat is resting and the bananas are freezing, make the breading. Place the rice krispies, breadcrumbs, self rising flour and cinnamon into a large ziplock bag. Crush the mixture until the rice krispies are broken down and it all takes on the texture of regular bread crumbs. Set aside.

2. **(A)** Beat the 2 eggs together in a bowl. Remove the bananas from the freezer, then dip them 1 at a time, into the egg wash. **(B)** Let the excess egg drip off of the banana, then coat with the breading. Place each breaded slice onto a large baking tray, lined with foil paper and coated with cooking spray. **(C)** Bake the bananas at 425 degrees for 12 minutes, then flip and **(D)** bake for 10 more minutes, or until browned. Remove from oven, set aside.

3. **(A)** Line a baking pan with foil and cooking spray. Use a measuring spoon to scoop even 1 Tablespoon scoops of meat into your palm. Form into small balls, then **(B)** place onto the baking pan. **(C)** Bake the meat at 425 degrees for 15 minutes, or until cooked through. Set aside.

4. **(A)** Use paper towels to pat your pineapple chunks dry. Heat a large pan over medium high heat, spray the pineapple with cooking spray, then cook for 3 minutes on each side, till charred. Set aside **(B)** Combine ALL of the sauce ingredients into the pan and bring to a low boil for 2 minutes, till thickened. **(C)** Toss the meatballs in the glaze, then set aside in a bowl. **(D)** Place the pineapple chunks into the glaze, toss to coat, then turn off heat.

5. Assemble by setting one cooled banana chip onto a plate. Set a meatball on top of the banana, then place a piece of pineapple on top of the meatball. Skewer with a toothpick and garnish with finely chopped fresh thyme.

NOTES:
A) You can use papaya or mango in place of the pineapple.
B) Adjust the level of spice, by adjusting the cayenne pepper.
C) Use real maple syrup, sugar, or actual Rum, if you wish, but adjust your points accordingly. You'll also need to increase the amount of Rum used, vs rum extract.

Appetizers • Page 83

Ok, in full disclosure, I have to admit that prior to this recipe, I had never made clams before in my life. Hopefully, that'll make you see how easy all these shellfish are to make. Anyways, this recipe is actually a famous Portuguese dish called "Amêijoas à Bulhão Pato" (Clams in White Wine Sauce). They have a delicious broth, typically made with white wine, butter, garlic and cilantro. I'm lightening it up by cutting the wine with water and white wine vinegar, to save points while retaining 90% of the flavor.

Servings Info.:
Yield: 2 pounds
Servings: 4
Serving Size: 7-8 clams

Point Values:
1 servings = 0 points
3-4 servings = 1 point

Ingredients:
- 2 pounds small variety Live clams (1-1/2" to 2" wide)
- 3 Tbsp white wine
- 1 Tbsp white wine vinegar
- 1 Tbsp water
- 1 tsp lemon juice
- 1 pinch black pepper
- 8 second spray, olive oil cooking spray
- 3-4 medium cloves fresh garlic, finely chopped or minced
- 1/2 cup fresh cilantro, chopped
- 1/4 cup flat leaf parsley, chopped

Pre-Soak:
- 1 large bowl or pot
- cold water
- salt
- 1 tsp cornmeal *(don't count for points, see notes)*

Directions:

1. At your local grocery store, there may be a few varieties of clams. We're going to avoid the larger ones for this recipe and choose a type that's on the smaller side, around 1-1/2 to 2 inches across. Otherwise we end up only getting around 12 clams for those 2 pounds, rather than 30-32. We want to fill up a medium serving bowl with small clams, not serve people 3 large ones.

2. **(A)** When you get home, pour all of the clams out into a large bowl. **(B)** In a cup, stir together 1 cup of water and 1 Tbsp of salt until dissolved. Fill the large bowl with the clams with enough cool water to cover them by a few inches, then pour in the salt water. Scoop 1 teaspoon of cornmeal into the water and slightly stir to distribute it. Let the clams soak for at least 1 hour. **(C)** Rinse off the clams, then **(D)** use a kitchen brush to clean each one, gently, they're ticklish. Set aside in the fridge.

NOTES:

A) The reason that I'm not counting the points for the 1 teaspoon of cornmeal is because of it's purpose. It is added to the water to act as debris. The theory being, that when the clams are soaking in the salt water, the gritty cornmeal particles in the water, encourage the clams to spit out any sand that they might have inside of their shells. Later, when you pour out the water and rinse off the clams, there's no reason to count the cornmeal as part of the actual recipe.

B) As stated earlier, make sure not to purchase large clams for this recipe. This is an appetizer for sharing. You CAN use larger clams if want, but you'll need to buy 4-5 pounds. $$$

C) MODIFY THIS RECIPE!!!! Feel free to replace the white wine and vinegar with chicken broth, bottled clam juice, anything you want. Add more garlic, add less garlic, add different herbs, add tomatoes... Use this as a template to make your own clam dish. It's super super simple. The only time consuming part is soaking the clams in the salt water.

3. (A) Mince the garlic cloves, chop the parsley and cilantro, set aside. (B) Spray 8 seconds of olive oil cooking spray into a large pan, over medium heat and immediately pour in the white wine, vinegar, water and pepper. Bring to a boil. (C) Once the liquid begins to boil, add the clams to the pan. Once the liquid begins to simmer again, (D) cover the pan and cook for 3 minutes. (E) Remove the lid and add the chopped herbs and garlic. Gently swirl the pan to spread the herbs around. (F) Replace the lid and cook for an additional 4 minutes, or until most all of the clams have opened wide. Use a spoon or tongs to place any opened clams into a serving bowl. If any clams have not opened, leave them in the pan, return the lid, and continue cooking for 2 more minutes to see if they open up. If they don't, they go in the trash. Otherwise, add ALL of the opened clams into the serving bowl and cover with the sauce. Done.

Rotolo di Lasagne

"Coiled" Mini Lasagna Rolls, With Delicate, Scratch-Made Pasta

Believe it or not, this appetizer was inspired by a commercial for... Olive Garden *gasp*. They showed a big hunk of lasagna that was rolled up and plated. But, rather than having it served on it's side, like you'd normally see, theirs is served standing upright. That immediately got the wheels turning. A 1/4 cup ball of fresh pasta dough can be made into a gigantic pasta sheet. So I wanted to try seeing how many servings I could get out of it. What you end up with is a mouthful of lasagna that's light, delicious and flavorful.

Servings Info.:
Yield: 19 rolls**
Servings: 19**
Serving Size: 1" thick rolls

Point Values:**
1 serving = 0 points
2-4 servings = 1 point
5-6 servings = 2 points

Ingredients:

Pasta Dough:
- 1/4 cup pasta dough ball. Make your dough as shown in my Low Point Pasta Guide, which can be downloaded for free in the "Cooking Guides" section of my website.

Lasagna Filling:
- 1 pound batch of my 0 point Italian Sausage. Recipe can be found in my FREE Meat Seasoning guide, in the "Cooking Guides" section of my website.
- 2 medium cloves garlic, finely chopped
- 1/2 cup diced onion
- 1/2 cup fresh basil, chopped **(optional)**
- 2 cups packed spinach, chopped
- 3/4 cup Greek yogurt
- 1 egg yolk
- 1 Tbsp reduced fat grated Parmesan cheese topping (Kraft)

5 Minute Marina Sauce:
- 1/2 cup diced onion
- 5 medim cloves roasted or regular garlic
- 1/2 cup chicken broth
- 1 tsp each, dried basil, oregano, parsley
- 1 Tbsp red wine vinegar
- 1 tsp 0 point sweetener
- 45oz canned tomato sauce (make sure it's a 0 point brand)

Topping:
- 1/4 cup shredded reduced fat mozzarella cheese

Directions:

1. **(A)** Take your batch of italian sausage and mix in the onions and garlic. Cook in a large pan, over med.-high heat. **(B)** When the meat is cooked through, add the spinach and basil. Cover and cook till wilted. **(C)** Place the meat, yogurt, egg yolk and parmesan into a food processor. **(D)** Pulse a few times until the filling is broken down, but not pureed. Set aside.

2. In a medium sized pot, heat all of the Marinara sauce ingredients, except for the tomato sauce, for 3 minutes over med.-high heat. Pour in the tomato sauce, then use a blender or hand blender to puree the mixture. Set aside.

4. **(A)** Spread a thin layer of marinara on top of the filling, then gently roll it all up, like a long jelly roll. **(B)** Use a sharp knife to gently cut 1" wide slices. I recommend using a slow back and forth sawing motion. Don't press down too hard or you'll smush the pasta. **(C)** After you cut a serving, lay it down flat, then use your fingers to gently shape it into a rounded shape, if needed. **(D)** Place a layer of marinara sauce on the bottom of a baking dish, then carefully use a fork to lift the rolls into the pan, 1 at a time. Slide the fork's prongs underneath the rolls while transfering them. Then place a small amount of marinara (about 1-2 tsp) on top of each slice. You want to keep the outside walls of pasta exposed to the heat of the oven, without sauce on them. **(E)** Sprinkle the mozzarella on top of the rolls. **(F)** Bake the rolls for 20-25 minutes at 375 degrees. You want to bake them until the pasta on the outside, gets slightly browned and firm to the touch. The inside is very soft, so having the outside pasta be browned and toasted is ideal. Garnish all of the plated "coils" with 1-1/2 tsp of grated parmesan topping and some fresh chopped parsley.

NOTES:
- If you use regular store bought lasagna noodles, boil them, follow the same process, but roll them up from end to end, then make slices. You'll only get 2 or 3" pieces per noodle, but it's still doable. Adjust points accordingly.
- I was able to make 19 servings from my pasta sheet. If you aren't able to get as many slices from your pasta, adjust your points accordingly.

3. **(A)** Take your large sheet of pasta, made from a 1/4 cup pasta dough ball and boil it for 2 minutes. **(B)** Remove it from the water, rinse it off (JUST DO IT!) then pat it dry with towels. **(C)** Lightly spray a large work surface with cooking spray, then place the pasta down and ladle some of the tomato sauce on top. **(D)** Cover with all the filling.

Appetizers • P

When I came up with this recipe, my original intention was to make some awesomely flavorful and low calorie/point CRAB CAKES!!! But when I went to the grocery store, 2 pounds of lump crab was $50. There ain't no way that this here cowpoke was spending $50 on an appetizer and there's no way I would ask you to... so... I swapped the crab for fresh salmon. Easy Peasy. This recipe makes 14 delicous 1/3 cup appetizer sized salmon cakes, though you could easily use Crab, Lobster, or any fish you'd like.

Servings Info.:
Yield: 14 salmon cakes)
Servings: 14
Serving Size: 1

Point Values:
1 serving = 0 points
2-5 servings = 1 point
6-8 servings = 2 points

Ingredients:
- 2 pounds fresh salmon, diced and chopped **(NOT THE CANNED STUFF!)**

Vegetable Mixture
- 1/3 cup finely diced red bell pepper
- 1/3 cup finely diced yellow bell pepper
- 1/3 cup finely diced red onion
- 1/3 cup finely diced celery
- 1/4 cup chopped flat leaf parsley
- 1/2 tsp salt
- 1/4 tsp black pepper
- 1/2 tsp old bay seasoning
- 1 egg
- 1/2 cup fat free Greek yogurt
- 1/2 tsp worcestershire sauce
- 1/4 tsp hot sauce (or more, to taste)
- 2 tsp dijon mustard

Breading:
- 1-1/4 cups rice krispies cereal (measure 1-1/4 cup, then crush it)
- 1-1/2 tsp regular breadcrumbs
- 2 tsp panko breadcrumbs

Directions:

1. **(A)** Spray a pan with cooking spray, then cook the red and yellow bell peppers, red onion, celery and flat leaf parsley over medium high heat. Cook till just softened, season with salt, pepper and old bay. Set aside, allowing to cool to room temperature. **(B)** Dice all of your salmon into bite sized chunks. You don't want perfectly uniform diced salmon, you want small chunks of varying sizes. **(C)** Place the cooled vegetables, chopped salmon, egg, yogurt, worcestershire, hot sauce and dijon mustard into a large mixing bowl. Mix until combined. **(D)** Place the rice krispies into a large ziplock bag and crush. Once they have the consistency of breadcrumbs, add all the breading ingredients into the salmon and mix together. Cover and allow to rest in the fridge for 30 minutes.

2. Line a sheet pan with parchment paper, then lightly spray with cooking spray. Preheat your oven to 425 degrees.

3. **(A)** Start off by slightly wetting your hands with some tap water, trust me. Using a measuring cup, scoop out an EVEN 1/3 cup portion of the salmon mixture into your palm. **(B)** Lightly press it together with your palms, you want to keep it as a tall mound. Place each one down onto the parchment paper, then gently press down on the top to slightly flatten the top. **(C)** Repeat until all of the salmon has been used, then coat the top of the patties with cooking spray.
(D) Bake at 425 degrees for 16 minutes.

4. **(A)** When the timer goes off, remove the pan from the oven and quickly, but gently, flip the salmon cakes over. Spray the tops with cooking spray, then return to the oven.
(B) Continue baking at 425 degrees for an additional 14 minutes, or until both the top and the bottom of the salmon cakes are nicely browned. Don't worry... they won't dry out, even at 30 total minutes in the oven, they'll still be awesome.

5. Remove salmon cakes from the oven and serve. Garnish with fresh chopped parsley and some lemon. They go great with my low point Tartar Sauce.

NOTES:
A) These babies may be appetizer sized, but they are very filling. However, if you would like to make these as more of an entree sized salmon cake, I'd use 1/2 cup scoops. You'll end up with 11 salmon cakes. If you do that, the first cake is still 0 points, and servings 2-5 are still 1 point. The servings for 2 points change though.
B) You can use this same recipe with most any seafood. This recipe was meant for Crab. You can definitely use any type of fish in place of the salmon, or even use crab, lobster, shrimp... the recipe doesn't change, just the protein.
C) You can definitely halve this recipe without any problems.
D) If you'd like a bit more texture in your patties, use 1/2 cup of each vegetable, rather than 1/3 cup.

Appetizers • Page 89

Stu...
Italian Saus...

This is my WW-erized, lower fat, calorie and point version of Ina Garten's famous sausage stuffed mushrooms. I used my 0 point Italian sausage in place of regular, swapped mascarpone for strained Greek yogurt, then used crushed rice crispies instead of breadcrumbs. Adios fat and calories!

Servings Info.:
Yield: 38 mushrooms**
Servings: 38**
Serving Size: 1 mushroom

Point Values:
1-3 serving = 0 points
4-11 servings = 1 point
12-18 servings = 2 points

Ingredients:
- (2) 24oz cartons, medium sized whole mushrooms. I used Cremini mushrooms, but you can use any variety, as long as they are "Legal" mushrooms. I'm lookin at you *@kingdayvid*!

Filling Mixture:
- 1 pound of my 0 point Italian Sausage
  (Recipe on my website and in my Low Point Cooking Guide)
- 1/2 cup diced onion
- 3 medium cloves garlic, minced
- 2 cups finely diced mushroom stems
- 1/2 tsp salt
- 2 tsp worcestershire sauce
- 1/2 cup chopped fresh basil (added at the end)

"Bread Crumbs": *(makes about 2/3 cup total)*
- 1-1/4 cups rice krispies cereal, crushed. *(makes around 1/2 cup)*
- 1-1/2 tsp plain breadcrumbs
- 2 tsp panko breadcrumbs
- 1/4 tsp black pepper
- 1/2 tsp italian seasoning
- 1/2 tsp dried basil
- 1/2 tsp onion powder
- 1/2 tsp garlic powder

"Cream Cheese Substitute":
- 1 cup plain fat free Greek Yogurt (I use Fage for this)
- 1/2 tsp garlic powder
- 1/2 tsp onion powder
- 1 tsp italian seasoning
- 1/4 tsp salt
- Paper Coffee Filters or Cheese Cloth, with a strainer

Garnish:
- 2 tsp reduced fat grated parmesan topping (like Kraft)
- Additional chopped fresh basil (or italian parsley)

Directions:

1. This needs to be done first, start it the night before. Let's make cream cheese substitute, boys and girls! Line a strainer with either cheese cloth or paper coffee filters. Scoop the Greek yogurt into the strainer, place over a bowl and cover with plastic wrap. Allow it to sit overnight. I highly recommend Fage brand for this.

2. YOU NEED TO CLEAN THE MUSHROOMS!!! Out of the package, they have dirt and yuck all over them. So, get 1 mushroom lightly wet at your sink, then gently scrub it with a kitchen brush. Gently pull off the stem, then use a small spoon to clean out a cavity for your filling. Save the stem in a bowl for later. Cover a large pan or plate with paper towels, then place the mushroom cap onto the paper towel, cavity facing down. Repeat with every mushroom till all are cleaned.

3. **(A)** Finely dice 2 cups of mushroom stems, set aside.
   (B) Add the italian sausage to a large pan, along with the onion and garlic. Cook over med-high heat until browned.
   (C) Add diced mushroom stems and cook for 3-4 minutes.
   (D) Stir in the crushed rice krispies "breading" and fresh chopped basil. Use a spoon to combine. Turn off the heat.

4. **(A)** Remove Greek yogurt from the fridge, scoop into a bowl and mix in the onion and garlic powders, italian seasoning and salt. **(B)** With the heat turned off, mix the yogurt, along with 2 teaspoons of worcestershire sauce, into the filling.
   (C) The finished mixture should be thick and hold together.
   (D) Using measuring spoons, scoop 1 even tablespoon into the large mushrooms and fill the smaller mushroom with less filling. Don't go over 1 tablespoon per mushroom though. The sizes of the 'shrooms vary, so your exact number of servings will vary, per batch. I made 38 before I ran out of filling.

5. **(A)** Line a baking pan with tin foil, then spray with cooking spray. Place the mushrooms tightly together on the pan, then spray the tops with cooking spray and lightly sprinkle 1 teaspoon of grated parmesan on top of the mushrooms.
   (B) Bake for 20-24 minutes at 375 degrees. **(C)** There will be a good deal of liquid at the bottom of the pan, so when you remove the pan from the oven, set one corner of the pan on a kitchen spoon or dish towel, to raise it up, and draw all of the liquid to one corner. **(D)** Use a slotted spoon to place each of the mushrooms onto a platter, allowing more of the liquid to run off. Garnish with fresh chopped basil and the rest of the parmesan cheese topping.

NOTES:
A) These can be fully assembled onto your sheet pan, up to 1 day before baking, WHICH IS AWESOME! Place all of the assembled mushrooms on your baking pan, like in step (5a), then wrap the entire pan in plastic wrap and store in the fridge, until ready to bake.

Appetizers • Page 91

For this recipe, we're using BIG jumbo scallops. Though you can definitely use smaller ones, which'll give you more bang for your buck, I wanted to come at these as a special occasion appetizer that you'd put out for a snazzy dinner party. For you folks who've never cooked scallops before, IT'S SO SIMPLE! They cook just as fast as shrimp, and have a wonderful natural flavor, that's like taking a bite of the ocean. The addition of a light and creamy lemon chive sauce is just frosting on the cake.

Servings Info.:
Yield: 16 Scallops
Servings: 16
Serving Size: 1 Scallop

Point Values:
1-3 servings = 0 points
4 - 11 servings = 1 point

Ingredients:

Scallops:
- 16 large (colossal) scallops
- 1 tsp olive oil
- olive oil cooking spray
- salt and pepper

Creamy Lemon Garlic Sauce:
- 1 Tbsp I Can't Believe It's Not Butter LIGHT *(melted in a cup)*
- 1/2 cup unsweetened plain almond milk
- 3 Tbsp lemon juice
- 1 tsp finely chopped lemon zest (optional, but awesome)
- 2 tsp Molly McButter fat free Butter Sprinkles (optional)
- 8 seconds spray, butter flavored cooking spray
- 1 tsp cornstarch
- 2 Tbsp finely chopped shallots
- 1 medium clove of garlic, crushed and finely chopped.
- 1 Tbsp finely chopped fresh chives. *(additional for garnish)*

Directions:

1. This isn't really a direction, but it's my book, so I can put random tidbits wherever I want. MUAHAHA! Ok, I'm going to start off by acknowledging that yes, colossal scallops are expensive. This is a high end, special occasion kind of appetizer. You can definitely use smaller, regular sized scallops, which would be less money and give you a lot more scallops per person. Feel free to make it that way if it makes the dish more accessible for you. Just remember to enter this into the recipe builder and adjust the number of scallops you are making, so that you can determine what the points per serving would be, as well as how many smaller scallops you'd consider a serving.

2. **(A)** Line a plate with 2 layers of paper towels, then place the scallops on top. **(B)** Cover the scallops with another layer of paper towels and set aside. We want to remove moisture from the top and bottom of the scallops, so that they get a good sear. We aren't using a lot of oil and butter in our pan, so this helps get a good sear. **(C)** Finely chop the shallot and garlic. You want around 2-3 tablespoons of shallot. Combine the shallots and garlic together in small bowl, set aside. **(D)** Finely chop a few tablespoons of the fresh chives, set aside. OMG!!, remind me to NEVER use a fuschia colored cutting board for recipe pictures again. My eye balls hurt just looking at that picture!

heat. Let the pan heat up for a minute, then place the scallops down onto the hot pan. DO NOT TOUCH THEM for 3 minutes!! Let them sit and develop a sear. Spray the top of the scallops with olive oil cooking spray, then **(B)** flip and sear for 3 minutes. **(C)** Pour the sauce over the scallops, along with 1 tablespoon of the chives. **(D)** Stir till the scallops are coated. Place the scallops onto a serving platter or bowl, pour extra sauce on top, garnish with extra chives.

NOTES:
A) You can use regular sized scallops instead of colossal ones, if you wish, but adjust your serving sizes and points accordingly. Additionally, the smaller scallops will cook faster.
B) If you don't mind your first 3 scallops being 1 point, rather than 0, feel free to use additional olive oil.
C) If you turn your flame higher than medium, there is a chance the cooking spray will start to burn, discoloring your sauce.

3. **(A)** In a bowl, whisk together the melted "ICBINB", almond milk, lemon juice, lemon zest (if using), molly mcbutter and 6 second spray of butter flavored cooking spray. Stir in the cornstarch, that has been dissolved in a little bit of water. Set aside. **(B)** In a small pot, sautee the chopped garlic and shallots over medium heat with olive oil cooking spray. Cook until the shallots are softened. **(C)** Pour the liquid mixture into the pot, stir, **(D)** then cook at a low simmer for 3-4 minutes. Remove from heat.

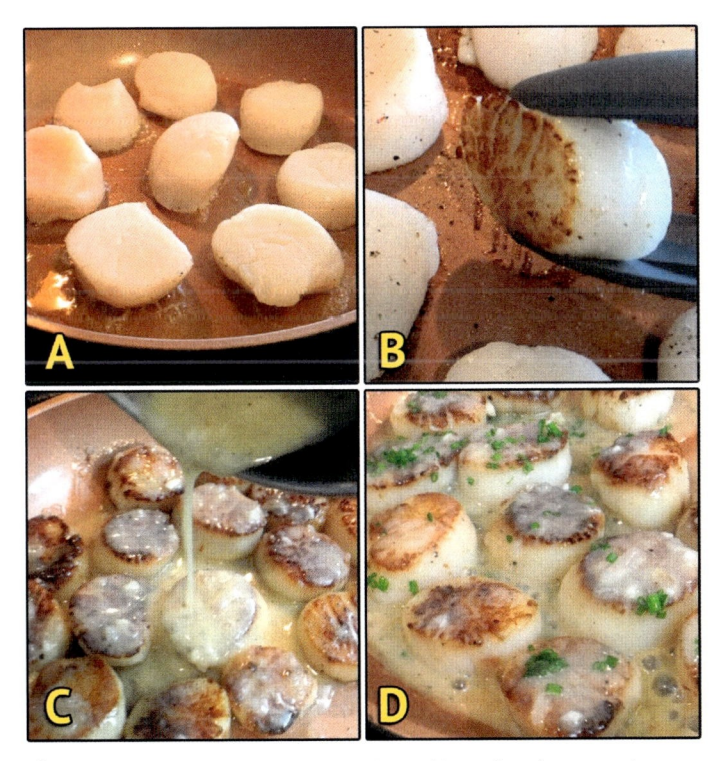

4. **(A)** Heat 1 teaspoon of olive oil and a 4 second spray of olive oil cooking spray in a large pan over medium

Shrimp Cocktail

Tender Poached Shrimp, with a Delicious Cocktail Sauce

I know that for a lot of you seasoned cooks out there, you're thinking "why is he putting shrimp cocktail in this? It's easy." Well, not everyone can cook as awesome as you. That's where I come in, because it's my mission to help talk people through how to cook stuff (cramming 50 pictures into each recipe doesn't hurt either). This recipe makes a good sized platter of poached, X-Large shrimp. You know when you go to those fancy buffets and see a big platter of shrimp on ice, with a big bowl of cocktail sauce? Well now you can make that fancy platter yourself, and the best part... it only takes 5 minutes once the water boils.

Servings Info.:

Yield: 2 pounds
Servings: 4
Serving Size: 1/2 pound

Point Values:

The shrimp is 0 points, so the points per serving is completely dependent on how much of my cocktail sauce you use.

Ingredients:

Shrimp:

- 2 lbs raw shrimp, cleaned and peeled, tail on. Buy decent sized shrimp, "16-20 count" is a good size for shrimp cocktail, though you can buy bigger if you'd like.
- 10 cups water, for boiling
- 2 Tbsp salt
- 2 Tbsp 0 point Natural sweetener of choice** (stevia, monkfruit, truvia, swerve, etc)
- 1 lemon
- Old Bay Seasoning, as much as you want *(OPTIONAL)*
- A goooood amount of ice. I used a 3lb bag from the grocery store

Additional:

- 1 batch of my low point cocktail sauce. Recipe can be found in the dips & spreads download at: www.theguiltfreegourmet.net, in the cooking guides section
- Lemon wedges and parsley for garnish

Shrimp Sizing Chart:

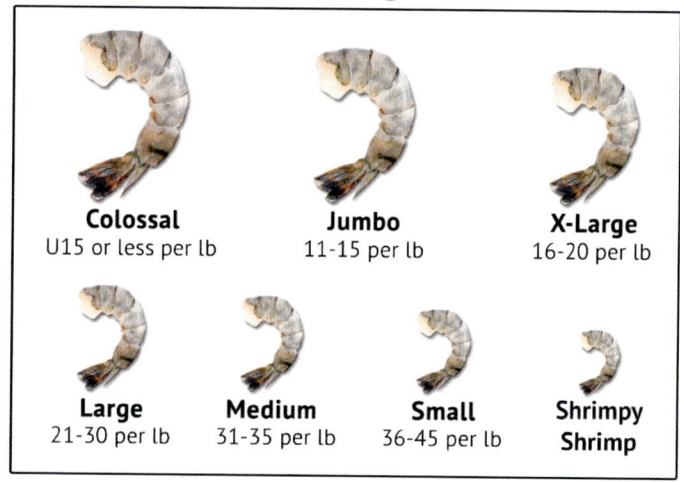

Colossal — U15 or less per lb
Jumbo — 11-15 per lb
X-Large — 16-20 per lb
Large — 21-30 per lb
Medium — 31-35 per lb
Small — 36-45 per lb
Shrimpy Shrimp

Directions:

1. This first step isn't really a direction, it's more of a little chat... go on, pull up a chair, I'll wait. Okay, this next part is for the newer cooks that aren't used to buying shrimp. When you go to the store, whether you're looking at fresh or frozen shrimp, there will be a number range listed on the bag or display. It'll be something like: 41-50, 31-35, 16-20, U15, U10.. etc, etc. Those numbers denote the size of the shrimp per pound. So if you get 41-50 shrimp, you're getting weeeee little fellas where it takes between 41-50 of them to make a pound. Shrimp with a U in front of the number are the big shrimp. U10 means that 10 or UNDER make a pound. For this recipe, you want size 16-20 shrimp, which are considered "Extra Large".

2. **(A)** Begin heating the water in a large pot, over high heat. Stir in the salt and sweetener, then slice the lemon in half and squeeze in the juice. Place the lemon halves in the water as well, don't worry if seeds got into the water. Bring the water to a rolling boil, then **(B)** turn off the heat and pour all of the raw shrimp into the hot water. Yes... turn off the heat. Let the shrimp cook in the scalding water for **3 minutes and 30 seconds**. If you are using shrimp larger than size 16-20, you will need to increase your cook time. **(C)** Immediately pour in the bag of ice. Allow the shrimp to sit in the ice bath for 10 minutes. **(D)** Remove the shrimp from the water and allow to drain, or pat dry with paper towels. **(E)** If serving on a large platter, place crushed ice on the bottom of the platter, then **(F)** lay the shrimp on the ice and serve with my awesome cocktail sauce and lemon wedges. Boom, done.

NOTES:
A) I didn't use Old Bay in my batch, but you can definitely add it to the boiling water if you want.
B) Rather than only serving a big platter of shrimp, you can also add some steamed, chilled mussels and clams to have a big ol' Miss Fancy Pants seafood platter, that'd make even Captain Ahab proud.
C) Know what else would go great with this? My Tartar Sauce.

Page 96 • Desserts

Dessert Section

Essential Ingredients ... pg 98-99
Cupcake Recipe, Guided Tutorial ... pg 100-105

Cupcakes

Blueberry Lemon ... pg 106-107
Boston Cream Pie ... pg 108-109
Caramel Apple Pie ... pg 110-111
Coconut Cream Pie ... pg 112-113
Death By Chocolate ... pg 114-115
Guinness and Baileys ... pg 116-117
Hostess-ish ... pg 118-119
Hummingbird ... pg 120-121
Kahlua Mudslide ... pg 122-123
Lemon Meringue ... pg 124-125
Mexican Hot Chocolate ... pg 126-127
Peanut Butter Bombs ... pg 128-129
Peanut Butter and Jelly ... pg 130-131
Pumpkin Pecan Butterscotch ... pg 132-133
Pumpkin Spice with Caramel ... pg 134-135
Reese's PB Cup ... pg 136-137
S'mores ... pg 138-139
White Chocolate Mocha ... pg 140-141

Cakes

Blueberry Lemon ... pg 142
Boston Cream Pie ... pg 143
Coconut Cream Cake ... pg 144
Death By Chocolate ... pg 145
Pumpkin Spice Cake ... pg 146-147
Raspberry Lemon White Chocolate ... pg 148-149
Reese's Peanut Butter Cup Cake ... pg 150
Steamed Cake ... pg 151

Essential Ingredients

Highlighting some of the specific ingredients that are used in these recipes

I know that a lot of you folks might be a intimidated by some of the weird, unfamiliar ingredients in my dessert. I want to be as helpful as possible, so figured that I'd showcase some of the most important ones to these recipes. Besides... every picture I add in this thing, is another minute that I'm not chasing toddlers around. So, it's a win win.

Flavored Baking Extracts:

- Newer cooks in the kitchen might have no idea what a flavored extract is, or where to get them, so... here'ya go. They are found in the spice or baking aisle at your grocery store. They are usually all lined up with Vanilla being the only one you may be familiar with. There are LOTS of flavors however and each of them gives a concentrated punch of flavor.
- Scan them. Some of them gain points once you hit 1 or 2 teaspoons of them, depending on the flavors and whether or not you get an imitation or natural flavored one. I personally use imitation vanilla extract, rather than natural, because imitation vanilla extract doesn't gain points.

Sugar Free Cake Mixes:

- For the sake of <u>convenience</u>, all of my cake and cupcake recipes were made with sugar free store bought cake mixes. My inspiration for trying to make my very first cake, in WW, was because of the beautiful cakes that @mlivinrn1 would post in Connect. If you don't follow her, you should. She inspired me to start making sweet treats early in my journey. If your local stores don't carry Sugar Free Pillsbury cake mixes, you can order them CHEAP off of Walmart.com. If you would like to use REGULAR cake mix, you can, but adjust your recipe points. **SWERVE** makes a **sugar free AND gluten free** cake mix, though it's pricey.

Sugar Free Pudding & Gelatin

- I use sugar free pudding in my cupcakes and cakes as both a flavor enhancer AND a thickening agent.
- The small box of Walmart "great value" brand, is lower in points than the Jello box of sugar free chocolate pudding.
- The small jello chocolate FUDGE box is lower in points than their regular sugar free chocolate pudding box.
- When you are entering a recipe in the WW app, if you search for sugar free pudding & pie mix, there is a huge issue. The app DOES NOT SPECIFY if you are selecting a large box, or a small box. You have no way of knowing unless you already know the point values.

Low-ish Point and Calorie Milk & Cream Alternatives

Because of calories and points, I don't really use regular milk or cream in ANYTHING. I pretty much use almond milk, soy milk, or CARBMaster brand (from Kroger stores) lactose free milk in everything. They are all extremely low in points and calories, but equally as important, they are all THICKER THAN REGULAR MILK, which makes them ideal for helping to thicken pudding and sauces.

My coconut cupcakes and cake, call for "coconut flavored beverage", rather than canned, Light coconut milk. I use Silk or So Delicious brands, because they are 2 points for an entire cup of thick and light coconut milk. If your local store doesn't have them (they can be found by the almond milk), you can most likely find an almond/coconut milk blend that you can use in its place. If you are allergic to nuts and can't use almond milk in one of my recipes that calls for it, use ANY low point and calorie milk you can find. Carbmaster is my top pick though.

Stevia, Truvia, Monkfruit & Erythritol-Based Sweeteners

Whether people agree with me or not about using them... I have absolutely no problem whatsoever with using Sweeteners. "They aren't natural!" There are plenty of natural sweeteners that are NOT white sugar. My personal favorite is Lakanto brand monkfruit. I have to warn you on one though... "Monkfruit In The Raw" brand is mixed with multidextrine, it has the worst artificial aftertaste ever, in my opinion. Putting "in the raw" behind monkfruit on that package, is horribly misleading. Organic Stevia is a 100% natural sweetener, that even the 2 old men from the muppets can't honestly complain about.

My primary reason for using them is calories. First and foremost, I am most concerned with using anything I can to cut calories from my recipes, without cutting flavor or portion sizes. Using sweeteners instead of sugar, if you have no food sensitivies to them, is a no brainer. 1 cup of sugar has nearly 800 calories... you'd be hard pressed to find any recipe for a sweet bread, pie, or cake, that doesn't require 2 cups of it. By contrast, an entire cup of most sweeteners has 0 calories. I didn't get fat by eating sweetener, and I'm not about to give up desserts or eat tiny portions.

How To Ensure That You Won't Binge Eat Cupcakes

Two words... FREEZE THEM!!! For all of the time I've been making my cupcakes, there has been one common comment, that has been repeated time and time again. "I can't make the cupcakes because I'd eat them all!" Hey, I have that same temptation, I always have. Thankfully there's a really simple and easy way to manage that. By Freezing the cupcakes, you pretty much make it impossible to binge eat them. You may WANT to shove 5 down your face... but it's kind of tough when they are frozen solid. Plus, you can't put them in the microwave, to thaw out faster... because you'll completely melt the topping, or turn the filling into liquid magma. You have to let them sit out to defrost, and it takes about an hour to an hour and a half.

"Well, how do you freeze them?" I use a super fancy method. It involved going to the 99 cent store and buying some cheap tupperware containers, that were tall enough to allow for the peak of frosting on the cupcakes. It cost maybe $5 for all the containers I'd need freeze an entire batch of 24 cupcakes. There's nothing to it. I don't wrap them in plastic, don't do any crazy voodoo chants over them... Just put the cupcakes in the containers, then put them in the freezer. That's what I do. Someone mentioned, in Connect, that because of limited freezer space, THEY freeze them, 1 plate at a time, then put the frozen cupcakes into gallon sized ziplock bags. Because once they are frozen, it doesn't matter if the frosting touches against others.

Each night, if you've done well that day and stayed on plan... take 1 or 2 out of the freezer, let them thaw out and enjoy. Even if you want to gorge, you have plenty of time to talk yourself out of it and put them back in, as they slowly defrost.

Recipe Tutorial

One of the things that separates my humble little cooking guides and recipe books apart, is that I honestly feel that it is my duty to show you how to not just cook differently, but also to make you comfortable preparing my recipes. Look, I know that most of you reading this are pretty new to the idea of having snazzy cupcakes on-plan. Most of you are used to just swapping yogurt, applesauce, a can of pumpkin, or a can of pineapple, for all of the oil, water, and sometimes even eggs, in a cake mix.

That's how I made them back when I first read about how to have low point cupcakes, in Connect. Someone said to swap out the oil and water, then use just as much Greek yogurt… "It'll make 2 point cupcakes!" they said. "They're wonderful!" they said. Well… they lied. They tasted like dense, flavorless, dry sadness.

My goal is to pack as much flavor and texture into a cupcake as humanly possible, without EVER going over my own personal rule for points. Namely, that I will NEVER make a cupcake that is higher than 3 points for the first 1. That way, you can have an insanely gourmet dessert, one that you can look forward to all day, one that makes you feel like you're not on a diet, one that makes you KNOW that you can beat the cravings… and only have to save 3 points for it. The purpose of this tutorial is to help the less experienced cooks, or even those of you who just want to step out of your comfort zones.

NOTE: This is not the recipe, this is a guided walkthrough.

Step 1: Making The Meringue

1. Crack an egg slightly till you can pull it apart in 2 halves Pull them apart, to put a little bit of space between them, then start sliding the egg back and forth, across the gap, like you're playing with a "Slinky". When the egg whites drop into the dish, put the egg yolks in a separate cup.

2. For this recipe, I used 4 egg whites, others call for 3. Use whichever the specific recipe calls for. The next step is to put the egg whites into a mixing bowl, I personally LOVE using an empty 32oz yogurt container for this step. Add 1/2 teaspoon of Cream of Tartar (no….. it's not tartar from teeth. Yes… I've been asked that a lot. lol)
to the egg whites, then beat with an electric hand mixer, on High, for 2-3 minutes.

3. When the egg whites form big, frothy, stiff peaks, they'll have fluffed up like firm whipped cream topping. Set the meringue aside for later. This meringue serves 2 purposes.
   1) It makes the cupcakes/cake MUCH lighter and fluffier, almost airy, verus not having it.
   2) It adds an extra 2 cups of volume into your batter, which allows you to fill each of the liners up 3/4 of the way.

Step 2: Making The Batter

4. Place all of the appropriate batter ingredients into a mixing bowl and combine until mixed together.

5. Now, take the meringue that you made earlier, and scoop about 1/3 of it into the cake batter. Gently fold it into the cake batter. Don't just stir it all forcefully, fold it gently. Then repeat, scooping and folding in another 1/3 of it, fold, then the rest.

6. When all of the meringue is folded into the batter, grats, you now have a lighter, fluffier, more awesome batter than if you just used straight applesauce, yogurt, or canned fruit. Cover the batter with plastic wrap and let it sit for 20 minutes. DO IT!! Walk away.

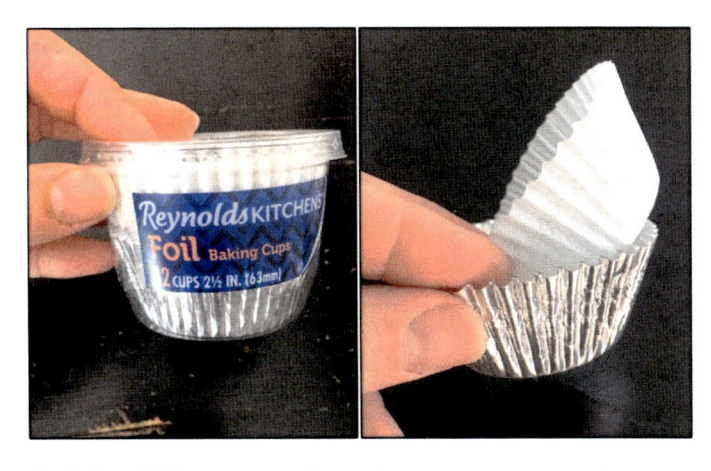

7. Using FOIL cupcake liners is my own personal preference. I AAAALWAYS remove the paper liners from them. I only use the foil, I never use paper liners. If your batter is wet, it fuses the liners to the cupcakes. You can use paper if you want, I don't.

8. After the batter has sat for 20 minutes, fill each of the 24 FOIL cupcake liners, 3/4 full, with batter. Where the back of cake boxes say to fill 24 liners up 1/2 way, because of the addition of the meringue, we can fill ours up 3/4 easily.

9. Bake the cupcakes for 22-25 minutes at 325 degrees, or until a toothpick inserted into them comes out clean. Remove them from the oven, and set them aside to cool to room temperature. You need them to cool before you try to fill or frost them.

Step 3: Making The "Jelly" Filling

10. The process for making all of my "jelly" fillings is pretty much the same, regardless of the cupcake, just change the fruit, extract, and flavored gelatin if that particular recipe calls for it. In THIS case... place the frozen strawberries, water, sweetener, strawberry gelatin packet and extract in a pot. Bring it up to a simmer and let it cook for a few minutes.

11. Use a blender or an immersion blender to blend the hot strawberry mixture into a smooth puree. If you are going to use an immersion blender, make sure that you are using a tall sauce pot, so that you don't accidentally send hot strawberry liquid magma flying across the room. Your kitchen should NOT resemble Pompeii when you are finished with this.

    When the strawberries are pureed, return them to the pot and bring the mixture back up to a low simmer.

12. Some of you have never worked with cornstarch before, so this might be intimidating, it's not. This is how we're going to thicken the puree into "jelly". Put the cornstarch in a small bowl and then mix it with a small amount of water, so that it dissolves completely. It doesn't take a lot.

13. With the strawberry puree bubbling over heat, pour in the cornstarch mixture and immediately start whisking. It will begin to thicken up almost immediately. Allow it to thicken, while whisking, for 3-4 minutes, then turn off the heat.

14. Pour the hot, thickened jelly into a dish that can withstand the high heat of the puree. Let it sit and cool on the counter for 15 minutes. Stir the puree, cover the dish with plastic wrap, and set it in the fridge to set for at least 2-3 hours. The longer it gets to cool, the better.

Step 4: Making The Frosting

Though all of my frostings have different recipes, they all follow a very similar process. This one happens to be based off of my standard sugar free pudding-based frostings.

15 Put the powdered peanut butter, pudding mixes, salt and coooooooold water into a mixing bowl (I love using empty 32oz yogurt containers). Use an electric hand mixer, and mix on high speed.

16 Mix until all of the ingredients are smooth and creamy. It should resemble a very thick pudding. Cover and set aside in the fridge, to set.

Step 5: Crushed Peanut Topping

17 Alright, this part is pretty much a no brainer, but if I'm going to go through the trouble to make a step by step tutorial... I might as well put this too. Fill a 1/3 cup measuring scoop with the peanuts. Don't forget your handy dandy Ziplock bag!

18 Now's the fun part. We're about to go medieval on these peanuts. Grab a mallet, a phone book, your replica of Thor's warhammer that you bought on eBay... and go to town. Beat the livin snot out of the peanuts. Yes, you actually DO want some of them beaten into dust. The majority will be small chunks, but you do want some fine powder.

Now we get to put it all together! Huzzah!

Cupcake Walkthrough • Page 103

ASSEMBLING THE CUPCAKES

19 Once eeeeeeverything is finished and the cupcakes are cooled, scoop out a roughly 1 inch diameter cavity from the cupcakes. Use whatever you want. I've used everything from toddler spoons and plastic picnic knifes (pictured), to an actual tool made specifically to core out cupcakes. Use any implement that you want.

20 Now we're going to move on to making a cheap piping bag, and filling up the cupcakes. Personally, I've found that I like to use ANY tall cup or container, like a tall drinking cup, or an empty 32oz yogurt container. Take an empty gallon sized Ziplock bag and push it down into the container, folding the extra length up and over the edges, like in the picture above.

Scoop the filling into the Ziplock bag, then pick it up and twist it into an arrowhead shape, like pictured. Squeezing all of the filling down to one corner.

21 Use a pair of sharp scissors to snip off a corner of the piping bag. As soon as you cut the corner off, rotate the bag, so that the cut corner is facing up. Otherwise, there's a chance that the filling will start oozing out onto your counter. Now, use your piping bag and fill up the cavity of each cupcake.

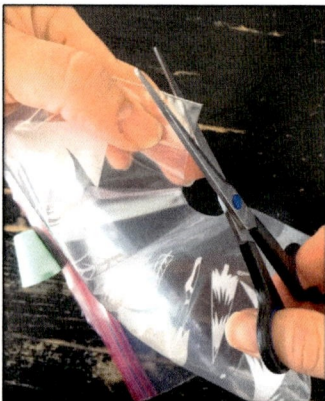

22 For the frosting, we're going to use "piping tip" insert, poor man's edition. This is a cheap $9 set from Walmart. Take your Ziplock bag and snip a hole in the bottom tip of the bag, just wide enough for the tip to aaaaalmost push through from the inside.

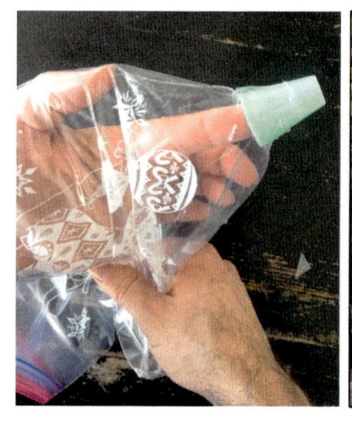

23 The hole that you cut should be a bit smaller than the piping tip, so that it won't pop out of the bag when you are pushing the frosting through it. Fill the bag with your frosting.

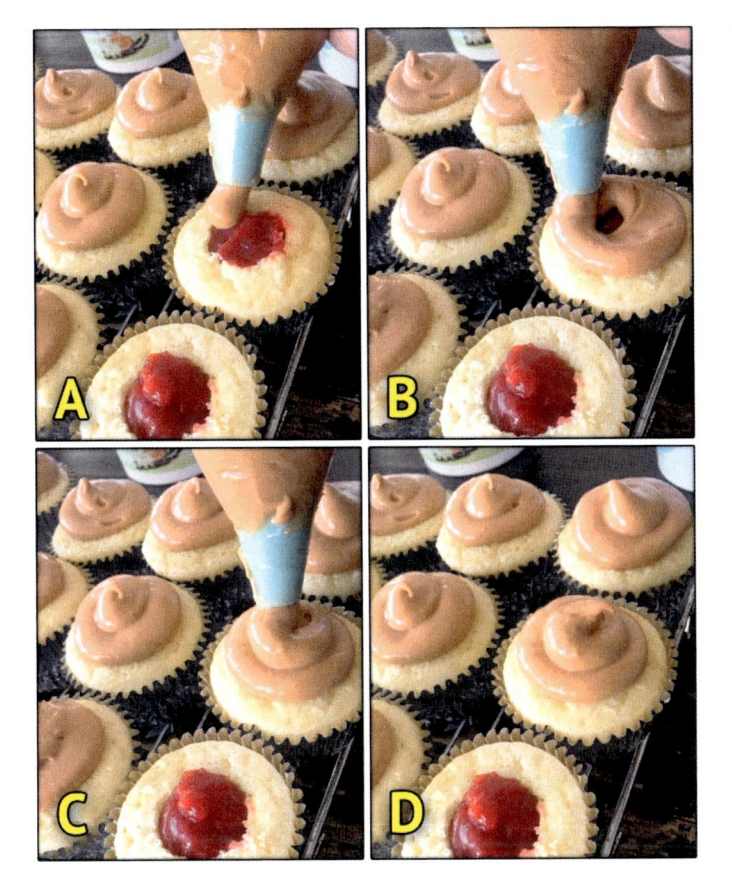

24 Now, for you folks that have never piped icing before, it can seem intimidating, but it's really not. Remember, using one of these nice piping tips for the bag is 100% optional. You can accomplish the same thing by simply snipping a hole at the end of the bag, just like how you piped the filling. So, pipe the filling down in a circular motion, around the cavitiy with the filling, building it up into a mound. Done. See? Easy peasy.

25 Now, use a 1/2 tsp measuring spoon, and scoop a 1/2 teaspoon of crushed peanuts into your palm (trust me, it's easier this way). Use your other hand and sprinkle some of the peanuts onto every cupcake until all of the peanuts have been used.

NOTES:
- Now that all of the cupcakes are frosted, filled, topped and finished... now comes the part where you have to put your big boy or girl pants on and be responsible. FREEZE THEM. Go to the 99 cent store, the Big Lots, wherever, and buy inexpensive, cheap tupperware, making sure that you buy containers tall enough to account for the frosting and toppings.
- Put all of the cupcakes in the freezer, they can stay there for mooooonths. Wonder how long they'll keep? I've pulled cupcakes out of the freezer half a year after baking them, thawed them out, and they were fine.
- To thaw them out, let them sit out UNCOVERED, for 1 hour, if the cupcake has no filling, or for 2 to 2.5 hours if it's a cupcake with filling. DO NOT THAW THEM COVERED!!!! If you do, it will destroy them. As they thaw, the ice crystals will thaw, releasing moisture. If you have these covered as they thaw, ALL of that moisture stays locked in with the cupcakes, and the cake will absorb ALL of that moisture. It turns the cupcakes into water-logged, soggy, disgusting piles of frosted sadness.
- Another option other than filling your freezer with tupperware, is to freeze them IN a few tupperware containers... but then remove them, once frozen, and place the frozen cupcakes into gallon sized ziplock bags. They will take up a lot less space in the freezer.

Blueberry Lemon

Fresh Blueberries? Check. Lemon? Check. White Chocolate? Check.

Vanilla lemon cake, filled with sweetened blueberry jam, frosted with white chocolate "cream cheese" and a fresh blueberry. All for 3 points? Can I get an Amen!

Serving Info.:

YIELDS: 24 cupcakes
Points:
1 cupcake = 3 points
2 cupcakes = 6 points
3 cupcakes = 9 points

Ingredients:

Cake:
- 1 sugar free yellow cake mix
- 1 cup plain fat free Greek yogurt
- 3 large eggs
- 1/3 cup water
- 1-1/2 tsp Lemon Extract (from the spice aisle)
- 1 tsp finely chopped lemon zest
- 1 tsp baking powder

Meringue:
- 4 egg whites
- 1/2 tsp cream of tartar

Blueberry Filling:
- 3 cups blueberries, frozen or fresh, no sugar added
- 1/2 cup water
- 2 Tbsp sugar
- 1 tsp lemon juice
- 4 Tbsp cornstarch

FROSTING:
- 1 cup cream cheese substitute, recipe on pg 13, in the Foundations section
- 2 (1oz) packages sugar free instant white chocolate pudding mix
- 1-1/4 cups cold water
- 3 Tbsp white chocolate chips
- 1 tsp water (for the chocolate chips)

Directions:

1. Preheat oven to 325.
2. Line cupcake pans with cupcake liners. Set aside.

*** MERINGUE DIRECTIONS

3. Place the egg whites and cream of tartar in a mixing bowl. Mix with an electric hand mixer set to High for until stiff peaks form, about 2-3 minutes. Set aside.

*** CAKE DIRECTIONS

4. In large mixing bowl, mix together the cake mix, yogurt, eggs, water, lemon extract, lemon zest and baking powder. Mix to combine. It's ok if the batter is a little thick.
5. Gently fold the Meringue into the cake batter till mixed well. GENTLY! Put on some smooth jazz and light candles if it helps... but be gentle. Don't tear it up.
6. WAIT!!!! Stop! Let the batter sit untouched for 20 minutes. It lightens, gets fluffier, adds volume, it's worth it to wait.
7. Fill 24 cupcake liners 3/4 full with batter. Bake at 325 for 23-25 minutes. Mine took 25.
8. Remove from oven and allow to cool to room temperature, so they won't melt the frosting when you put it on.

*** FILLING DIRECTIONS

9. In a medium saucepan or pot, heat the blueberries, sugar, water and lemon juice over medium heat till boiling. Reduce heat and allow to cook at a low simmer for 3-4 minutes.
10. In a small dish, combine the cornstarch with enough water to dissolve it into a thin white liquid mixture.
11. Pour the dissolved cornstarch into the hot blueberry mixture and bring to a low simmer for 5 minutes, stirring while the sauce thickens.
12. Remove from heat and allow the thickened blueberry mixture to cool to room temperature. It will continue to thicken as it cools. Stir with a spoon every 15 minutes or so, to ensure that a firm layer doesn't develop on the top as it cools.

13. Store the filling in the fridge while you prepare the rest of the recipe. (Note: this can also be used as a low point blueberry jelly or spread).

*** FROSTING DIRECTIONS

14. In a 32oz empty yogurt container, or a mixing bowl, use an electric hand mixer to beat the "cream cheese" till soft.
15. Put the 3 Tbsp of white chocolate chips in a small microwave safe dish with 1 tsp of water and microwave for 25 seconds. Stir to melt the chips and microwave longer, if necessary. When the chips are completely melted and mixed with the water, pour the mixture into the cream cheese and mix together with the electric hand mixer. Set aside.
16. In a second container, mix together the 2 packets of instant jello pudding and 1-1/4 cups of COLD water till well combined and smooth.
17. When combined, pour the thick pudding into the cream cheese container, and mix until combined. Add a little extra water, if necessary, to get the mixture juuuuuust smooth, but still thick. Set aside.

*** ASSEMBLY

18. When your cupcakes have cooled completely on a wire rack, use a spoon to carefully scoop down into the middle of each one. Scoop out a cavity about the same size as if you were to stick your thumb down into the middle of it.... But don't use your thumb for God's sake... that's unsanitary.

Filling Assembly:

19. Take your blueberry mixture out of the fridge and scoop it all into a large ziplock bag. Squeeze all the blueberry mixture down to one corner of the bag so that you can use it like a big piping bag, then use scissors to snip a medium sized hole (like poking your index finger through the bag) out of the tip of the bag's corner.
20. Pipe some of the blueberry filling into each cupcake's cavity to fill it up to the top.

Frosting Asembly:

21. In a similar fashion, spoon the frosting into a ziplock bag and make a piping bag out of it as well. Pipe some frosting onto the top of each cupcake, building the frosting up into a peak.
22. Place a fresh blueberry on top of each frosting peak. Enjoy!

I know that most of you ladies are all going to say the best thing to come out of Boston has been Marky Mark and the Funky Bunch, or maybe the Red Sox and Big Papi. But... you're wrong. It's Boston Cream Pie, Baby! Vanilla cake filled with custard cream and topped with chocolate! Thanks to a hybrid of real custard mixed with sugar free vanilla pudding, we're able to keep this baby tasting legit, while keeping it low in points.

Serving Info.:

YIELDS: 24 cupcakes
Points:
1 cupcake = 3 points
2 cupcakes = 6 points
3 cupcakes = 9 points

Ingredients:

Cake:
- 1 sugar free yellow cake mix
- 3 large eggs
- 1 cup plain fat free Greek yogurt
- 1/3 cup water
- 1-1/2 tsp imitation vanilla extract
- 1/2 tsp baking powder

Meringue:
- 4 egg whites
- 1/2 tsp cream of tartar

Vanilla Custard Filling:
- 1 cup unsweetened vanilla almond milk
- 3/4 cup water
- 3 egg yolks
- (1) 1oz box sugar free instant vanilla pudding
- 1 tsp imitation vanilla extract
- 3 Tbsp cornstarch, dissolved in a little water
- 3 Tbsp sweetener of choice
  (swerve, monkfruit, splenda, stevia, etc.)

FROSTING:
- 1 small box, sugar free instant chocolate pudding
- 1 Tbsp cocoa powder
- 1 cup COLD water
- 6 Tbsp Lily's Dark Chocolate Chips + 3 Tbsp water

Directions:

1. Preheat oven to 325.
2. Line cupcake pans with cupcake liners. Set aside.

*** MERINGUE DIRECTIONS

3. Place the 4 egg whites and cream of tartar in a mixing bowl. Mix with an electric hand mixer set to High for around 2 minutes, until stiff peaks form. Set aside.

*** CAKE DIRECTIONS

4. In large mixing bowl, mix together the cake mix, eggs. yogurt, water, extract and baking powder. Mix to combine. It's ok if the batter is a little thick.
5. Gently fold the Meringue into the cake batter till mixed well. GENTLY! Put on some smooth jazz and light candles if it helps... but be gentle. Don't tear it up.
6. WAIT!!!! Stop! Let the batter sit untouched for 20 minutes. It lightens, gets fluffier, adds volume, it's worth it to wait.
7. Fill 24 cupcake liners 3/4 full with batter. Bake at 325 for 23-25 minutes. Mine took 25.
8. Remove from oven and allow to cool to room temperature, so they won't melt the frosting when you put it on.

*** CUSTARD CREAM FILLING DIRECTIONS

9. In a small stock pot, whisk together almond milk, water, yolks, pudding mix extract, cornstarch and sweetener.. Whisk until smooth and free of lumps.
10. Bring the mixture to a low boil, while whisking. Allow to simmer for 3-4 minutes, whisking the entire time. When the custard has thickened to easily coat a spoon, remove from heat and pour into a container. Cover with plastic wrap and then set in the fridge to cool.

*** FROSTING DIRECTIONS

11. In a mixing bowl, mix packet of sugar free chocolate pudding and cocoa powder with 1 cup of very cold water, using an electric hand mixer.
12. In a small microwave safe dish, combine the 6 Tbsp of chocolate chips with 3 Tbsp of water. Microwave for 25 seconds, then remove and stir. Microwave for another 25 seconds, then stir again until the chocolate chips and water are a thick, velvety, dark chocolate sauce.
13. Use the hand mixer to mix the chocolate pudding with the dark chocolate sauce. Cover and set in the fridge to cool and set.

*** ASSEMBLY

14. When your cupcakes have cooled completely, use a spoon or other scooping implement to carefully scoop down into the middle of each cupcake. Remove a cavity about 1 inch in diameter and MOST of the way down into the cupcake. We're not digging to China here folks, stop before you hit the cupcake liner.

Filling Assembly:

15. Take your custard mixture out of the fridge and scoop it all into a large ziplock bag. Squeeze all the filling down to one corner of the bag so that you can use it like a big piping bag. Use scissors to snip a medium sized hole (like poking your index finger through the bag) out of the tip of the bag's corner.
16. Pipe some of the custard filling down into each cupcake's cavity, to fill it up to the top.

Dark Chocolate Frosting Assembly:

17. In a similar fashion, spoon the frosting into a ziplock bag and make a piping bag out of it as well. Pipe some frosting onto the top of each cupcake, building the frosting up into a SHALLOW peak. Don't use a ton of frosting per cupcake, or you'll run out before you cover all 24. This doesn't make as much as my regular recipes. Look at the picture for reference.
18. Grab a cupcake, chat about the Founding Fathers, and the Pat's winning the Superbowl *grumble*... and enjoy a low point Boston treat that won't kill your points.

These are seriously amaze-balls. Spiced yellow cake, filled with chunks of sauteed granny smith and honey crisp apples. Topped with cinnamon cream cheese and drizzled with caramel. It's a shame this isn't a scratch and sniff book.

Serving Info.: Yields: 24 cupcakes
Points: 1 cupcake = 3 points
2 cupcakes = 6 points

Ingredients:

Cake:
- 1 sugar free yellow cake mix
- 3 large eggs
- 1/2 tsp baking powder
- 1-1/2 tsp ground cinnamon
- 1/2 tsp nutmeg
- 1/4 tsp ground allspice
- 1/4 tsp ground cardamom (OPTIONAL, it's hard to find)
- 1 cup no sugar added Apple Sauce (0 point kind)
- 1 tsp maple extract (found by the vanilla extract)
- 1/4 cup water
- SPICED APPLE MIXTURE *(see below)*

MERINGUE MIXTURE *(just roll with it)*
- 4 egg whites
- 1/2 tsp cream of tartar

SPICED APPLE MIXTURE:
- 1 LARGE honeycrisp apple, peeled and diced into small pieces
- 1 LARGE granny smith apple, peeled and diced into small pieces *(the 2 apples chopped up together make about 2.5 cups of diced apples)*
- 1 Tbsp sugar free maple (pancake) syrup
- 1 tsp ground cinnamon
- 1/4 tsp ground nutmeg
- 1/8 tsp ground allspice
- 1/2 cup water
- 2 tsp Molly McButter butter sprinkles (optional)
- 1/4 cup sweetener of choice (swerve, monkfruit, splenda, stevia)
- 1/2 tsp maple or caramel extract

FROSTING:
- 3 cups cream cheese substitute, recipe on pg 13 of the Foundations section
- 1/2 cup powdered sugar (or sweetener of choice)
- 1 tsp ground cinnamon
- 1/2 tsp maple extract
- 1/2 cup unsweetened almond milk

CUPCAKE TOPPING:
- 20 pieces Werther's Original Sugar Free Chewy Caramel Candies
- 1 Tbsp water, plus more if needed
- Additional ground cinnamon for dusting

Directions:
1. Preheat oven to 325.
2. Line cupcake pans with foil cupcake liners (NOT PAPER). Set aside.

*** MERINGUE DIRECTIONS
3. Place the 4 egg whites and cream of tartar in a mixing bowl. Mix with an electric hand mixer set to High for around 2 minutes till stiff peaks form. Set aside

*** SPICED APPLE DIRECTIONS:
4. In a decent sized pan, combine the diced apples, pancake syrup, cinnamon, nutmeg, allspice, water, Molly McButter, sweetener and maple extract. Heat over medium heat until it comes to a simmer, then lower heat and allow to cook for 5-10 minutes, until the apples are fairly tender and most of the liquid has reduced. Set aside and allow to cool.

*** CAKE DIRECTIONS:
5. In large mixing bowl, mix together the cake mix, baking powder, cinnamon, nutmeg, allspice, cardamom (if using), Apple Sauce, maple extract, water, and 3 large eggs with the egg yolk, until well combined.
6. Fold the Spiced Apple mixture into the batter.
7. Gently fold in the Meringue, until just mixed in with the batter.
8. Allow the cake batter to sit for 20 minutes!!!! Seriously, fold in the egg whites, then walk away! Do not touch! Go get a mani-pedi, eat some Halo Top... but do not touch that batter.
9. Fill 24 cupcake liners 3/4 full with batter. If you have additional batter (it makes more than 24 cupcakes but I can't remember how many it actually made, it was a month or so ago.)

10. Bake at 325 for 22-25 minutes. Mine took 23 minutes.
11. Remove cupcake pans from the oven and allow to cool on counter for 5 minutes in the pans. Remove cupcakes and place onto a wire rack to cool completely.

*** Frosting Directions:
12. Take your strained suuuuper thick greek yogurt out of the fridge. It should now have the texture of firm cream cheese that is juuuuust spreadable. Put the "cream cheese" into a new mixing bowl. Pour out the drained liquid, you won't be using it.
13. Add ALL of the other listed frosting ingredients into the mixing bowl with the thickened greek yogurt. Use an electric hand mixer to mix it. Pulse it at first so that you don't throw powdered sugar everywhere.... Seriously, if you start off on high speed your kitchen is going to look like a kilo of coke exploded. Set aside in the fridge.

*** ASSEMBLY
14. When your cupcakes are pretty much cooled, put all of the frosting into a gallon sized ziplock bag, squeeze all the frosting into one corner of the bag and use scissors to snip an index finger sized hole out of the bottom corner. Grats, you now have a piping bag on a budget.
15. Squeeze some of the frosting onto the top of each cupcake in a clockwise motion to create an upwards cone-like mound with the frosting.

*** CARAMEL SAUCE
16. Take ALL of the chewy caramel candies and 1 Tablespoon of water, put it all into a microwave safe dish, then microwave for 30 seconds.
17. Microwave again at 50% power for 30 seconds. Remove from microwave and use a spoon to press on the caramels to try to spread them a bit.
18. Repeat this process over and over at 30% power for 20 seconds at a time. Remove them, stir, then put them back in at 30% power a few more times until you can completely stir them around into a thick goopy caramel mixture. If it starts to firm up almost immediately, stir in extra water, 1/2 teaspoon at a time. You don't want it to seize up when it cools. You want a thick caramel sauce.
19. Scoop the caramel INTO a small ziplock bag, run all of the caramel to one corner, then use scissors to snip a tiny hole out of the bag's edge.
20. Move over all of the cupcakes, squirting the thick caramel over each and every one of them. It will firm up as it cools.
21. Lastly, put a little bit of additional ground cinnamon into a wire mesh strainer (or figure out some other way to do it) and liiiiiightly dust the frosting of each cupcake with a very very very light dusting of ground cinnamon.

Coconut Cream Pie

This is a completely brand new and revised recipe. My original one was posted over a year ago, but in truth, I always though they could be better. I absolutely LOVE this revised recipe. By using strained greek yogurt, instead of fat free cream cheese for my frostings, I was able to free up a bunch of points for additional toasted coconut flakes and extract.

Serving Info.:

YIELDS: 24 cupcakes
Points:
1 cupcake   = 3 points
2 cupcakes = 7 points
3 cupcakes = 10 points

Ingredients:

Cake:
- 1 sugar free yellow cake mix
- 1/3 cup fat free greek yogurt
- 1 cup low calorie coconut beverage
  (*silk 45, soy delicious, coconut almond milk...*)
- 3 large eggs
- 1 tsp baking powder
- 2-1/2 tsp imitation coconut extract

Meringue:
- 4 egg whites
- 1/2 tsp cream of tartar

Filling & Frosting:
- 3 cups "cream cheese" substitute, pg 13
- 1 (1oz) box sugar free instant cheesecake pudding
- 1 (1oz) box sugar free instant vanilla pudding
- 1-1/3 cup low calorie coconut beverage
  (*silk 45, soy delicious, coconut almond milk...*)
- 1-1/2 tsp imitation coconut extract

Topping:
- 3/4 cup sweetened flaked coconut

Directions:

1. Preheat oven to 325.
2. Line cupcake pans with FOIL cupcake liners. Set aside.

*** MERINGUE DIRECTIONS
3. Place the egg whites and cream of tartar in a mixing bowl. Mix with an electric hand mixer, set to High, until stiff peaks form, about 2 minutes. Set aside.

*** CAKE DIRECTIONS
4. In large mixing bowl, combine the cake mix, yogurt, coconut beverage, eggs, baking powder and imitation coconut extract.
5. Gently fold in the egg whites until just mixed together.
6. Allow the batter to sit, untouched, for 20 minutes, which will let it fluff up a bit.
7. Fill the cupcake liners 3/4 full with batter, then bake at 325 degrees for 20-25 minutes. Mine took 24.
8. Remove cupcake from the oven and allow to cool completely.

*** FILLING & FROSTING DIRECTIONS
9. In a mixing bowl, combine the contents of the 2 pudding boxes with the cold coconut beverage. Mix together, with an electric hand mixer, until thick and smooth. Set asidie.
10. Add the "cream cheese" substitute and coconut extract to the mixing bowl with the pudding. Mix together until thick and creamy. Cover and place in the fridge to set.

*** Toppings:

11. Heat the coconut flakes in a saucepan over medium heat, stirring occasionally with a rubber spatula until you begin to notice they are juuuust starting to get a little toasted in coloring. **Immediately reduce the heat to low.**
12. Stir the flakes, then stop and let them stay put for 10 seconds, then stir... then stop and let them sit again for 10 seconds, then stir. Rinse and repeat the process until the majority of flakes take on a nice toasted color, but don't burn 'em.
13. Remove from the pan and let cool/harden in a little dish. Set aside.

*** ASSEMBLY

14. When your cupcakes are cooled to room temperature, use a little spoon or utensil, to scoop out a cavity, down and into the middle of each cupcake. You want it to be about 3/4 inch wide.
15. Do whatever you want with the scooped out cake... I won't tell. Dailies be damned.
16. Put all of the frosting into a large ziplock bag. Squeeze all of the it into one corner, then use scissors to snip a hole out of the bags tip. Grats! You've made a piping bag! Wooot!
17. Pipe frosting into each cupcake, filling the cavities.
18. Using a circular motion, pipe frosting onto the top of the cupcakes, moving upwards as you get closer to the center, so that you can form a peak in the center.
19. Take your bowl of toasted coconut flakes and sprinkle them liberally over the cupcakes. By liberally, I don't mean "allow the flakes to start protesting and sitting in traffic, while decrying their mistreatment in the kitchen"... I mean, cover the cupcakes with a bunch o' flakes. Done.

Death By Chocolate

Chocolate cake, filling, frosting, crumbles and chips. *mic drop*

Of all of my cupcakes, this is the one that people have made more than any other. This was made specifically to trigger chocoholics to flee to the nearest "safe space."

Serving Info.:

YIELDS: 24 cupcakes
Points:
1 cupcake = 3 points
2 cupcakes = 7 points
3 cupcakes = 10 points

Ingredients:

Cake:
- 1 sugar free devil's food cake mix
- 3 large eggs
- 1 cup diet cola, or regular water
- 3/4 cup fat free Greek yogurt
- 1 tsp baking powder
- 1/2 tsp instant coffee grounds (optional)
- 1 (1.4oz) box sugar free instant chocolate pudding
- 1 Tbsp cocoa powder

Meringue:
- 4 egg whites
- 1/2 tsp cream of tartar

Fudge Pudding Filling:
- 2 (1.4oz) boxes sugar free instant chocolate pudding
- 1 Tbsp cocoa powder
- 1-3/4 cups cold water

Chocolate Cream Cheese Frosting:
- 2 (1.4oz) boxes sugar free instant chocolate pudding
- 1 Tbsp cocoa powder
- 1 cup of "cream cheese" substitute, page 13, OR 8oz of fat free cream cheese
- 1-1/2 cups cold water
  (add more water if too thick, 1 tsp at a time)

Cupcake Topping:
- 1/2 tsp of Ghirardelli MINI premium semi sweet chocolate chips **PER CUPCAKE.** Which is 18 mini chips per cupcake (around 432 chips in total, or 1/4 cup all together)
- 1 finely crushed, Honey Maid Chocolate Graham Cracker sheet *(all 4 small crackers that make up 1 full sheet)*

Directions:

1. Preheat oven to 325.
2. Line cupcake pans with FOIL cupcake liners, no paper. Set aside.

*** MERINGUE DIRECTIONS

3. Place the egg whites and cream of tartar in a mixing bowl. Mix with an electric hand mixer set to High for around 2 minutes till stiff peaks form. Set aside.

*** CAKE DIRECTIONS

4. In large mixing bowl, mix together the cake mix, eggs, pudding mix, seltzer water *(or other liquid)*, yogurt, instant coffee (optional), cocoa powder and baking powder.
5. Gently fold the Meringue into the cake batter till mixed well. GENTLY! Don't beat it up.
6. WAIT!!!! Stop! Let the batter sit untouched for 20 minutes. It lightens, gets fluffier... it's worth it to wait.
7. Fill 24 cupcake liners 3/4 full with batter. Bake at 325 for 20-25 minutes. Mine took 23.
8. Remove from oven and allow to cool so that they won't melt the frosting when you put it on.

*** FILLING DIRECTIONS

9. Mix the 2 boxes of pudding and the cocoa powder with COLD water, until the mixture is smooth and thick, about 2 minutes.
10. Set aside in the fridge to cool and set.

*** FROSTING DIRECTIONS

11. In an old 32oz yogurt container (seriously... they are awesome for this stuff), use an electric hand mixer to mix together the "cream cheese" with the cocoa powder.
12. In a separate container, mix the 2 pudding packets with the cold water, until combined and thick.
13. Scoop the pudding into the cream cheese container and then mix the 2 together with the mixer until smooth. Set aside in the fridge.

*** TOPPING DIRECTIONS

14. Put 1/4 cup of the mini chips in a bowl. You will be using a 1/2 tsp of chips per cupcake. Scooping 1/2tsp of chips will yield right around 18 chips. It's not going to kill anyone if one cupcake has 15 chips and the next has 18.... you'll be fine. Just use 1/2 tsp.
15. Take 1 full chocolate graham cracker sheet, break it in half, and then grind it up into a bowl. Not crumbled like for pie crust where there are chunks... I mean... GRIND it up to chocolate graham cracker dust. Set aside.

*** ASSEMBLY

16. When your cupcakes have cooled completely on a wire rack, use a spoon to carefully scoop down into the middle of each cupcake to scoop out a cavity about the same size as if you were to stick your thumb down into the middle of it.... But don't use your thumb for God's sake... that's unsanitary.

Filling Assembly:

17. Take your filling out of the fridge and scoop it into a large ziplock bag. Squeeze all the pudding down to one corner of the bag so that you can use it like a big piping bag. Use scissors to snip a medium sized hole (like poking your index finger through the bag) out of the tip of the bag's corner.
18. Pipe the filling down into each cupcake's cavity.

Frosting Assembly:

19. In a similar fashion, spoon the cream cheese frosting into a ziplock bag and make a budget piping bag out of it as well. Pipe some frosting onto the top of each cupcake, building the frosting up into a peak.

Topping Assembly:

20. Scoop 1/2 tsp of the mini chips (a level scoop) into your palm. Use your other hand to pick up the chips and sprinkle/place them over the frosting of each cupcake, so that they fall onto the frosting and adhere to it.
21. Finally, pick up a pinch of the crushed graham cracker dust and sprinkle it over each cupcake all over the frosting. Enjoy.

Guinness & Bailey's

Guinness chocolate cupcakes with Bailey's white chocolate frosting

For years, it's been a popular cake mix hack in WW, for people to replace the oil, water and eggs in cake mixes with soda. I figured, why not use a carbonated Ale instead?

The deep flavor of these cupcakes comes from using an extra stout dark ale mixed in with the cake mix. Then we up the Irish theme by making a frosting with Bailey's Irish Cream, white chocolate pudding, and strained greek yogurt, dusted with cocoa powder.

Serving Info.:

Yields: 24 cupcakes
Points: 1 cupcake = 2 points
        2 cupcakes = 5 points
        3 cupcakes = 7 points

Ingredients:

Cake:
- 1 sugar free devil's food cake mix
- 1-3/4 cup Guinness Extra Stout Ale
- 1 egg
- 1/2 tsp baking powder
- 1 Tbsp cocoa powder

MERINGUE MIXTURE (just roll with it)
- 4 egg whites
- 1/2 tsp cream of tartar

FROSTING:
- 1-1/2 cups cream cheese substitute (recipe on pg 13), or use 1-1/2 cups of reduced fat cream cheese, but adjust points accordingly
- 1 (1oz) box sugar free instant white chocolate pudding
- 2 Tbsp Cold Water
- 1/3 cup + 1 Tbsp Bailey's original Irish cream liqueur

TOPPING:
- 1 tsp cocoa powder

Directions:

1. Preheat oven to 325.
2. Line cupcake pans with FOIL cupcake liners. I personally HATE using paper liners, my cupcakes always stick to them. I always use foil liners, and remove the paper inserts that are in them. DO NOT USE THE PAPER LINERS!! Just the foil.

*** MERINGUE DIRECTIONS

3. Place the egg whites and cream of tartar in a mixing bowl. Mix with an electric hand mixer set to High for around 2-3 minutes, until stiff peaks form. Set aside.

*** CAKE DIRECTIONS:

4. In a large mixing bowl, combine the cake mix, egg, baking powder, cocoa powder and Guinness. Mix to combine.
5. GENTLY fold the meringue into the cake batter until it's well combined. Don't beat it to death, fold it in gently.
6. Now the tough part.... wait. Seriously, wait 20 minutes, I beg you. There is a HUGE difference with mixed instant cake batter if you wait 20 minutes and then stir it again. In that time, it becomes more airy and fluffy.
7. Pour the batter into the cupcake liners, filling each one 3/4 full. Bake for 22-25 minutes at 325 degrees, until a toothpick comes out clean. Remove from the oven, set aside to cool.

*** FROSTING DIRECTIONS:
8. In a large mixing bowl... or an empty 32oz yogurt container, use an electric hand mixer to mix the cream cheese substitute, water, pudding mix and extract. Mix until smooth. Add the Bailey's liqueur and mix until smooth. Set aside in the fridge, allowing the mixture to set.

*** FINAL ASSEMBLY
9. Once the cupcakes are cooled and your frosting has had time to set up in the fridge, get ready to do a happy little riverdance cupcake jig.
10. Spoon all of your Bailey's frosting into a large gallon sized ziplock bag. Squeeze all of the frosting down towards a corner of the bag, then use a pair of scissors to snip a hole out of the bottom corner tip. No, you aren't making bagpipes, you're making a piping bag. Huzzah!!
11. In a clockwise or counter clockwise motion (seriously... it doesn't matter) pipe frosting onto each cupcake moving towards the middle and upwards to create a layered, raised peak, in the center.
12. When you're all done with that, scoop the cocoa powder into a fine mesh wire strainer. Hold the strainer over the top of each cupcake and gently tap it, dusting the frosting of each cupcake in a light coating.
13. Done.

*** NOTES
- You can use any type of beer, lager, or stout for this recipe in place of the Guinness.
- I used little bottles of Bailey's, because I don't need a big ol' expensive bottle. A 6 pack of the lil guys was 1/3 of the price.
- These cupcakes were cool for St. Paddy's day, though in full disclosure, my wife didn't like them. If you aren't a fan of beer or ale, you may not like the flavor of the cake. You can always replace the beer with something else if you don't have any proper Irish hooligans in your abode.
- These cupcakes are magically delicious.

These are just plain out freaking awesome-sauce. Chocolate cupcakes filled with a mixture of marshmallow fluff and "cream cheese". Frosted with a mixture of chocolate pudding and melted dark chocolate chips, then finished with swirls of white chocolate pudding mixed with "cream cheese".

Serving Info.:

YIELDS: 24 cupcakes
Points:
1 cupcake = 3 points
2 cupcakes = 6 points
3 cupcakes = 10 points

Ingredients:

Cake:
- 1 sugar free devil's food cake mix
- 3 large eggs
- 1/4 cup water
- 1-1/2 cup plain fat free Greek yogurt
- 2 Tbsp cocoa powder
- 1/2 tsp baking powder

Meringue Filling:
- 4 egg whites
- 1/2 tsp cream of tartar

Marshmallow "Cream Cheese" Filling:
- 3-1/2 oz Jet Puffed Marshmallow Creme (1 container is 7 ounces, use 1/2 of it)
- 1 cup of "cream cheese" substitute, from page 13 of the Foundations section

Dark Chocolate Frosting:
- 1 (1.4oz) box sugar free instant chocolate pudding
- 1 Tbsp cocoa powder
- 1 cup COOOOOOLD water
- 1/3 cup Lily's sugar free dark chocolate chips
- 3 tsp water, to melt with chocolate chips

White Chocolate Cream Cheese Swirl:
- 1/2 cup of "cream cheese" substitute, from page 13 of the Foundations section
- 1/4 packet (2 tsp) sugar free instant white chocolate pudding mix

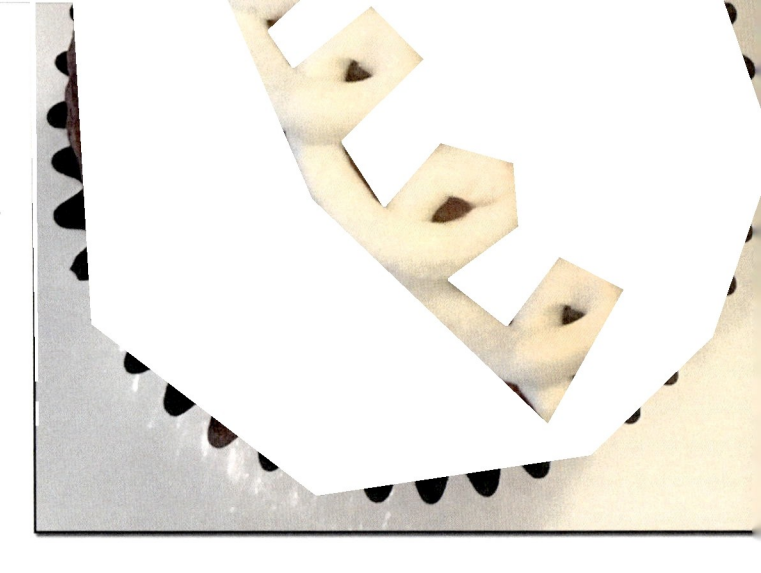

Directions:

1. Preheat oven to 325.
2. Line cupcake pans with FOIL cupcake liners, no paper. Set aside.

*** MERINGUE DIRECTIONS

3. Place the egg whites and cream of tartar in a mixing bowl. Mix with an electric hand mixer set to High for about 2-3 minutes, until stiff peaks form. Set aside.

*** CAKE DIRECTIONS

4. In large bowl, mix together the cake mix, eggs, water, yogurt, cocoa and baking powder.
5. Gently fold the Meringue into the cake batter till mixed well. GENTLY! Don't beat it up.
6. WAIT!!!! Stop! Let the batter sit untouched for 20 minutes. It lightens, gets fluffier… it's worth it to wait.
7. Fill 24 cupcake liners 3/4 full with batter. Bake at 325 for 20-25 minutes. Mine took 23.
8. Remove from oven and allow to cool so that they won't melt the frosting when you put it on.

*** FILLING DIRECTIONS

9. Take the 7oz container of marshmallow fluff, use a rubber spatula to cut down directly into the container, dividing the contents in half. Scoop out half of the fluff, into a mixing bowl.

10 In the same mixing bowl, add the 1 cup of cream cheese substitute and use an electric hand mixer to combine. Set aside.

*** FROSTING DIRECTIONS:
11 Use an electric hand mixer to mix together the instant pudding mix, cocoa powder and COOOOLD water.
12 In a microwave safe dish, heat the dark chocolate chips and 3 teaspoons of water for 25 seconds. Stir, heat for another 25 seconds, stir until the mixture is melted.
13 Mix the melted dark chocolate into the pudding, set aside.

*** WHITE SWIRL DIRECTIONS:
14 In a small bowl, add the 1/2 cup of cream cheese substitute with the 2 teaspoons of white chocolate pudding mix. Mix to combine, the mixture will be thick, almost dough-like. That's ok. Set aside.

*** ASSEMBLY
15 When your cupcakes have cooled completely, use a spoon to carefully scoop down into the middle of each cupcake, scooping out a cavity about 1 inch wide.

Filling Assembly:
16 Take your filling out of the fridge and scoop it into a large ziplock bag. Squeeze all of it down to one corner of the bag, so that you can use it like a big piping bag. Use scissors to snip a medium sized hole (like poking your index finger through the bag) out of the tip of the bag's corner.
17 Pipe the filling down into each cupcake's cavity.

Frosting Assembly:
18 In a similar fashion, spoon the chocolate frosting into a ziplock bag and make a piping bag out of it as well. Pipe some frosting onto the top of each cupcake, building the frosting up into a low peak.

White Swirl Assembly:
19 Scoop the swirl frosting into a small ziplock bag and make a little piping bag with a smaller opening. Pipe a little swirl going across the top of each cupcake. Don't worry if it doesn't look perfect.

Hummingbird

A Low Point Take On A Traditional Southern Favorite

No, sickos, this doesn't contain real hummingbirds. Hummingbird cake is a luxuriously rich Southern cake made with pineapple, bananas and walnuts. This lightened version is the bomb.com and won't make your pants pop a button.

Serving Info.:

YIELDS: 24 cupcakes
Points:
1 cupcake   = 2 points
2 cupcakes = 4 points
3 cupcakes = 7 points

Ingredients:

Cake:
- 1 sugar free yellow cake mix
- 4 large eggs
- 1-1/2 tsp ground cinnamon
- 1/2 tsp baking powder
- 1/2 tsp maple extract (or vanilla)
- 3 Tbsp water
- 3/4 cup crushed pineapple, rinsed and drained (canned)
- 3/4 cup of mashed up ripe bananas (2 medium)

Meringue:
- 4 egg whites
- 1/2 tsp cream of tartar

Cinnamon Cream Cheese Frosting:
- 1-1/2 cups "cream cheese" substitute, recipe on page 13 of the Foundations section
- (1) 1oz box sugar free instant cheesecake pudding
- 2/3 cup **COLD** water
- 1/2 tsp vanilla extract
- 1/4 tsp lemon juice
- 1/4 tsp ground cinnamon

Cupcake Topping:
- 2 Tbsp crushed pecans, toasted.*

Directions:

1. Preheat oven to 325.
2. Line cupcake pans with FOIL cupcake liners, no paper. Set aside.

*** MERINGUE DIRECTIONS

3. Place the egg whites and cream of tartar in a mixing bowl. Mix with an electric hand mixer set to High for around 2 minutes, till stiff peaks form. Set aside.

*** CAKE DIRECTIONS

4. In a large mixing bowl, combine the cake mix, drained crushed pineapple, the mashed bananas, baking powder, cinnamon, water, eggs, and maple extract. Mix to combine.
5. When it's all combined, GENTLY fold the 4 beaten egg whites into the batter until just combined. Mix it together, but don't beat the snot out of it.
6. STEP AWAY! Wait 20 minutes, I beg you. There is a HUGE difference with mixed instant cake batter if you wait 20 minutes. In that time, it becomes more airy, fluffy, and expands a little bit. The cupcakes will bake up lighter and fluffier as a result of having that extra bit of time to rise.
7. Pour the batter into the cupcake liners to fill each one 3/4 of the way full. Bake the cupcakes at 325 for 20-25 minutes. Mine took 23.
8. Remove from oven and allow the cupcakes to cool to room temperature so that they don't melt the frosting.

*** FROSTING DIRECTIONS

9. In a large mixing bowl, or empty 32oz yogurt container, use an electric hand mixer to mix the "cream cheese," cinnamon, vanilla extract, and lemon juice till smooth.
10. In another large mixing bowl… or an empty 32oz yogurt container, use an electric hand mixer to mix the 1oz packet of sugar free instant cheesecake flavored pudding with the 2/3c of COLD water until thickened and smooth.
11. Use a rubber spatula to scoop the "cream cheese" into the container with the pudding. Use a hand mixer to mix the "cream cheese" and the pudding together until well combined. Move container to the fridge and allow it to set.

*** TOASTED PECAN DIRECTIONS

12. Heat a small sauce pan over medium heat for 1 minute. Take a handful of pecans.... listen, just do it, no arguing, don't measure, just trust me. Put a handful of pecans into the heated sauce pan.
13. Heat the pecans over medium heat, no cooking spray, no butter, nothing... for a few minutes. Stir them around in the pan so that they start to warm up and toast. Continue for a few minutes, but don't allow them to burn.
14. Once you start to smell the fragrance of the pecans warming up in the pan, lower the heat. Continue stirring for a minute until the pecans begin to get a toasted color.
15. Remove from heat and put the pecans in a bowl to cool.
16. Take the toasted pecans and put them in a large ziplock bag. Use a kitchen mallet, hammer, a pot, or small lap dog, to beat the snot out of the pecans, crushing them. Seriously, crush them into a fine consistency. You don't want chunks, crush them to the consistency of panko bread crumbs.
17. Use a measuring spoon to scoop out an even 2 Tablespoons of crushed toasted pecans, then put them into a little dish or cup. THAT is what you will be using for the topping. Set aside

*** ASSEMBLY

18. Once the cupcakes are cooled and your cream cheese mixture has had time to set up in the fridge, get ready for cupcake bliss.
19. Spoon all of your cream cheese/pudding mixture into a large gallon sized ziplock bag, then squeeze all of it down towards one corner. Using a pair of scissors, snip a hole at the bottom tip of the bag, about as wide as your index finger... Unless you have little girlie hands, then... use your thumb, I guess. Congrats!... you just made a piping bag!
20. In a circular motion, pipe cream cheese onto each cupcake, moving in towards the middle and upwards to create a raised peak in the center.
21. Once all the cupcakes are frosted, take a pinch from the 2 Tablespoons of toasted pecans and sprinkle them over the frosting of all the cupcakes. Repeat until the pecan crumbs have been used. Done.

Make sure to ALWAYS have some of these on hand in case your in-laws come to visit unannounced. Instead of looking like a lush and taking shots to make them more tolerable, you'll be eating cupcakes. Cope like a boss and sauce it up, baby.

Serving Info.:
Yields: 24 cupcakes
Points: 1 cupcake = 3 points
 2 cupcakes = 6 points
 3 cupcakes = 9 points

Ingredients:

Cake:
- 1 sugar free devil's food cake mix
- 1 (1oz) box sugar free instant chocolate pudding
- 3 large eggs
- 2 tsp rum extract (in the spice aisle, by the vanilla)
- 1/2 tsp baking powder
- 2 tsp cocoa powder
- 1-1/2 cups plain fat free Greek yogurt
- 1/4 cup water

Meringue:
- 4 egg whites
- 1/2 tsp cream of tartar

Kahlua Cream Cheese Frosting:
- (2) 1oz boxes sugar free instant cheesecake pudding
- 1-1/4 cup **VERY** cold water
- 1 cup "cream cheese" substitute, recipe on page 13, in the Foundations section
- 6 Tbsp powdered sugar
- 1/4 tsp Rum Extract
- 2 tsp of bottled, pre-mixed Kahlua Mudslide *(see note)*

Topping:
- 1 tsp cocoa powder

THE BLESSED INGREDIENT:
- (1) 200ml bottle of pre-mixed Kahlua Mudslide (see note**)

Directions:
1. Preheat oven to 325.
2. Line cupcake pans with **FOIL** cupcake liners only! **DO NOT USE PAPER LINERS!!!! DON'T DO IT!!!!!**

*** MERINGUE DIRECTIONS
3. Place the egg whites and cream of tartar in a mixing bowl. Mix with an electric hand mixer set to High for around 2-3 minutes till stiff peaks form. Set aside.

*** CAKE DIRECTIONS
4. In large bowl, combine the cake mix, pudding, eggs, rum extract, baking powder, cocoa powder, yogurt and water. Mix until well combined.
5. Gently fold in the meringue, until just mixed in with the batter.
6. WALK AWAY. Allow the batter to sit untouched for 20 minutes.
7. Fill 24 cupcake liners 3/4 full with batter.
8. Bake at 325 for 20-25 minutes or until toothpick comes out dry.
9. Remove cupcake pans from the oven and allow to cool on counter.

*** FROSTING DIRECTIONS
10. Use an electric hand mixer to mix the 2 packets of cheesecake instant pudding with the **COLD** water until combined into a thick mixture. Add a liiiiittle bit more water if needed, 1 tsp at a time. You want the pudding to be thick enough to hold it's shape as a frosting.
11. Set aside in the fridge.
12. In another container, use the hand mixer to mix the cream cheese, powdered sugar, rum extract and Kahlua Mudslide beverage until smooth and creamy.

13 Add the cheesecake pudding to the cream cheese and use an electric hand mixer to combine them till smooth. If the taste of the cheesecake pudding is a little too sharp for your taste, add a little vanilla extract to the frosting.
14 Set aside and allow to cool in fridge.

*** ASSEMBLY
15 Wait for the Angels to stop singing.
16 When the cupcakes are completely cooled, take a toothpick and pierce the top of each one a bunch of times. Seriously, pretend they're that ex boss you hate. Go full-on voodoo doll on them suckers, just like in Fatal Instinct... minus the rabbit.
17 Empty the contents of 1 bottle of the Kahlua Mudslide drink into a glass. Use a measuring spoon to scoop and pour 2 teaspoons of liquor onto the top of each cupcake. It will quickly be absorbed into the cupcakes through all the holes you poked. There will be some booze leftover after you finish saucing up the cupcakes. Feel free to use it as stress relief medication. Dr. Daniel's orders.
18 Put all of the frosting into a large ziplock bag, then squeeze it all into one corner. Using scissors, snip an index finger sized hole out of the corner of the bag. Woohoo! You just made a piping bag!! Then use your index finger to point at your in-laws. to remind yourself that THEY are the reason you need the booze. Get off our backs, Karen... we don't want kids yet!
19 Pipe frosting onto the top of each cupcake, to create a rounded peak. It will cover up most of the evidence from your toothpick assault.
20 Once all of the cupcakes are frosted, take a fine metal mesh strainer and put the cocoa powder in it. Gently tap the strainer with your finger while holding it up above each cupcake. This will make a small bit of the powder fall down and dust the tops.

*** NOTES
- You are looking for 200ml bottles of pre-mixed Kahlua Mudslide. They have it at grocery stores. If you want to know specifically what I used, go to **walmart.com** or look in google for *"Kahlua Mudslide 4 pack cocktail"*.
- We are using THIS instead of regular Kahlua Liquor, because 1 200ml bottle of this stuff is only 5 points, whereas 200 ml of full strength Kahlua is 33 points. REGULAR kahlua mudslide MIX is 18 points for 200 ml. So using a bottled mix like the ones pictured below is VITAL to this recipe.
- You can use any type of Kahlua 200 ml bottle drink. Just make sure that what you use comes to no more than 5 points. Stretch it with some water or coffee if you need to.
- We are using 1 entire 200ml bottle in this recipe.

Cupcakes • Page 123

Lemon Meringue

Lemon Cake filled with Lemon Curd, topped with fluffy meringue

To call these delicious would be like saying Darth Vader has minor issues with parenting. Ultra moist lemon cake is filled with a tart and sweet lemon curd, then topped with a fluffy meringue. I've also included steps to make the cupcakes with a baked crust and without the meringue.

Serving Info.:

YIELDS: 24 cupcakes
Points: *(varies based on cupcake version)***
1 cupcake = 3 points
2 cupcakes = 7 points
3 cupcakes = 10 points

Ingredients:

Cake:
- 1 Pillsbury sugar free yellow cake mix
- 4 large eggs
- 1 cup fat free plain Greek Yogurt
- 1/3 cup water
- 2 tsp lemon extract (found online, or in the baking aisle of most grocery stores, by the vanilla extract)
- 1/2 tsp baking powder
- 1 tsp lemon zest, finely chopped

Meringue (for batter):
- 4 egg whites
- 1/2 tsp cream of tartar

Low Point Lemon Curd Filling:
- 3 large eggs
- 1/4 tsp lemon extract
- 1/2 cup lemon juice
- 1/4 cup I Can't Believe It's Not Butter! Light
- 6 Tbsp natural sweetener of choice (stevia, monkfruit, etc.)
- 1 (1oz) box sugar free instant lemon pudding
- 3/4 cup cold water
- 1 tsp lemon zest, minced

Meringue Topping: (used for version 1)
- 4 egg whites
- 1 tsp cream of tartar
- 1/4 cup regular powdered sugar, OR "swerve" brand 0 point powdered sugar substitute

OPTIONAL PIE CRUST: (used for version 2)
- 1-1/3 cup Kellog's All Bran or Fiber One cereal
- 1-1/2 Tbsp sugar free syrup (pancake syrup)
- 3 Tbsp fat free plain Greek yogurt
- 1/2 tsp ground cinnamon
- 1 Tbsp 0 point natural sweetener of choice (stevia, truvia, etc.)

Directions: -- For version 1, with meringue --

1. Preheat oven to 325.
2. Line cupcake pans with FOIL cupcake liners, not paper! Set aside.

*** MERINGUE DIRECTIONS (for batter)
3. Place the egg whites and cream of tartar in a mixing bowl. Mix with an electric hand mixer set to High for around 2 minutes, till stiff peaks form. Set aside.

*** CAKE DIRECTIONS
4. In large mixing bowl, combine the cake mix, eggs, yogurt, water, lemon extract, lemon zest and baking powder. Mix together until well combined.
5. Gently fold the Meringue into the cake batter till mixed well. GENTLY! Don't beat it up.
6. WAIT!!!! Stop! Let the batter sit untouched for 20 minutes. It lightens, gets fluffier... it's worth it to wait.
7. Fill 24 cupcake liners 3/4 full with batter. Bake at 325 for 20-25 minutes. Mine took 23.
8. Remove from oven and allow to cool completely to room temperature.

*** LEMON CURD FILLING
9. Beat the eggs together in a bowl, set aside. In a separate microwave safe dish, microwave the butter spread until softened/melted, set aside.
10. In a small pot, heat the beaten eggs, lemon juice, extract, butter and sweetener. Stir frequently with a rubber spatula.
11. When thickened, remove from heat and pour through a wire strainer (to remove any clumps) into a glass bowl.

12. Allow the mixture to cool for a few minutes, then cover with plastic wrap directly onto the surface of the hot curd. Set in fridge to cool.
13. In a separate bowl, mix together the lemon pudding and lemon zest with the 3/4 cup COLD water to make pudding. Set aside in the fridge.

*** MERINGUE TOPPING
14. Place the egg whites and cream of tartar into a large mixing bowl (or a 32oz yogurt container works great). Beat with an electric hand mixer for 1 minute, then add the powdered sugar. Continue mixing for 2-3 more minutes until it becomes a big ol' fluffy bowl of stiff peaks, just like the meringue for the batter. Set aside.

*** OPTIONAL PIE CRUST: (for version 2)
15. Place the bran cereal, syrup, yogurt, sweetener and ground cinnamon into a food processor. Pulse the power on/off a few times, until similar to graham cracker crust.

16. Scoop 2 teaspoons of the crust mixture into the bottom of each foil liner (DON'T USE PAPER!) and use your fingers or a spoon to spread the crust to the edges. Done.

*** ASSEMBLY (for version 1)
17. When your cupcakes have cooled completely, scoop down into the middle of each cupcake, to carve out a cavity about 1 inch in diameter, for the filling.

Filling Assembly:
18. Take your lemon curd out of the fridge and mix it with the lemon pudding, until well combined.
19. Scoop the lemon filling into a large ziplock bag. Squeeze all the pudding down to one corner, so that you can use it like a big piping bag. Use scissors to snip a hole out of the tip of the bag's corner.
20. Pipe filling down into each cupcake's cavity.

Meringue Topping Assembly:
21. In a similar fashion, spoon the sweetened meringue into a ziplock bag and make a piping bag out of it as well. Pipe the meringue onto the top of each cupcake, building into a peak. Use a kitchen torch to toast the meringues, or place the cupcakes on a large baking pan and bake at 400 degrees for 5-10 minutes, or until meringues are toasted.

OPTIONAL DIRECTIONS (For Version 2:)
- Pour the cake batter onto the rice krispies crust, filling each liner 3/4 of the way. Bake like normal.
- Instead of filling the cupcakes with lemon curd, pipe the curd onto the top of each cupcake, using it as a frosting.
- Do not make a meringue topping, these have no filling. With crust, they remain the same points. Dust with a little powdered sugar.

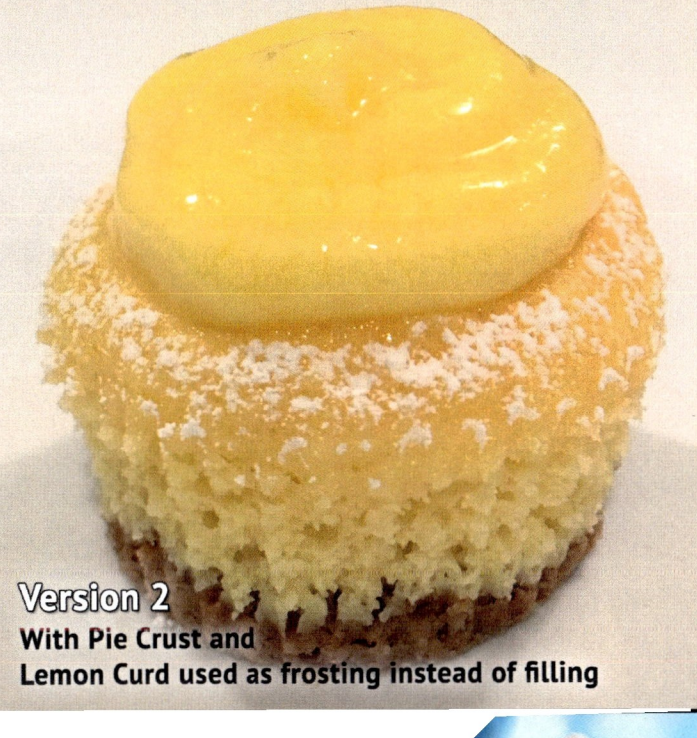

Version 1
With Lemon Curd Filling
and Plain or Toasted Meringue topping

Version 2
With Pie Crust and
Lemon Curd used as frosting instead of filling

Cupcakes • Page 125

Mexican Hot Chocolate

Chocolate, Cinnamon and Chili Powder... Viva Los Cupcakes

If you're like me, you grew up thinking that hot chocolate was packaged "Swiss Miss" instant cocoa. Well, that was true until I had Mexican Hot Chocolate. A deliciously deep cocoa flavored drink with strong notes of cinnamon and a slight kick of chili to wake you up. This is my cupcake version of that drink. Even your Abuelita won't be able to complain about these babies, once she sees her waistline shrinking.

Serving Info.:

YIELDS: 24 cupcakes
POINTS: 3 points per cupcake, period

Ingredients:

Cake:
- 1 sugar free devil's food cake mix
- (1) 1.4oz box sugar free instant chocolate pudding
- 3 large eggs
- 1/2 tsp instant coffee
- 1-1/2 tsp ground cinnamon
- 1 tsp McCormicks chipotle chili powder, OR ancho chili powder
- 1-1/4 cup plain fat free Greek yogurt
- 1/2 cup water
- 1/2 tsp baking powder

Meringue:
- 4 egg whites
- 1/2 tsp cream of tartar

Cinnamon & Chili Cream Cheese Frosting:
- 2 (1.4oz) boxes sugar free instant cheesecake pudding
- 1 cup COLD water
- 1 cup "cream cheese" substitute, recipe on page 13
- 1 tsp ground cinnamon
- 1 tsp imitation vanilla extract
- 1/8 tsp chipotle (or ancho) chili powder

Topping:
- 2 tsp cocoa powder
- 1 tsp powdered sugar

Directions:

1. Preheat oven to 325.
2. Line cupcake pans with **FOIL** cupcake liners only! **DO NOT USE ANY PAPER LINERS!!!! DON'T DO IT!!!!!**

*** MERINGUE DIRECTIONS

3. Place the egg whites and cream of tartar in a mixing bowl. Mix with an electric hand mixer set to High for 2 minutes till stiff peaks form. Set aside.

*** CAKE DIRECTIONS

4. In large bowl, mix the cake mix, chocolate pudding, eggs, coffee, cinnamon, chili powder, yogurt, water and baking powder, until well combined.
5. Gently fold in the meringue, until just mixed in with batter. Fold it in gently, don't kill it.
6. WALK AWAY. Allow the batter to sit untouched for 20 minutes.
7. Fill 24 cupcake liners 3/4 full with batter.
8. Bake at 325 for 20-25 minutes or until toothpick comes out dry.
9. Remove cupcake pans from the oven and allow them to cool to room temperature.

*** FROSTING DIRECTIONS

10. Use an electric hand mixer to mix the 2 boxes of cheesecake pudding, with the vanilla extract and **COLD** water until they are a thick mixture. Add a liiiittle bit more water if needed 1 tsp at a time. The finished pudding should be smooth, but thicker than regular pudding.
11. Add the 1 cup of 0 point cream cheese substitute, cinnamon and chipotle (or ancho) chili powder. Use the hand mixer to mix the pudding and "cream cheese" together until smooth.
12. Set aside in the fridge.

*** TOPPING:
13 In a small container, stir together the cocoa powder and the powdered sugar until combined. Set aside.

*** ASSEMBLY
14 When the cupcakes are completely cooled, put all of the frosting into a large ziplock bag. Squeeze the frosting into one corner of the bag, then use scissors to snip a medium sized hole in the corner. Congrats, mis amigos! It's a piping bag!!
15 Squeeze some frosting onto the top of each cupcake, in a circular motion, to create a raised and rounded peak.
16 Once all of the cupcakes are frosted, take a fine metal mesh strainer and put the cocoa powder and powdered sugar mixture into it. Hold the strainer a few inches over each cupcake and gently tap it with your finger. This will make a small bit of the powder fall down and dust the top of the cupcakes.

*** NOTES
- Snack responsibly!!!
- Bake these bad boys, eat 1 or 2, then freeze the rest in regular tupperware containers to avoid gorging on them. Enjoy one every night, as a 3 point sweet treat to look forward to.
- To thaw them out, just place one of the cupcakes onto the counter, uncovered, and allow them to sit for 1 to 1.5 hours.
- Chipotle powder isn't as spicy as cayenne powder. It has a slight smokiness to it. Ancho chili powder is a little spicier than chipotle, but doesn't have as much smokiness to it. Cayenne powder is just pure heat. Regular "chili powder" that you find in the spice aisle has more of a savory flavor, as well as some saltiness to it. I wouldn't recommend using regular chili powder for these.
- Some people have mentioned that they don't like the taste of the cheesecake instant pudding… If you don't like the flavor, feel free to use sugar free vanilla or white chocolate flavored instant pudding. However, while white chocolate instant pudding will retain the white color of the cheesecake flavored pudding mix, vanilla pudding mixes have a yellow colored hue to them. It will affect the finished look of the cupcakes, but will still taste good.

¡My cupcakes are delicioso!

Alright folks, first thing's first... if you are going to make these more than 1 time, ever, you should consider buying stock in a powdered peanut butter company. Heck, if you have nut allergies, you'll explode within 15 feet of these.

These cupcakes were a special request from *@kygoatgirl* on Connect. They're chocolate cake, loaded with powdered peanut butter and filled with a creamy butterscotch, peanut butter center. Finally, they are frosted with peanut butter flavored pudding, topped with crushed peanuts and drizzled with caramel sauce.

Serving Info.:

YIELDS: 24 cupcakes
Points:
1 cupcake = 3 points
2 cupcakes = 6 points
3 cupcakes = 10 points

Ingredients:

Cake:
- 1 sugar free devil's food cake mix
- 3 large eggs
- 1-1/2 cups fat free plain Greek yogurt
- 1/2 cup water
- 1/2 tsp baking powder
- 1/4 cup powdered peanut butter

Meringue:
- 4 egg whites
- 1/2 tsp cream of tartar

Peanut Butter Butterscotch Filling:
- 1 cup "cream cheese" substitute, recipe on pg 13
- (1) 1oz box sugar free instant butterscotch pudding
- 1 cup powdered peanut butter
- 1 cup cold water, plus more if needed

Peanut Butter Pudding Frosting:
- 2 (1oz) boxes sugar free instant butterscotch pudding
- 1 cup powdered peanut butter
- 1-3/4 cups COLD water, plus more if needed

Toppings:
- 1/4 cup crushed salted/roasted peanuts.
- 3 Tbsp Smucker's sugar free caramel sundae syrup

Directions:

1. Preheat oven to 325.
2. Line cupcake pans with FOIL cupcake liners, no paper. Set aside.

*** MERINGUE DIRECTIONS
3. Place the egg whites and cream of tartar in a mixing bowl. Mix with an electric hand mixer set to High for around 2-3 minutes till stiff peaks form. Set aside.

*** CAKE DIRECTIONS
4. In large mixing bowl, combine the cake mix, eggs, yogurt, water, baking powder and powdered peanut butter. The mixture MAY be thick because of all the peanut butter powder. Add water if necessary, 1 Tbsp at a time, so that it isn't crazy thick.
5. Gently fold the Meringue into the cake batter till mixed well. GENTLY! Don't beat it up.
6. WAIT!!!! Stop! Let the batter sit untouched for 20 minutes. It lightens, gets fluffier... it's worth it to wait.
7. Fill 24 cupcake liners 3/4 full with batter. Bake at 325 for 20-25 minutes. Mine took 23.
8. Remove from oven and allow to cool to room temperature.

*** FILLING DIRECTIONS
9. In a mixing bowl, use an electric hand mixer to combine the cream cheese substitute with the packet of butterscotch pudding until smooth. Slowly add the water, 1/4 cup at a time, mixing until smooth. Add the peanut butter powder and mix until well combined. It should have the consistency of thick pudding. Add more water if necessary.
10. Set aside in the fridge to cool and set.

*** FROSTING DIRECTIONS

11. In an old 32oz yogurt container (seriously... they are awesome for this), use an electric hand mixer to mix together the 2 packets of pudding mix and powdered peanut butter with the COLD water. The mixture will be pretty thick. You want it to end up about as thick as softened cream cheese. Add more water if needed, 1 Tablespoon at a time. Set aside in the fridge.

*** TOPPING DIRECTIONS

12. Put a handful of the salted, roasted peanuts (you don't need to measure, trust me), into a ziplock bag. Now grab a mallet, a small pot, or a typical CVS Pharmacy receipt and start playing whack-a-mole. Seriously, crush them up. You don't want large chunks, the finished product needs to be able to be scooped into a teaspoon sized measuring spoon.
13. Squeeze the Caramel sauce into a small snack-sized ziplock bag, making a little piping bag. Set aside.

*** ASSEMBLY

14. When your cupcakes have cooled completely, scoop down into the middle of each cupcake, creating a roughly 1 inch diameter cavity.

Filling Assembly:

15. Take your filling out of the fridge and scoop it into a large ziplock bag. Squeeze it all down to one corner of the bag so that you can use it like a big piping bag. Use scissors to snip a medium sized hole (like poking your thumb through the bag) out of the tip of the bag's corner.
16. Pipe the filling down into each cupcake's cavity.

Frosting Assembly:

17. In a similar fashion, spoon the frosting into a ziplock bag and make a piping bag out of it as well. Using a circular motion, pipe some frosting onto the top of each cupcake. Build the frosting up into low peaks.

Topping Assembly:

18. Scoop up 1 even teaspoon of the crushed peanuts and place them in your palm (trust me, it's easier this way).
19. Use your other hand and pick up half of the mixture, then sprinkle it over the frosting of one cupcake. Sprinkle the other 1/2 onto another cupcake. Repeat until all of the cupcakes are covered.
20. Use scissors to slice a tiny hole in the corner of the small ziplock bag with the caramel sauce. Carefully drizzle a little bit of caramel over each cupcake.

** NOTES:

- Though you are crushing a handful of peanuts, you will only end up using 1/4 cup of them. There are 12 teaspoons in 1/4 cup, and you are putting 1/2 tsp on each cupcake.
- If you want to go overboard, you can put 1/4 cup of Hershey's sugar free chocolate syrup into a little piping bag, then drizzle the caramel sauce AND chocolate syrup on top, it won't change the points.

Peanut Butter & Jelly

Strawberry Jelly filled, Peanut Butter Frosted cupcakes.

I... love... peanut butter and jelly sandwiches. That being said, since I started WW, I have RARELY ever had one because of how high in points they are. Even if you use low point bread, PB2 and sugar free jelly... you're still looking at 5-6 points. So you can imagine just how ecstatically happy I am about these.

Serving Info.:

YIELDS: 24 cupcakes
Points:
1 cupcake = 3 points
2 cupcakes = 7 points
3 cupcakes = 10 points

Ingredients:

Cake:
- 1 sugar free yellow cake mix
- 3 large eggs
- 1-1/4 cups fat free plain Greek yogurt
- 1/2 cup water
- 1/2 tsp baking powder

Meringue:
- 4 egg whites
- 1/2 tsp cream of tartar

Strawberry "Jelly" Filling:
- 3 cups strawberries, fresh or frozen
- 1/2 cup water
- 1 (0.6oz) box sugar free strawberry gelatin
- 1/2 tsp strawberry extract (can use vanilla if unable to find strawberry extract)
- 1/4 cup sweetener of choice
- 1/2 tsp lemon juice
- 4 Tbsp cornstarch, dissolved with some water

Peanut Butter Butterscotch Pudding Frosting:
- 2 (1oz) boxes of sugar free instant butterscotch pudding
- 1-1/4 cup powdered peanut butter
- 1/8 tsp salt
- 1-3/4 cups COLD water, plus more if needed

Toppings:
- 1/3 cup salted roasted peanuts, crushed. (measure the 1/3 cup whole peanuts, then crush them.)

Directions:

1. Preheat oven to 325.
2. Line cupcake pans with FOIL cupcake liners, no paper. Set aside.

*** MERINGUE DIRECTIONS

3. Place the egg whites and cream of tartar in a mixing bowl. Mix with an electric hand mixer set to High, for 2-3 minutes, until stiff peaks form. Set aside.

*** CAKE DIRECTIONS

4. In large mixing bowl, combine the cake mix, eggs, yogurt water and baking powder until well mixed.
5. Gently fold the Meringue into the cake batter till well combined. GENTLY! Don't beat it up.
6. WAIT!!!! Stop! Let the batter sit untouched for 20 minutes. It lightens, gets fluffier... it's worth it to wait.
7. Fill 24 cupcake liners 3/4 full with batter. Bake at 325 for 22-25 minutes. Mine took 25.
8. Remove from oven and allow to cool to room temperature.

*** FILLING DIRECTIONS

9. In a sauce pot, heat the strawberries, water, gelatin, extract, sweetener and lemon juice. Bring to a low boil, turn down heat and allow to simmer for 3-4 minutes, so the fruit can soften and break down.
10. Use either a blender or an immersion blender to process the strawberry mixture until smooth. If you had to pour the puree into another container to do this, pour the puree back into the pot. Return it to a low simmer.
11. Pour the dissolved cornstarch into the bubbling puree, whisking as it thickens. Allow to simmer for 2-3 minutes, stirring and whisking continuously. Pour into a large bowl.

12. Allow the jelly to cool for 15 minutes, stir, then cover with plastic wrap. Place in the fridge to cool for 2-3 hours.

*** TOPPING DIRECTIONS
13. Fill a 1/3 cup measuring scoop with the dry, roasted peanuts. Pour the peanuts into a ziplock bag.
14. Now's the great part. All that pent up frustration about your boss, that you keep inside? The neighbor's chihuahua that keeps digging up your daisies? That anger you carry in your soul about how disappointing Superman vs. Batman and The Justice League movies were???.... The time for vengeance is nigh!!
15. Grab a kitchen mallet, a phone book, a typical receipt from CVS Pharmacy... and beat the everloving snot out of those peanuts. Go full-blown whack-a-mole on them.
16. Place the crushed bits of peanut destruction into a small bowl, set them aside for later.
17. Now that your kitchen looks like an episode of "Dexter" was filmed in it... catch your breath and get ready to put these low point morsels of PB&J glory together.

*** ASSEMBLY
18. When your cupcakes have cooled completely, scoop down into the middle of each one, creating a roughly 1 inch diameter cavity.

Filling Assembly:
19. Take your strawberry filling out of the fridge and scoop it into a large ziplock bag. Squeeze it all down to one corner of the bag, so that you can use it as a piping bag. Use scissors to snip a 1/2" hole from the bag's corner.
20. Pipe the filling down into each cupcake's cavity.

Frosting Assembly:
21. In a similar fashion, spoon the frosting into a ziplock bag and make a piping bag out of it as well. Pipe some frosting onto the top of each cupcake, in a circular motion, building it into rounded peaks.

Topping Assembly:
22. Using a measuring spoon, scoop 1/2 teaspoon of the crushed peanuts into your palm (trust me).
23. Use your other hand and pick up half of the mixture, then sprinkle it over the frosting of one cupcake. Sprinkle the other 1/2 onto another cupcake. Repeat until all of the cupcakes are covered.

** NOTES:
- If your local stores do not have strawberry extract, feel free to use vanilla.
- If you cannot find sugar free strawberry gelatin mix, you can also use raspberry, black cherry, or any other flavor.
- Make sure to give the hot strawberry puree a few hours in the fridge to set. It will continue to thicken as it cools. It will eventually have the texture of spreadable jam. You will end up with around 1/2 cup of leftover Jelly, which is 0 points.

Pumpkin Pecan

These babies are not just beautiful as a snazzy display, they are also incredibly indulgent. This moist chocolate pumpkin cupcake is filled with pumpkin spice pudding then frosted with a caramel butterscotch pudding. Doesn't sound delicious enough? Then let's top them with crushed pecans and a crispy wedge of turkey bacon. Yeah... that's how I roll.

Serving Info.:
YIELDS: 24 cupcakes
Points:
1 cupcake = 3 points
2 cupcakes = 5 points
3 cupcakes = 8 points

Ingredients:

Cake:
- 1 sugar free devil's food cake mix
- 3 large eggs
- 1/2 tsp baking powder
- 1-1/2 tsp maple extract
- (1) 15oz can of 0 point pumpkin puree (scan the can)
- 1 Tbsp unsweetened cocoa powder

Meringue:
- 4 egg whites
- 1/2 tsp cream of tartar

Pumpkin Spice Pudding Filling:
- (1) 15oz can, 0 point pumpkin puree (scan the can)
- (1) 1oz box sugar free instant free vanilla pudding
- 1/2 tsp pumpkin pie spice
- 1/2 tsp ground cinnamon
- 1/4 cup COLD water

Butterscotch Caramel Frosting:
- (2) 1oz boxes sugar free instant butterscotch pudding
- 1/4 cup Smucker's sugar free caramel sundae syrup
- 1-1/4 cup COLD water + more water if needed, 1 Tbsp at a time. (You want **THICK** pudding consistency)

Cupcake Toppings:
- 1/4 cup of seeeeeeriously crushed pecans. Not joking, seriously... take out your workplace frustrations on 'em.
- 3 full strips of uncooked turkey bacon. Make sure it's 1 point per slice

Directions:
1. Preheat oven to 325.
2. Line cupcake pans with FOIL cupcake liners, no paper. Set aside.

*** MERINGUE DIRECTIONS
3. Place the egg whites and cream of tartar in a mixing bowl. Mix with an electric hand mixer set to High, until stiff peaks form, around 2 minutes. Set aside.

*** CAKE DIRECTIONS
4. In large mixing bowl, combine the cake mix, eggs, baking powder, maple extract, pumpkin puree and cocoa powder, until well mixed.
5. Gently fold the Meringue into the cake batter, until well combined. GENTLY! Don't beat it up.
6. WAIT!!!! Stop! Let the batter sit untouched for 20 minutes. It lightens, gets fluffier... it's worth it to wait.
7. Fill 24 cupcake liners 3/4 full with batter. Bake at 325 for 20-25 minutes. Mine took 23.
8. Remove from oven and allow to cool until they reach room temperature.

*** FILLING DIRECTIONS
9. Use an electric hand mixer to combine the pumpkin puree, pudding mix, pumpkin pie spice, cinnamon and COLD water. Mix until thick, smooth and creamy. Cover and set aside in the fridge for later.

*** FROSTING DIRECTIONS

10. In an old 32oz yogurt container (seriously... they are awesome for this stuff), use an electric hand mixer to mix together the 2 packets of butterscotch pudding, caramel sundae syrup and COLD water. If needed, add more water, 1 tsp at at a time. You want it to be thick, about the same consistency as softened cream cheese.
11. Once the mixture is smooth and thick, set aside in the fridge to firm up.

*** TOPPING DIRECTIONS

12. Put a handful of pecans into a large ziplock bag. Use a rolling pin, mallet, whatever... and beat the bajeezus out of them until they are broken down into nicely crushed pieces. No large chunks, you want to be able to scoop the crushed pecans with a teaspoon measuring spoon. Set aside.
13. Take the 3 uncooked slices of turkey bacon and place them onto a cutting board. Use a knife to cut the slices into 4 equal-sized squares of bacon.
14. Using cooking spray, cook the bacon squares until they are slightly crispy and firm. Not TOO crispy, or they'll crumble when you cut them.
15. Remove the bacon squares and cut across them diagonally, to create 2 little crispy triangles from each one. You'll now have 24 little crispy bacon triangles from the 3 pieces of bacon.

*** ASSEMBLY

16. When your cupcakes have cooled completely on a wire rack, carefully scoop down into the middle of each cupcake, creating a 1 inch cavity in each one.

Filling Assembly:

17. Take your filling out of the fridge and scoop it into a large ziplock bag. Squeeze all the pudding down to one corner of the bag so that you can use it like a big piping bag. Use scissors to snip a medium sized hole (about the width of your thumb) out of the tip of the bag's corner. Grats, you now have a piping bag.
18. Pipe the filling down into each cupcake's cavity.

Frosting Assembly:

19. In a similar fashion, spoon the butterscotch caramel frosting into a ziplock bag and create a piping bag out of it as well. Pipe some frosting onto the top of each cupcake, building the frosting up into a small peak.

Topping Assembly:

20. Use a measuring spoon to scoop an even 1/2 tsp of crushed pecans into your palm, then use sprinkle it over the top of 2 cupcakes. It's easier this way, trust me. Each cupcake is supposed to only get 1/4 tsp of pecans, but it's a lot easier to scoop them up, 1/2 tsp at a time vs 1/4 tsp. Roll with it.
21. Finally, pick up a single crispy wedge of bacon and place it down into the frosting of each cupcake, partially down into the filling. Enjoy.

NOTE: The bacon does not freeze well. If you plan to freeze cupcakes for later, freeze them without the bacon wedges. Cook fresh bacon when you plan to serve/eat them.

Cupcakes • Page 133

Pumpkin Spice

I know how completely nutjob crazy you all go in Fall, once pumpkin spice lattes are back in season. I thought I should make a cupcake to go with your $8 small, I mean "tall" hipster coffees, served by handle-bar mustached barristas.

I wanted to put a filling in these, but decided to try and keep them at no more than 2 points for the first one. There are so many people making simple 2 point plain cupcakes out of a can of pumpkin puree and some cake mix, so I wanted to show that you could make something completely over-the-top for the same low points. When Charlie Brown was looking for the Great Pumpkin, he really just wanted a low point and calorie cupcake. It's a Peanuts thing.

Serving Info.:
YIELDS: 24 cupcakes
Points:
1 cupcake   = 2 points
2 cupcakes = 5 points
3 cupcakes = 7 points

Ingredients:

Cake:
- 1 sugar free yellow cake mix
- 3 large eggs
- 1/2 tsp baking powder
- 2 tsp pumpkin pie spice
- 1 tsp ground cinnamon
- 1 (15oz) can, pumpkin puree (Use a 0 point can. Scan it.)
- 2 tsp pumpkin pie spice EXTRACT ***
- 1-1/2 tsp maple extract

Meringue:
- 4 egg whites
- 1/2 tsp cream of tartar

Cinnamon Cream Cheese Frosting:
- (1) 29-30oz can of pumpkin puree (Use a 0 point can. Scan it.)
- (2) 1oz boxes sugar free instant vanilla pudding
- 1 tsp pumpkin pie spice
- 1/2 tsp ground cinnamon
- 1/4 tsp pumpkin pie spice EXTRACT ***

Cupcake Topping:
- 1/4 cup Smucker's sugar free caramel sundae syrup
- 1/2 tsp ground cinnamon

Directions:
1. Preheat oven to 325.
2. Line cupcake pans with FOIL cupcake liners, no paper. Set aside.

*** MERINGUE DIRECTIONS
3. Place the egg whites and cream of tartar in a mixing bowl. Mix with an electric hand mixer set to High, until stiff peaks form, around 2-3 minutes. Set aside.

*** CAKE DIRECTIONS
4. In a large mixing bowl, combine the cake mix, eggs, baking powder, pumpkin pie spice, cinnamon, pumpkin puree and the two extracts. Mix to combine.
5. Gently fold the meringue into the batter... GENTLY! Put on some soft Jazz and dim the lights if it helps.
6. STEP AWAY! Wait 20 minutes, I beg you. There is a HUGE difference with mixed instant cake batter if you wait 20 minutes. In that time, it becomes more airy, fluffy and expands a little bit. The cupcakes will bake up lighter and fluffier as a result of having that extra bit of time to rise.
7. Pour the batter into the cupcake liners to fill each one 3/4 of the way full. Bake the cupcakes at 325 for 20-25 minutes. Mine took 23.
8. Remove from oven and allow the cupcakes to cool to room temperature so that they don't melt the frosting.

*** FROSTING DIRECTIONS
9. In a large mixing bowl, use an electric hand mixer to mix the pumpkin puree, vanilla pudding packets, pumpkin pie spice, cinnamon, and pumpkin pie extract, until smooth. If necessary, add a little bit of water to thin it. You are trying to get the consistency of softened cream cheese so that it will stay firm when used as a frosting.
10. Cover and set aside in the fridge.

*** TOPPING DIRECTIONS
11. Pour the caramel sundae sauce into a 1/4 cup measuring cup. Set aside.
12. Scoop the 1/2 tsp of ground cinnamon into a fine mesh wire strainer. Set aside.

*** ASSEMBLY
13. Once the cupcakes are cooled and your pumpkin pie spiced frosting has had time to set up in the fridge, get ready for some cupcake bliss.
14. Spoon all of your frosting into a large gallon sized ziplock bag. Squeeze all of the frosting down towards a corner of the bag, then use a pair of scissors to snip a hole at the bottom tip of the bag.
15. In a circular motion, pipe the frosting onto each cupcake, moving in towards the middle and upwards to create a raised peak in the center.
16. When all of the cupcakes are frosted with the pudding mixture, take the wire mesh strainer that has the ground cinnamon in it, then gently tap it a few times over each cupcake. You want to lightly dust each cupcake.
17. In the same manner as the frosting, pour the caramel sauce into a small ziplock bag, but snip a tiny little hole out of the corner, so that the caramel doesn't just run out of it.
18. Drizzle a tiny bit of caramel sauce over the top of each cupcake.
19. Done.

** NOTES:
- You can order pumpkin spice extract, online from Walmart, then have it shipped for free to your local store for in-store pickup.
- If you cannot find pumpkin spice extract, you can use caramel or maple extracts in its place, though the flavor of the cupcakes will obviously be changed.
- Not ALL canned pumpkin purees are 0 points, a lot of them have added sugars and are higher in points. Make sure to scan the cans at your local store (located in the baking aisle). The Walmart "great value" brand is 0 points, as is Libby's and a few others. Canned pumpkin pie FILLING has lots of sugar added into it. You want puree.

I ❤ Pumpkin

These cupcakes are moist chocolate cake, filled with a delicious, salted, peanut butter and butterscotch "cream cheese" pudding. Then they are FROSTED with that saaaaame peanut buttery awesomeness, as if by divine intervention. Then, an entire mini Reese's peanut butter cup stands atop our mountain of peanut butter frosting, gazing out from atop Mt. Peanut Butter, like an ancient monolith, casting it's shadow of low point judgement upon the world.

Serving Info.:

YIELDS: 24 cupcakes
Points:
1 cupcake = 3 points
2 cupcakes = 7 points
3 cupcakes = 10 points

Ingredients:

Cake:
- 1 sugar free devil's food cake mix
- 1 (1.4oz) box, sugar free instant chocolate pudding
- 3 large eggs
- 1 cup fat free plain Greek yogurt
- 3/4 cup water
- 1 tsp instant coffee (optional)
- 2 Tbsp cocoa powder
- 1/2 tsp baking powder

Meringue:
- 4 egg whites
- 1/2 tsp cream of tartar

Chocolate Peanut Butter Frosting & Filling:
- 2 cups "cream cheese" substitute, pg 13
- 2 (1oz) boxes, sugar free instant butterscotch pudding
- 1/2 tsp salt
- 7 Tbsp (1/4 cup + 3 Tbsp) powdered peanut butter
- 1-1/3 cup COOOOOOLD water

Cupcake Topping:
- 24 sugar free Reese's peanut butter cup miniatures

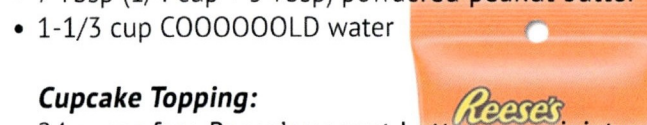

Directions:

1. Preheat oven to 325.
2. Line cupcake pans with FOIL cupcake liners, don't use paper liners. DON'T DO IT!! Paper, baaaad! Set aside.

*** MERINGUE DIRECTIONS
3. Place the egg whites and cream of tartar in a mixing bowl. Mix with an electric hand mixer, set to High, until stiff peaks form, about 2 minutes. Set aside.

*** CAKE DIRECTIONS
4. In large mixing bowl, combine the cake mix, pudding, eggs, yogurt, water, instant coffee, cocoa powder and baking powder. Mix till well combined.
5. Gently fold the meringue into the cake batter till mixed well. GENTLY! Don't beat it up.
6. WAIT!!!! Stop! Let the batter sit untouched for 20 minutes. It lightens, gets fluffier... it's worth it to wait.
7. Fill 24 cupcake liners 3/4 full with batter. Bake at 325 for 20-25 minutes. Mine took 23.
8. Remove from oven and allow to cool, so that they won't melt the frosting.

*** FROSTING DIRECTIONS
9. Use an electric hand mixer to mix together the 2 boxes of pudding, salt and COLD water, until thick and smooth. Allow the pudding to set in the fridge.
10. Use an eletcric hand mixer, to mix together the "cream cheese" and powdered peanut butter, until thick and smooth.
11. In a large mixing bowl, fold the butterscotch pudding together with the peanut butter "cream cheese", till well combined. Set aside in the fridge.

*** TOPPING DIRECTIONS
12. Place 24 of the sugar free peanut butter cups in a bowl, still in the wrappers. Set aside.
13. The hardest part of the recipe...... DON'T EAT ALL OF THE REST OF THE PEANUT BUTTER CUPS!!!!!! Seriously! Ok, who are we kidding, you know that you're going to eat a couple of them. But stay strong and throw them in the freezer. Save the rest of them for later on, when you're out of cupcakes and need a 1 point sweet treat.

*** ASSEMBLY
14. When your cupcakes have cooled completely, take your frosting out of the fridge and scoop it into a large ziplock bag. Squeeze all the pudding down to one corner, then use scissors to snip a thumb-size hole out of the tip of the bag. Grats! You've made a piping bag! Set it aside.
15. Use a spoon, knife, or miniature Hoover upright vacuum and scoop out a cavity, down into the center of the cupcake. Make it about 1 inch across. Try not to eat the cake scraps. Trust me... I know that the struggle is real.

Frosting Assembly:
16. Pipe the cavity full of frosting. Then, pip the frosting up into mid-sized peak on every cupcake. You don't need to make the frosting very tall, it's going to get squished down by a peanut butter cup.

Topping Assembly:
17. Unwrap 1 peanut butter cup, then push it down, halfway into the frosting. Done.

** NOTES:
- For the love of God, snack responsibly. After you make these, you will not be able to eat just one. Freeze them!!! Trust me. My wife and I murdered half of these in almonst 1 day, by ourselves. Our kitchen looked like an episode of **CSI: Keebler Elves** had been filmed at our house.
- The Sugar Free peanut butter cups are available at some major grocery stores, however the only place where I have personally had any luck finding them regularly, has been at Walmart. If your local walmart does not have them, you can always purchase them online at walmart.com, they are cheapest there. You can then select to have them shipped free, for in-store pickup.
- A HUGE thank you to the ever wonderful @missvw40 with this recipe. Earlier this year (March 2019) she convinced me that I should try to completely redo this recipe. It originally was chocolate cake, no filling, and a thin smear of chocolate pudding on top, with the pb cup on top. She suggested and was 100% right, that not only would it look better in a picture, to have the frosting be peanut butter-ish instead of chocolate... But that I could probably stretch it with the "cream cheese" hack, to allow for filling AND frosting. Thanks Misty... yet again.
- And a biiiiiig "sorry honey!!!!" to my wife, because I only ever made these one single time, over a year ago... even though I knew they were her favorite. I had to cook more stuff! lol. The books done, I'll make another batch now. :-)

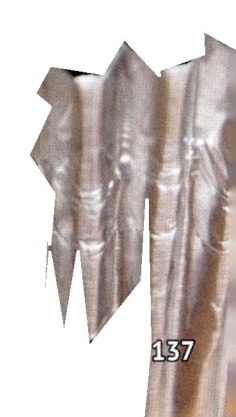

S'mores

These are amazeballs. A rich chocolaty cupcake, with a faux graham cracker crust, chocolate fudge pudding frosting and topped with a toasted marshmallow. These are pure, decadent, awesome-sauce. These are so eye catching that anywhere you take them, people will comment on how awesome they look. Followed closely by asking if they can have one yet.

Serving Info.:
YIELDS: 26 cupcakes
Points:
1 cupcake = 3 points
2 cupcakes = 6 points
3 cupcakes = 9 points

Ingredients:

Cake:
- 1 sugar free devil's food cake mix
- 3 large eggs + 1 egg yolk
- 1-1/4 cup plain fat free Greek yogurt
- 1/2 cup water
- 2 Tbps cocoa powder
- 1/2 tsp baking powder

Meringue (for batter):
- 4 egg whites
- 1/2 tsp cream of tartar

Dark Chocolate Pudding Frosting:
- 3 (1.4oz) boxes sugar free instant chocolate pudding
- 1 Tbsp + 1 tsp cocoa powder
- 2 cups COLD water

Faux "Graham Cracker" Crust
- 1-1/2 cups Kellogs All-Bran or Fiber One cereal
- 1/4 cup graham cracker crumbs
- 1 Tbsp sugar free pancake (maple) syrup
- 3 Tbsp 0 point sweetener of choice***
- 1/4 cup fat free plain Greek yogurt
- 1/2 tsp ground cinnamon
- 1 tsp molly mcbutter fat free butter sprinkles OR a few sprays of butter flavored cooking spray

Marshmallow Topping:
- 13 regular sized marshmallows, sliced in half to make... 26 marshmallow halves

Directions:
1. Preheat oven to 325.
2. Line cupcake pans with FOIL cupcake liners, don't use paper liners!! Set aside.

*** PIE CRUST
3. Place the bran cereal and graham crackers into a gallon sized ziplock bag. Crush them down, then pour into a mixing bowl. Mix the crumbs with the syrup, sweetener, yogurt, cinnamon and butter flavored cooking spray or molly mcbutter. Blend until crumbly and well mixed, similar in texture to a graham cracker crust.

4. Scoop 2 teaspoons of the crust mixture into the bottom of each cupcake liner (DON'T USE PAPER!). Use your fingers or a spoon to spread the crust to the edges of each liner, then lightly press down to bind them together. Set aside.

*** MERINGUE DIRECTIONS (for batter)

5. Place the egg whites and cream of tartar in a mixing bowl. Mix with an electric hand mixer set to High for 2-3 minutes, until stiff peaks form. Set aside.

*** CAKE DIRECTIONS

6. In large mixing bowl, mix together the cake mix, eggs, egg yolk, water, yogurt, cocoa powder and baking powder. Mix together until well combined.
7. Gently fold the Meringue into the cake batter till just combined. GENTLY!!! Don't beat it up.
8. WAIT!!!! Stop! Let the batter sit untouched for 20 minutes. It lightens, gets fluffier... it's worth it to wait.
9. Scoop batter into each liner, over the inserted crusts. Fill 26 cupcake liners 3/4 full with batter. Bake at 325 for 20-25 minutes. Mine took 23.
10. Remove from oven and allow to cool completely to room temperature.

*** DARK CHOCOLATE PUDDING FROSTING

11. Pour the 3 boxes of pudding, cocoa powder and COLD water into a mixing bowl or an empty 32oz yogurt container (they work GREAT for this), then combine with a hand mixer at high speed until thickened and smooth.
12. Cover and set aside in the fridge to set.

*** ASSEMBLY

13. When your cupcakes have cooled completely, get ready to have some fun.

Filling Assembly:

14. Scoop the chocolate frosting into a large ziplock bag. Squeeze all the pudding down to one corner of the bag so that you can use it as a big piping bag. Use scissors to snip a medium sized hole (like poking your thumb through the bag) out of the tip of the bag's corner.
15. Pipe the pudding onto the top of each cupcake, building into a small peak.

Toasted Marshmallow Options:

Option 1: (easiest, but time consuming)
- Use a skewer to toast each marshmallow half, one at a time, over the flame of your stove. When each one is lightly toasted, remove it from the skewer and press it down into the frosting.

Option 2: (fastest, but most likely to result in 911 calls)
- Place the untoasted marshmallows down onto the top of each cupcake's frosting.
- Use a kitchen torch to quickly toast each marshmallow. Done.

Option 3: (requires ninja-like reflexes)
- Place the cupcakes onto a large baking pan, turn on your stove's Broiler function and try toasting them that way.

NOTES:

- If you plan to store these in the freezer or fridge for a few days, DO NOT TOP THEM WITH MARSHMALLOWS YET! The marshmallows will deflate and look fuggly. Top them with the toasted marshmallows the day you'll be serving them.

Cupcakes • Page 139

This delicious chocolate cake is infused with enough coffee to make you slap'yo momma, then arm wrestle a grizzly bear. The white chocolate frosting, on its own, is de-freaking-licious. Seriously... this frosting makes you feel like Winnie The Pooh, laying on his back in Rabbit's house, with a jar of honey stuck to his face. That honey being a jar of this amazeballs frosting, of course.

Serving Info.:

Yields: 24 cupcakes
Points: 1 cupcakes = 3 points
          2 cupcakes = 6 points
          3 cupcakes = 10 points

Ingredients:

Cake:
- 1 sugar free devil's food cake mix
- 3 large eggs
- 1/2 cup water
- 1-1/4 cup fat free plain Greek yogurt
- 1/4 cup instant coffee powder... yes, an entire 1/4 cup. In the words of Obi Wan Kenobi, *"Remember, a Jedi can feel the Caffeine flowing through him."*
- 1/2 tsp baking powder
- 1 Tbsp cocoa powder

MERINGUE MIXTURE (just roll with it)
- 4 egg whites
- 1/2 tsp cream of tartar

FROSTING:
- 1 cup "cream cheese" substitute, recipe on pg 13
- 2 (1oz) boxes sugar free instant white chocolate pudding
- 1-1/2 cups COLD water
- 1/4 cup white chocolate chips. I used "toll house morsels, premier white", it's what my local store had.
- 1/2 cup powdered sugar

CUPCAKE TOPPING:
- 1/2 tsp cocoa powder
- 1/2 tsp crushed up instant coffee

EXTRAS: (optional, but completes the look)
- 8 regular sized, green Starbucks straws, cut into thirds. This one's fun, because you get to look like a weirdo, running into Starbucks, grabbing a fist full of straws, then sprinting back out the door. You'll look like the Hamburglar, but with straws. The Millennials won't know what's happening and will flee to the nearest safe space.

Directions:

1. Preheat oven to 325.
2. Line cupcake pans with FOIL cupcake liners. I personally HATE using paper liners, my cupcakes always stick to them. I always use foil liners, and remove the paper inserts that are in them. DO NOT USE THE PAPER LINERS!! Just the foil.

*** MERINGUE DIRECTIONS

3. Place the egg whites and cream of tartar in a mixing bowl. Mix with an electric hand mixer, set to High, until stiff peaks form, about 2 minutes. Set aside.

*** CAKE DIRECTIONS:

4. In a large mixing bowl, combine the cake mix, eggs, water, yogurt, instant coffee powder, baking powder and cocoa powder. Mix to combine.
5. GENTLY fold the meringue into the cake batter until well combined. Don't beat it to death, fold it in gently.
6. Now the tough part.... wait. Seriously, wait 20 minutes, I beg you. There is a HUGE difference with mixed instant cake batter if you wait 20 minutes and then stir it again. In that time, it becomes more airy and fluffy. Please wait the 20 minutes, it'll help add volume to your cupcakes.
7. After waiting 20 minutes like a good little boy/girl, pour the batter into the cupcake liners, filling each one 3/4 full. Bake for 22-25 minutes at 325 degrees, until a toothpick comes out clean. Remove from the oven, set aside to cool.

*** FROSTING DIRECTIONS:

8 In a large mixing bowl, or an empty 32oz yogurt container, use an electric hand mixer to mix the cream cheese substitute until smooth. Add the powdered sugar, 1/4 cup at a time, then mix until smooth.
9 In a separate mixing bowl, mix the 1-1/2 cups COLD water, with the 2 packets of pudding mix. Mix until smooth and creamy, then fold the pudding into the "cream cheese" mixture.
10 In a microwave safe dish, melt the white chocolate chips with 1 teaspoon of water, for 20 seconds. Stir, then microwave for 20 more seconds, repeat until smooth. Then mix the melted white chocolate into the "cream cheese" and pudding mixture.

*** FINAL ASSEMBLY

14 Once the cupcakes are cooled and your cream cheese and white chocolate frosting is ready, let's get ready for a colossal crescendo of caffeinated cupcake bliss!!!!
15 Spoon all of your frosting into a large gallon sized ziplock bag. Squeeze all of the frosting down towards one corner then use a pair of scissors to snip a corner off of the tip. Grats, you just made bagpipes, or a piping bag... whatever.
16 In a clockwise, or counter clockwise motion (seriously... it doesn't matter), pipe frosting onto each cupcake, moving towards the middle and upwards. You want to create a raised peak in the center, like an edible Mt. Kilimanjaro.
17 When all of the cupcakes have been frosted, take the dish with the cocoa powder/coffee powder mix and put it into a fine wire mesh strainer. Hold the strainer a little bit above the tops of each cupcake and gently tap the strainer with your finger, causing some of the powder to cascade down onto the frosting, then move to the next cupcake, rinse and repeat.
18 Take your little Starbucks green straw sections and spear down at an angle into each cupcake's beating heart. You've probably seen a Dracula movie at one point in your life, just pretend your Van Helsing, sent to dispatch a nest of slumbering vampire coffee cupcakes. Done.

*** NOTES

- If you don't like coffee, but still feel the need to ask "what can I use instead of coffee?" You DO realize that these are coffee cupcakes..... right?
- Fiiiiiiiiiine *eye roll*. You can always use DECAF instant coffee instead of regular, it has 1/10th the caffeine of regular coffee. That's pretty much like having black water, but, least it has some of the flavor though.
- Make sure that you don't live in one of the west coast hippie towns when you make these. They'll chase you down with torches and hacky sacks if you post a picture with a plastic straw. If you start getting lip about it.... you need to stand your ground, look the hippies in the eye, and calmly tell them that your straws are "organic, free-range straws, that are made from recycled vegan hemp and they were harvested humanely." Hippies like that kinda jive-talk.

This cake is a layered variant of my Blueberry White Chocolate Cupcakes. Yeeees, I know the blackberry and blueberry cupcake recipes are nearly identical, but the fruit and the steps for making the filling are different. I personally like blueberry more than blackberries (I don't like seeds), so I chose to make this cake.

Changes:

Cake:
- For the "Meringue" step of the recipe, use **ONLY** 2 egg whites and 1/4 tsp cream of tartar. Also, you do NOT need to let the batter rest for 30 minutes.
- Line the bottom of (2) 9" pie pans with parchment paper, then spray with cooking spray.
- Divide the batter between the pans, then bake at 325 for 30-35 minutes. Allow to cool.

Blueberry Jelly Filling:
- Add an additional 1 Tbsp of cornstarch, for a total of 5 Tbsp.
- The cupcake recipe calls for 1/2 cup water, reduce that amount to 1/4 cup of water instead.
- The regular recipe calls for 2 Tbsp sugar. If you'd like to use sweetener, use 1/4 cup, due to the reduced points from sugar to sweetener.

Frosting:
- Remove 1 of the 2 boxes of sf white chocolate pudding. You will only be using 1 now.
- Reduce the amount of COLD water to 3/4 cup, instead of the listed 1-1/4 cup.

Serving Info.:
Servings: 12 slices
Serving Size: 1 slice
1 slice = 7 points
2 slices = 14 points

Notes:
- We reduced the amount of frosting by 3/4 cup, to have the extra points to make the filling thicker. It was needed, so that it could stand up to the weight of the top cake layer.
- You can use any piping tip that you would like for the frosting, or, if you want to try a different way of decorating it, try having the jelly cover the entire top, from edge to edge. Then use a rubber spatula to put a thin layer of frosting around the sides of the cake.

Boston Cream Pie

Variation of the Cupcake Recipe on page 108

One of my absolute favorite desserts, pre WW (aka fat me), was the Boston Cream Pie Cake at a local grocery store. I'd get that baby as often as I could. What's not to love? Fluffy cake, custard and thick chocolate ganache. Unfortunately, the real deal has enough fat and calories to kill a grey whale.

Changes:

Cake:
- For the "Meringue" step of the recipe, use **ONLY** 2 egg whites and 1/4 tsp cream of tartar. Also, you do NOT need to let the batter rest for 30 minutes.
- Line the bottom of (2) 9" pie pans with parchment paper, then spray with cooking spray.
- Divide the batter between the pans, then bake at 325 for 30-35 minutes. Allow to cool.

Serving Info.:
Servings: 12 slices
Serving Size: 1 slice
1 slice = 6 points
(5 points, if portioned into 16 slices, as pictured)

Vanilla Egg Custard:
- Add an additional 1 Tbsp of cornstarch, for a total of 4 Tbsp, to the custard.
- The regular recipe calls for 3 Tbsp of sweetener in the custard. This custard is not overly sweet. If you'd like it sweeter, add more of your sweetener of choice, but adjust points accordingly.

Frosting:
- Add an additional 1 Tbsp of water while melting the chocolate chips, so that it spreads across the surface of the cake easier. Unlike the cupcakes, for this cake version, we don't need the frosting to stay up in a peak. We're adding extra water, so that it's easier to spread across the top of the cake.

Notes:
- *Making a Spiderweb Pattern, is COMPLETELY optional. It's incredibly easy to do though All I did, was go to youtube and searched "how to make a spiderweb cake pattern." It's really easy.*
- *Traditionally, Boston Cream Pie's DON'T have anything on the top, other than the chocolate frosting. However... if you DO choose to put the custard on top (which is optional...), know that having pudding mixed into the topping, will cause it to slowly "leech" color from any other surrounding frostings or liquids, over time. 1 day after taking the pictures to the right, the yellow-ish custard, had sucked in the brown color from the dark frosting and turned it dark beige in color. It took 2 days for the custard to completely change to brown.*

I have never really been that big a fan of coconut cake or coconut cream pie, but that being said… I flippin' loved this cake. I never thought that I'd be able to make a "perdified" cake like this, with the toasted flakes on the side and ya'know what? It's not that hard. Even more surprising is that I was able to do it with only the 3/4 cup of flakes.

Changes:

Cake:
- For the "Meringue" step of the recipe, use **ONLY** 2 egg whites and 1/4 tsp cream of tartar. Also, you do NOT need to let the batter rest for 30 minutes.
- Line the bottom of (2) 9" pie pans with parchment paper, then spray with cooking spray.
- Divide the batter between the pans, then bake at 325 for 30-35 minutes. Allow to cool.

Filling & Frosting:
- Ok, this is going to be a little out of most folks comfort zones, it was for me. I piped a double thick layer of filling in the middle of the cake, because the top and sides of the cake will be getting a thin layer. More for the filling!!! Woot.
- After you put the top cake layer on, cover it with a thin layer of frosting, all the way to the edge. Then frost the sides, all around the cake, with a thin layer. Really… not joking, a thin layer. Some of the filling will bulge out a little from the center of the cake, but that's ok. Use your spatula to smooth it back out.

Toasted Coconut:
- This step is messy. Put some of the toasted coconut in your palm, then lightly press it against the side of the cake. Don't cram it on, that 3/4 cup has to spread all the way around.
- Most of the flakes will fall off, just keep working your way all around the cake, palming more flakes up onto the sides. Eventually, you'll be able to apply a thin layer all the way around the circumference of the cake. Lightly press all around the sides.

Notes:
- *An easier option for applying the toasted coconut, that's just as pretty, is to frost the sides of the cake with a slightly thicker layer of frosting. Then, rather than covering the sides of the cake with the flakes, frost the top of the cake. It's much easier, less messy and is also really pretty.*

Serving Info.:
Servings: 12 slices
Serving Size: 1 slice
1 slice = 7 points
2 slices = 14 points

Death By Chocolate

Variation of the Cupcake Recipe on page 114

The changes for converting this particular cupcake into a cake get a little confusing, so bear with me. I took the Frosting from the cupcakes, which is a chocolate "cream cheese" frosting and instead, used it as the Filling for this cake. I then took the Filling for the cupcakes and used it as the cake's frosting. I swapped the two. Remember that.

Changes:

Cake:
- For the "Meringue" step of the recipe, use **ONLY** 2 egg whites and 1/4 tsp cream of tartar. Also, you do NOT need to let the batter rest for 30 minutes.
- Line the bottom of (2) 9" pie pans with parchment paper, then spray with cooking spray.
- Divide the batter between the pans, then bake at 325 for 30-35 minutes. Allow to cool.

Chocolate "Cream Cheese" Filling:
- Use the cupcake recipe's FROSTING, as the cake's filling.
- Apply a double thick layer of filling.

Dark Chocolate Pudding Frosting:
- Use the cupcake recipe's FILLING, as the cake's frosting.
- Apply a thin coat around the sides of the cake, then put a thicker layer on top.

Toppings:
- Sprinkle the top of the cake with the 1/4 cup of mini chocolate chips, then
- with the crushed chocolate graham crackers.

Notes:
- Remember, the original filling for the cupcakes, gets modified with the above changes, and is used as the cake's filling. The cupcake filling gets modified, then gets used as the cake's frosting. I know it's confusing, but if this is the weirdest thing you have to deal with today, you're doing pretty good.

Serving Info.:
Servings: 12 slices
Serving Size: 1 slice
1 slice = 7 points
2 slices = 14 points

Pumpkin Spice Cake

This is, hands down, one of my favorite cakes. It's insanely easy to make, comes together REALLY quickly and is so moist and fluffy that you won't believe it. I loved it, my wife, who can't stand pumpkin pie spice anything, still didn't like it... So that's how I knew it was juuuust right 😊. Imagine if you will, a sexy pumpkin pie, going out to a club, having a few drinks, then hooking up with a tall dark and handsome pumpkin cake. The two elope to Vegas... then 9 months later, this cake would be the logical byproduct of said-union.

Serving Info.:
YIELDS: 12 slices
Points: 1 slice = 5 points
        2 slices = 9 points
        3 slices = 14 points

Ingredients:

Cake Batter:
- 1 sugar free yellow cake mix
- 1 (15oz) canned pumpkin puree *(Pick a 0 point can, scan it)*
- 1 egg *(optional though HIGHLY recommended for texture)*
- 1 tsp baking powder
- 2 tsp ground cinnamon
- 2 tsp pumpkin pie spice
- 1 tsp McCormick's maple extract (or other brand)
- 2 tsp McCormick's Pumpkin Pie Spice EXTRACT
- 1-1/3 cup carbonated water or diet soda (root beer)

Pumpkin Spice Puree Frosting
- 2 (15oz) cans pumpkin puree *(pick 0 point cans, scan them)*
- 1 (1oz) box sugar free Jello instant butterscotch pudding
- 1 (1oz) box sugar free Jello instant vanilla pudding
- 2 tsp pumpkin pie spice
- 1-1/2 tsp ground cinnamon
- 1-1/2 tsp McCormick's Pumpkin Pie Spice EXTRACT

Topping:
- 1/4 tsp ground cinnamon
- fine mesh, wire strainer

Directions:
1. Preheat oven to 325.
2. Line the bottom of 2 round 9" cake pans with parchment paper. Spray the sides with cooking spray, set aside.

*** CAKE DIRECTIONS
3. In a large mixing bowl, combine the cake mix, egg, pumpkin puree, baking powder, cinnamon, pumpkin pie spice, and the extracts. Pour in the carbonated liquid of choice (I used seltzer water) and mix.
4. Pour the batter into the 2 prepared 9" round cake pans. Use a measuring scoop to try and fill each pan with a relatively equal amount, so that they bake up close to the same height.
5. Bake at 325 for 30-35 minutes, or until a toothpick inserted into the center comes out clean. Cooking times may vary depending on your oven, altitude... or attitude.
6. When the toothpick comes out dry, remove the cakes from the oven and allow to cool to room temperature.

*** FROSTING DIRECTIONS
7. Using an electric mixer, mix together the 2 cans of pumpkin puree, instant pudding packets, pumpkin pie spice, cinnamon and pumpkin pie spice EXTRACT. Mix until well combined and smooth.
8. Cover and place in the refrigerator for 30 minutes to set.

*** ASSEMBLY

9. Remove one of the cake layers from the pans and place it on a serving dish or platter, flat side down.
10. Scoop all of your pumpkin puree frosting into a 1 gallon sized ziplock bag. Twist the bag, while forcing all of the frosting down to 1 corner of the bag. Use scissors to snip an index finger-width hole in the bag's corner, to make a piping bag.
11. Cover the bottom cake layer with a layer of frosting, about as tall as your pinky finger is wide. Pipe a second layer of frosting on top of the first, to create a thick layer of filling for the cake.
12. Take your second cake layer, and flip it upside down, so that the perfectly flat bottom, which was on the bottom of the cake pan, will now be the top of your cake. Gently push down on the top cake layer, to sliiiiightly press it down into the pumpkin filling.
13. Frost the top of the cake, from edge to edge, with a thin layer of the pumpkin puree. You want to try and leave enough puree to pipe more around the entire edge of the cake. So just spread a thin layer on top.
14. Put the remaining 1/4 tsp of cinnamon into a small wire strainer and dust all over the top of the cake, to lightly coat the frosting.
15. Pipe small mounds of the pumpkin puree all around the outer edge of the cake. You can use a decorative piping tip if you'd like it to look snazzier.

*** NOTES

- If you cannot find pumpkin pie spice EXTRACT at your local grocery stores, you might be able to purchase it online at walmart.com. You can then have it delivered to a local walmart for free in-store pickup.
- IF you have no luck, you can always just use maple extract. The final flavor will be different, but it will still be very tasty.
- You can leave out the 1 egg from the batter if you wish, however, the cake WILL be light and fluffy, but extremely delicate. When I made it without the egg, it was light, fluffy and delicious, but it would start to break when I'd pick up the finished cake layers. Adding 1 egg helps hold it together, though it's not absolutely necessary. I care about you ultra strict vegan hipsters too. 😄

This is hands down, one of the most amazingly delicious cakes I've ever had in my entire life... and it's WW friendly. I wanted to make something extra special for Thanksgiving this past year, so I thought I'd make a cake version of my raspberry white chocolate cupcakes. I decided to kick it up a few notches by infusing the raspberry jam with lavender, then upping the heck out of the lemony flavor in the cake.

Serving Info.:

YIELDS: 12 slices
Points:
1 slice = 7 points
2 slices = 13 points
3 slices = 20 points

Ingredients:

Lemon Cake:
- 1 sugar free yellow cake mix
- 3 large eggs + 1 yolk
- 1/2 cup lemon juice
- 1 cup plain fat free Greek yogurt
- 1 tsp baking powder
- 1 (0.3oz) box sugar free Jello Lemon flavored gelatin
- 1 (1oz) box sugar free Jello instant Lemon pudding mix

Meringue:
- 4 egg whites
- 1/2 tsp cream of tartar

Raspberry Lavender Filling:
- 12oz fresh or frozen raspberries. You can use frozen berries, but make sure to buy "no sugar added" 0 point ones.
- 3 cups water
- 1 (0.6oz) box sugar free raspberry flavored gelatin.
  You can use strawberry gelatin if you can't find raspberry.
- 1/2 cup 0 point sweetener of choice
  (splenda, swerve, monkfruit, truvia, stevia, etc.)
- 1 tsp fresh lavender, finely chopped (optional)
  You can use dried lavender, or "herbs de provence" in a pinch.
- 1/4 cup cornstarch, dissolved in a little water

White Chocolate "Cream Cheese" Frosting:
- 1 (35oz) container of FAGE fat free plain Greek yogurt. You will be straining it to make cream cheese substitute, recipe on page 13.
- 1/3 cup Tollhouse premium white chocolate baking chips +2 tsp water for melting
- 1/3 cup powdered sugar
- 1 tsp imitation vanilla extract

Directions:

1. Preheat oven to 325.
2. Spray the bottom of 3 round 9" cake pans with cooking spray, to coat. Set aside.

*** MERINGUE DIRECTIONS

3. Place the 4 egg whites and cream of tartar in a mixing bowl. Mix with an electric hand mixer set to High for 3 minutes till stiff peaks form. Set aside.

*** CAKE DIRECTIONS

4. In a large mixing bowl, combine the cake mix, eggs, yolk, lemon juice, yogurt, baking powder and the contents of the lemon flavored pudding and gelatin packets. Mix to combine.
5. When it's all combined, GENTLY fold the meringue into the batter until just mixed together. Did I mention GENTLY??
6. Unlike most all of the other cake recipes, you do NOT have to wait 20 minutes. Just go ahead and go to step 7.
7. Pour the batter into the 3 separate 9" round cake pans. Scoop it out in equal amounts, into each pan, to ensure that they each get close to the same amount of batter.
Bake at 325 for 20-23 minutes, or until a toothpick inserted into the center comes out clean. Cooking times may vary depending on your oven, altitude... or attitude.
8. When the toothpick comes out dry, remove the cakes from the oven and allow to cool to room temperature.
9. When the cakes cool completely, the layers can be wrapped in plastic, to be stored in the fridge.
10. If you are going to make the cake over the course of a few days, store the wrapped cake layers in the freezer. But make sure to unwrap the layers when thawing the cake out. Let them thaw out uncovered, or the texture will turn mushy.

Note: If your cakes happened to have baked with a "dome" on the top, use a serrated knife to cut it off. You want relatively flat layers.

*** RASPBERRY LAVENDER FILLING

11. Place the raspberries (fresh or frozen), water, lavender, raspberry gelatin and sweetener into a sauce pot. Heat on medium-high heat, until the fruit breaks down. Remove from heat.
12. Pour the mixture through a fine wire strainer and into a bowl, to remove all of the raspberry seeds and lavender. We want a smooth seed-free puree. Pour the strained mixture back into the sauce pot, return to heat, and stir in the dissolved cornstarch. Bring to a boil.
13. Reduce heat and allow the mixture to simmer and thicken for 4-5 minutes. Remove from heat and pour into a bowl. Lay plastic wrap directly onto the surface of the warm filling. Place the filling into the fridge to cool and set.

*** WHITE CHOCOLATE "CREAM CHEESE" FROSTING

14. In order to proceed, you must have strained 1-1/2 cups of FAGE (preferred brand) Greek yogurt, as instructed on page 26 of my Low Point Cooking Guide.
15. In a microwave safe dish, microwave the white chocolate chips and teaspoon of water for 20 seconds. Stir, then microwave for another 20 seconds and stir. Repeat until the mixture is completely melted and smooth. Set aside.
16. In a medium mixing bowl, combine the "cream cheese" yogurt substitute, melted white chocolate, vanilla extract and powdered sugar. Use an electric hand mixer to mix the ingredients together until smooth... it should be thick enough to where it can stay firm on the sides of a cake. Return to the fridge to set.

*** ASSEMBLY

17. Take one of your cake layers and spread some of the raspberry lavender jam across it from edge to edge. Place the 2nd cake layer on top, spreading more jam and then repeat the process on the top layer.
18. Scoop the cream cheese frosting into a gallon sized plastic bag, then snip the tip off to create a piping bag. You can use a decorative tip insert if you want to go all fancy.
19. Pipe small mounds of frosting around the top edge of the cake. Done.

*** NOTES

- Though my assembly instructions give directions to make a "naked" cake, with exposed sides, this recipe makes enough frosting to frost around the sides of the cake.
- You can use "Swerve" brand 0 point powdered sugar in the frosting, instead of regular powdered sugar. Freeing up the extra points would allow up to a total of 3.5 ounces (by weight) of white chocolate to be melted into the frosting.
- You can make a lot of versions of this cake, with a few simple tweaks. For a strawberry version, simply use fresh or frozen strawberries and sugar free strawberry flavored gelatin, instead of raspberry. Want blueberry? Same thing. Replace the raspberries with blueberries. There is unfortunately no sugar free blueberry gelatin mix, but you can try using black cherry, though it might give the blueberry puree a purple tint. However, you can leave out the gelatin with no ill effects to the cake. It's just there for some extra flavor.

Reese's PB Cup Cake

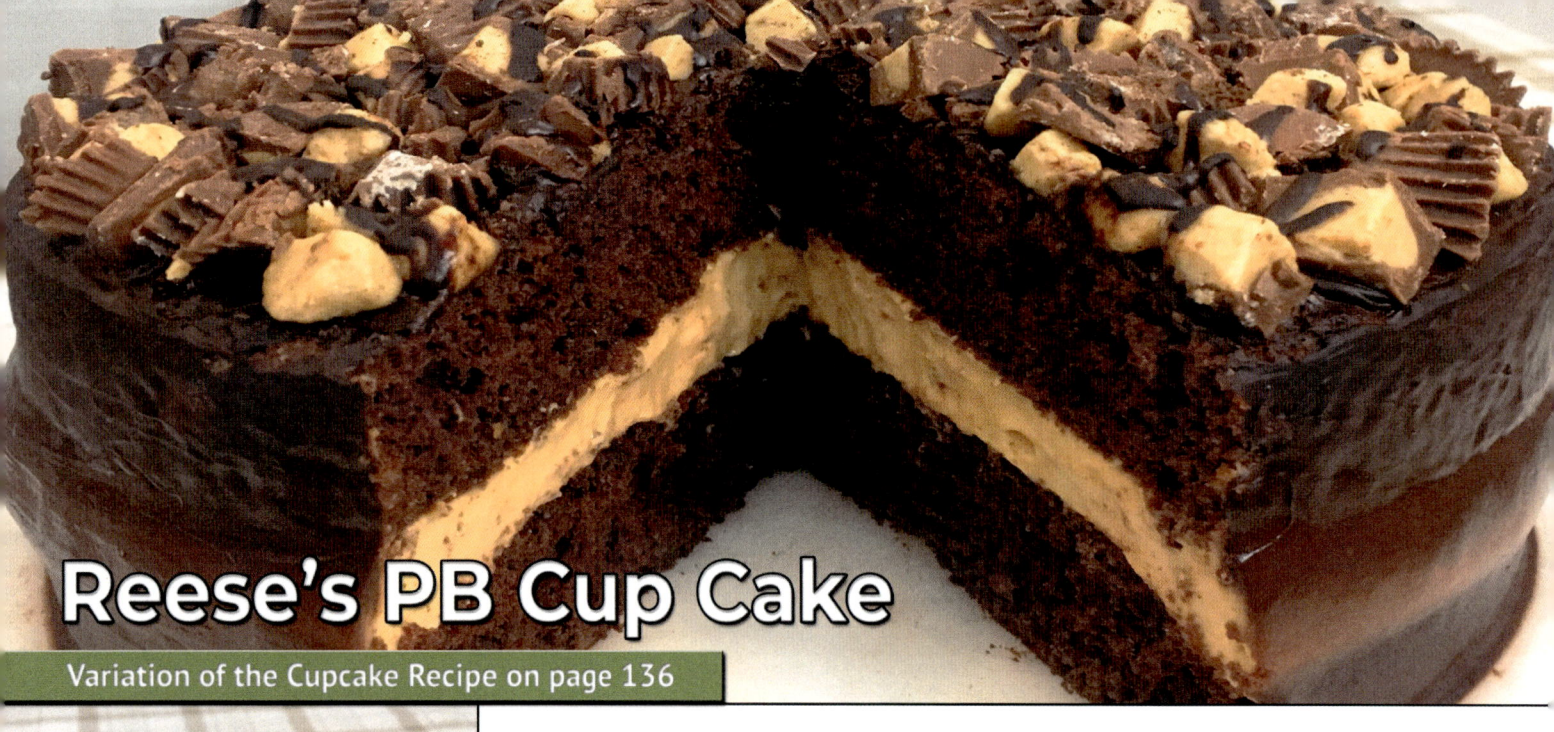

Variation of the Cupcake Recipe on page 136

This is my favorite of all the cakes. I could probably get news that all of the world's Super Powers have launched all of their nukes… but as long as I had this cake and a tall glass of cold milk, everything would be just fine for the next 8 minutes. This cake is absolute, peanut butter and chocolate perfection.

Changes:

Cake:
- For the "Meringue" step of the recipe, use **ONLY** 2 egg whites and 1/4 tsp cream of tartar. Also, you do NOT need to let the batter rest for 30 minutes.
- Do not put the 2 Tbsp of cocoa powder into the cake, they'll be going into the frosting. (see below)
- Line the bottom of (2) 9" pie pans with parchment paper, then spray with cooking spray.
- Divide the batter between the pans, then bake at 325 for 30-35 minutes. Allow to cool.

Peanut Butter Filling:
- Apply a double thick layer of the peanut butter "cream cheese" filling between the two layers of cake. You'll have leftover filling, unless you want to keep piling it in.

Dark Chocolate Pudding Frosting:
- For this cake version, we are going to add 1 (1.4oz) box of sugar free instant chocolate pudding to the recipe. Use an electric mixer to mix together the pudding and 2 Tbsp cocoa powder, with 1/2 cup plus 2 Tbsp COOOLD water, until thick and smooth. It doesn't sound like a lot, but it works. Use a rubber spatula to spread a VERY thin layer of frosting onto the sides and top of the cake.

Toppings:
- You will ONLY be using 20 peanut butter cups for the cake. We took away 4 of them to allow for the addition of the chocolate pudding.
- Rough chop all of the peanut butter cups on a cutting board and then sprinkle the chopped bits all over the top of the cake. You won't be able to cover every single nook and cranny, but trust me… it'll be amazing anyways.
- (OPTIONAL) Drizzle 2-3 Tbsp of Hershey's sugar free chocolate syrup over the top of the cake. The cake tastes insane without it, but it makes it look snazzier.

Serving Info.:

Servings: 12 slices
Serving Size: 1 slice
1 slice = 7 points
2 slices = 14 points

Steamed Cake

Prepare yourself for a super moist, light and fluffy cake

This cake is simplistic perfection. It sounds crazy, but it's awesome. By using a big pot, with a deep steamer insert, you can STEAM a cake. The end product is ultra moist, spongy... and with a texture that's a cross between a souffle and a cake.

Ingredients:

** CAKE BATTER
- 1 sugar free devil's food cake mix
- 1-3/4 cups seltzer water or diet soda
- 2 large eggs
- 1 tsp baking powder
- 1 Tbsp cocoa powder

Serving Info.:

Yields: 12 scoops
Servings: 12
Serving Size: 2/3 cup scoop**

Points Value:

1 serving = 3 points
2 servings = 7 points

Directions:

1. Fill a large pot (that has a deep DEEP steamer insert) with enough water to stop about 1/2 inch below the insert. Remove the insert (trust me) and bring the water to a boil.
2. Mix all of the cake ingredients together in a large mixing bowl, until well combined.
3. Pour the batter into a 1.5qt round baking dish that fits into the insert. It's a tight-ish squeeze, which is why you've removed the insert from the pot before you start boiling the water. Otherwise it'll burn your hands.
4. Set the batter-filled baking dish into the steamer insert.. Lower the insert into the pot, then cover with the lid. Crank up the heat to high, and steam over a rolling boil for 10 minutes.
5. Reduce the heat to medium-low and continue steaming the cake for another 25 minutes. Done.

*** NOTES

- The servings are very hard to gauge with this. By default I have the points and calories per serving calculated, assuming that you will take 12 scoops. It is hard to gauge how many servings you will ACTUALLY get, because it will be completely dependent on how big of a scoop you take, versus how much your cake puffed up.
- This is a very, very simple and inexpensive cake to make. However, it might take you 2-3 times to get the actual cook time to be exaaaaactly what you want. If you steam it a few minutes too long, it will stay forever-moist, but it will be completely cooked through. Steam it a few minutes less and you have freakin' amaze-balls lava cake. The cake is cooked all around, but the very bottom is juuuuust almost firm, giving you the most amazingly hot, chocolaty gooey sauce. Mmmmmmm.
- When you add water into the pot, make sure that you put enough in to just barely miss coming into contact with the underside of the insert. You don't want all of the water to evaporate before it's finished steaming... then it's just baking in the pot.

Nutritional Values

All those crazy macro-thingies, that you folks jabber-on about.

One of the biggest reasons for cooking and preparing meals like I do, is because I want to eat amazingly snazzy food, without having to reduce my portions. A prime example being my salad dressings and dips. My wife and I had a busy day, so we ordered delivery for dinner. There was a small packet of creamy dressing that came with my salad. According to the packet, 1/4 cup of that dressing had 440 calories and 48 grams of fat!!! By comparisson, my creamy roasted garlic and onion dressing, for the same 1/4 cup portion, has 45 calories and 1 gram of fat. If you look, you'll notice that ALL of my serving sizes, for everything, are huge. Most all food bloggers and cookbooks have tiny serving sizes for their sauces, dips and dressings. In equal amounts, theirs are usually twice the calories of mine.

MEAT SEASONINGS (with 99% FF ground turkey)	POINTS (1st serving)	SERVING SIZE	CALORIES	FAT (grams)	CARBS (grams)	SUGAR (grams)	PROTEIN (grams)	PAGE #
"Savory" Ground Turkey	0	1/2 cup	70	1	2	1	14	24
Asian	0	1/2 cup	100	6	2	1	11	20
Bratwurst	0	1/2 cup	80	1	3	1	14	20
Breakfast Sausage	0	1/2 cup	70	1	3	2	14	21
Chorizo	0	1/2 cup	70	1	2	0	14	21
Cuban Picadillo	0	1/2 cup	100	3	4	1	13	22
Italian Sausage	0	1/2 cup	100	4	1	0	12	22
Jerk Seasoning	0	1/2 cup	70	1	2	1	14	23
Lebanese Kafta	0	1/2 cup	80	1	4	1	14	23
Linguica	0	1/2 cup	60	1	1	0	13	24

DIPS & SPREADS	POINTS (1st serving)	SERVING SIZE	CALORIES	FAT (grams)	CARBS (grams)	SUGAR (grams)	PROTEIN (grams)	PAGE #
Artichoke Spinach	0	1/4 cup	40	1	4	1	4	28
Awesome Ketchup	0	1/4 cup	15	0	5	2	1	38
Black Bean Puree	0	1/4 cup	90	0	15	1	5	29
Cheddar Cheese & Beer	1	1/4 cup	40	0	6	3	3	30
Chik-Fil-A Copycat	1	1/4 cup	60	1.5	11	7	2	31
Chocolate Hummus	0	1/4 cup	130	3	27	4	7	37
Cocktail Sauce	0	1/4 cup	40	3	6	3	1	33
Creamy Chimichurri	1	1/4 cup	70	4.5	4	1	4	32
French Onion Dip	0	1/4 cup	80	2	13	9	4	34
Herbed "Cream Cheese"	1	1/4 cup	60	1.5	4	2	9	36
Holy Guacamole	1	1/4 cup	40	3	4	1	1	35
Hummus	1	1/4 cup	70	2.5	9	2	3	37
Roasted Pepper Balsamic	1	1/4 cup	40	0	7	5	2	39
Smoked Salmon	0	1/4 cup	70	2	8	6	6	40
Tartar Sauce	0	1/4 cup	70	2	11	9	3	42
Thai Peanut Dip	1	1/4 cup	60	1.5	12	2	5	43
Thai Sweet and Sour Sauce	0	1/4 cup	15	0	33	0	0	41

SALAD DRESSINGS	POINTS (1st serving)	SERVING SIZE	CALORIES	FAT (grams)	CARBS (grams)	SUGAR (grams)	PROTEIN (grams)	PAGE #
Apple Vinaigrette	1	1/4 cup	35	0	8	7	0	46
Blue Cheese	1	1/4 cup	60	2.5	6	4	4	46
Carrot Ginger	1	1/4 cup	35	1.5	3	0	1	47
Catalina	1	1/4 cup	25	1.5	9	1	0	47
Hail Caesar!	1	1/2 cup	60	3.5	4	3	3	48
Creamy Chipotle	1	1/4 cup	60	1.5	10	7	4	49
Creamy Cilantro	0	1/4 cup	50	1	9	5	3	49
Creamy Garlic and Onion	1	1/4 cup	45	1	6	4	2	50
Feta, Dill and Cucumber	1	1/4 cup	30	0	5	4	2	50
French	0	1/4 cup	15	0	10	1	1	51
Italian	1	1/4 cup	35	1.5	3	1	1	51
Peppercorn & Parmesan	1	1/4 cup	60	1.5	8	5	4	52
Russian (look out for collusion!)	0	1/4 cup	45	0	7	6	3	52
Sesame Ginger	1	1/4 cup	60	2	8	5	3	53
Thousand Island	0	1/4 cup	45	1	7	5	3	53

APPETIZERS	POINTS (1st serving)	SERVING SIZE	CALORIES	FAT (grams)	CARBS (grams)	SUGAR (grams)	PROTEIN (grams)	PAGE #
Arancini	1	1 rice ball	90	2.5	9	1	7	56
Bolitas de Tamale	2	1 tamale ball	80	1.5	10	5	8	58
Breaded Calamari	1	1 cup	200	4.5	18	1	25	60
Chicken Croquettes	0	1 croquette	60	1	4	1	10	62
Chicken Satay	0	1 skewer	30	0.5	1	0	5	64
Chorizo Stuffed Peppers	0	1 pepper	25	0	3	1	3	66
Crab Mac and Cheese	3	3/4 cup	170	1.5	20	2	18	68
Crispy Onion Rings	1	1/4 tray	100	2.5	15	4	5	80
Cuban Meatballs	0	1 meatball	50	1.5	3	2	7	70
Focaccia	1	1 slice	30	0	7	1	1	72
Garlic Mushrooms	0	1/2 cup	25	0.5	4	2	3	74
Kafta Kababs	0	1 skewer	50	0.5	2	1	10	76
Mussels with Saffron	0	1/2 lb mussels	140	6	7	1	13	78
Pineapple Jerk Skewers	0	1 skewer	45	0.5	6	2	4	82
Portuguese Clams	0	7-8 clams	120	3	6	0	28	84
Rotolo il Lasagne	0	1 roll	90	2.5	10	3	7	86
Salmon Cakes	0	1 cake	130	3.5	9	3	15	88
Seared Scallops	0	1 big scallop	60	1	2	2	10	92
Shrimp for Shrimp Cocktail	0	1/2 lb shrimp	110	2	4	0	18	94
Stuffed Mushrooms	0	1 mushroom	20	0	3	1	2	90

CUPCAKES	POINTS (1st serving)	SERVING SIZE	CALORIES	FAT (grams)	CARBS (grams)	SUGAR (grams)	PROTEIN (grams)	PAGE #
Blueberry Lemon	3	1 cupcake	140	2	26	6	4	106
Boston Cream Pie	3	1 cupcake	120	3	20	1	4	108
Caramel Apple Pie	3	1 cupcake	150	2	31	11	4	110
Coconut Cream Pie	3	1 cupcake	190	6	28	9	5	112
Death By Chocolate	3	1 cupcake	120	3	19	4	4	114
Guinnes and Baileys	2	1 cupcake	110	2	20	4	3	116
Hostess-ish	3	1 cupcake	140	3.5	24	6	5	118
Hummingbird	2	1 cupcake	120	2	21	4	4	120
Kahlua Mudslide	3	1 cupcake	140	3	23	8	4	122
Lemon Meringue	3	1 cupcake	170	3	30	8	8	124
Mexican Hot Chocolate	3	1 cupcake	110	2.5	18	3	4	126
Peanut Butter Bombs	3	1 cupcake	200	5	27	6	10	128
Peanut Butter & Jelly	3	1 cupcake	150	3.5	27	3	7	130
Pumpkin Pecan	3	1 cupcake	140	1	25	1	3	132
Pumpkin Spice	2	1 cupcake	120	1.5	25	1	3	134
Reese's PB Cup	3	1 cupcake	170	5	27	4	7	136
S'mores	3	1 cupcake	120	3	24	4	3	138
White Chocolate Mocha	3	1 cupcake	140	3	25	7	4	140

CAKES	POINTS (1st serving)	SERVING SIZE	CALORIES	FAT (grams)	CARBS (grams)	SUGAR (grams)	PROTEIN (grams)	PAGE #
Blueberry Lemon	7	1/12 slice	260	4.5	49	12	7	142
Boston Cream Pie	6	1/12 slice	240	6	41	2	7	143
Coconut Cream Pie	7	1/12 slice	370	11	56	18	9	144
Death By Chocolate	7	1/12 slice	230	6	39	7	7	145
Pumpkin Spice Cake	5	1/12 slice	220	2	51	4	4	146
Raspberry Lemon Cake	7	1/12 slice	350	5	68	21	14	148
Reese's PB Cup Cake	7	1/12 slice	330	10	52	8	12	150
Steamed Cake	3	1/12 scoop	160	4.5	29	0	3	151

Acknowledgments

Well, it's that time again. Here we are are the end of book 2, never in a million years would I have thought that I'd be here doing this. I can't even begin to express what a complete and utterly surreal ride this entire past year has been. The response that I received from the first book, which wasn't really a cookbook, but was more of a cooking guide, was so insanely positive and overwhelming. You people have completely changed my life, my family's lives and you've continued to give me the opportunity to help people by doing something that I love.

I'd like to take this time to thank a small handful of people. There are a ton of you that are in Connect, who KNOW that I view you as a friends, but these are the people that I have to thank directly, for helping me with this project. If I was going to thank all of my in-system buddies, it'd put "war and piece" to shame.

Of course I have to start off with the most obvious, @andmatsmom. I know that we don't always see eye to eye about butter, sugar and sweeteners, (you'll come around someday....) but that doesn't take away from the fact that you've always been encouraging and kind to me. Nevermind the fact that you recently tried to murder me with a box of angry lobsters. Enjoy the goat slippers and be thankful Amazon doesn't deliver cattle.

Mudhustler. Thank you for being an encouragement to me from the very beginning of all this, back in Fall 2018. I appreciate how you've always taken the time out of your busy schedule to let me get your opinion on things, no matter how small.

MariaRachael12, Jody and Missvw40. Thank you. Earlier this year, when I was at a low point, due to Cruella Deville, you three helped get me out of it. You allowed me, a stranger, to be a part of your lives. You THEN made me start thinking about making appetizers... and here we are. Thank you.

69gabygal. Lady... there ain't enough space in a stack of blank journals, to let me properly express how thankful I am for everything you've done for me over the past year. I don't know how you haven't turned into a raging alchy by now. But booooy do I know that I'm in trouble if you ever write those "tell-all" memoires. You've got some serious blackmail cred.

Kygoatgirl and EmilyBronte, thank you for being 2 of the people who were the most encouraging to me, in Connect, back when I first started sharing recipes and was being verbally ripped apart every time over it. It was completely against the thought process of so many members back then, that there was value to truly digging into recipes, like I do. You 2 would always stick up for me and my style of cooking. It kept me going back then.

Oh goodness... how could I forget. I HAVE to thank all of the wonderful therapists and staff at Pediatric Therapy of Santa Clarita and all the awesome Behavioral Therapists at California Psych-Care, that not only TREAT my 2 kiddos.... but allow me to use their office spaces during treatments, so that I can set up my laptop and get some work done. You have no idea how much of this book was only made possible because of that little bit of time I'd get, once per week.

Aaaaaaaand my wife, who has had to share her husband with the hungry masses. Who has had to deal with only having half a husband, for almost an entire year now. I'm taking a gooooooood few months break after this gets published. Thankfully, next year when Jesse's in school with normal hours, I can get work done during the day... and not have to stay up till 3-4am every night. You deserve a whole lot of attention to be showered on'ya for a good while. Thank you for your patience, understanding and allowing me to work on this grand project. Te Amo, chica.